Prison of Grass

Trent Native Series No. 1

This book is the first in a series published by new press jointly with Trent University, Peterborough, Ontario. The general aim of the series is to publish books by and about native peoples of Canada. Founding members of the editorial board are Don McCaskill (chairman), Joan Vastokas, William L. Morton, Harvey McCue, and James Bacque.

The author gratefully acknowledges the assistance of the Ontario Arts Council in the preparation of this book.

Prison of Grass

Canada from the native point of view

Howard Adams

new press Toronto 1975

ISBN 0-88770-211-2

Printed in Canada

In memory of my great grandfather,
Maxime Lépine, a guerilla warrior who
sacrificed his life in the struggle
against imperialism.

Contents

Two: Halfbreed Resistance to Imperialism

Three: The Native Plight in White-Supremacy Canada

Four: Towards Liberation

Preface

To the whites of Canada, "Métis" means a light-coloured Indian. In Canadian history, "halfbreed" refers specifically to the group of people who are part Indian and part white. These halfbreed people did not have a choice as to whether they would be Indians or whites or in-between; society defined them as members of the native society and it still does today. Halfbreed was the original name used by white traders in the early fur-trading years, but today this word has become unacceptable to mainstream society. To whites, halfbreed became a vulgar expression, so they adopted the name Métis – the French expression for mixed blood – which seems to be a more polite term. Most hinterland natives, however, still use halfbreed or simply "breed", while urban natives use Métis. Even this name is subject to different pronunciations. Most native people pronounce it *may-tee*. However, many English Métis are inclined to pronounce it *met-iss*. The old native people use still another pronunciation, *met-chiff*, which seems to have its historical origins among the Fort Garry halfbreeds. Halfbreed does not mean that these native people live half in the white world and half in the Indian world – they live largely in the native world. Society segregates and isolates Métis as rigidly as it does Reserve Indians and, like them, most halfbreeds see themselves as separate from the white mainstream world. There is no independent halfbreed society separate from the Indian nation: the Métis are part of the total native world.

Although this book deals primarily with the Indians and Métis of the western plains of Canada, the ideas relating to colonization apply to all native people in Third World colonies. The reason for dealing with the Canadian natives in this particular region is their unique historical development, which is based on the specific economic factors of that region. The plains Métis became a definite political group as a result of their involvement in the conflict between the Hudson's Bay Company and the North West Company and their long struggle against British imperialism or "industrialism", by which I mean the industrial capitalist system that was emerging in the western nations. It included the aims, policies, and ideology of the rising bourgeois ruling class. It does not mean that an industrial society was in existence in western Canada in the nineteenth century. It means, however, that the new white rulers were forging an industrial society. Historically, plains Indians and Métis had a flourishing culture that played an important role in the development of western Canadian society. For several decades in the mid nineteenth century their native government was one of the major governing forces on the prairies.

Although there is little discussion in this book of the economics of imperialism, there is considerable discussion of the cultural, psychological, and racial aspects of colonialism. The economics of imperialism have been well developed by several capable scholars whose works are listed in the bibliography. Up to now, the cultural, historical, and psychological aspects of colonialism for Indians and Métis have not been explored in depth.

Since I am a Métis, I have developed the historical discussion as much as possible from a native viewpoint. I hope that this interpretation will unmask both the white-supremacist and the white-liberal view that the natives were warring savages without any government, who craved white civilization. Three hundred years of white supremacy, imperialism, colonization, and capitalism are discussed in terms of their effect on the native people and their nation. Racism and colonization are analysed as both subjective and objective conditions in order to show how imperialism operates to conquer and colonize Indians and Métis, while seizing their land and resources at the same time.

The historical interpretation contained in this book takes the following into account: objective conditions and consequences of historical colonization, the present circumstances of Indians and Métis, discussions with senior native people, primary documents, and secondary sources. One study I have used extensively is *L'Histoire de la Nation Métisse dans l'Ouest Canadien*, by A. H. de Trémaudan, a book based on documents and statements collected from the Métis people in the Red River and Batoche areas between 1910 and 1925. A historical committee organized by Ambroise Lépine accumulated "a mass of writings, letters and official documents and conducted minute investigations among the people actually involved in the revolt". Fortunately some of these valuable documents have been preserved by the L'Union Nationale Métisse Saint-Joseph du Manitoba.

Since colonized, indigenous people are deterred from compiling records on the history of their nation and from writing their own history, documentary material is scarce. Furthermore, some government documents that have been represented as authentic, official historical documents apparently were invented by officials of the federal government and are therefore misleading. I include an explanation of how it was possible to forge these documents, which have been used by historians and writers to distort the true history of the Métis and Indian people of the plains.

Finally, I wish to give special acknowledgement to Kristine Anderson, who was most helpful in research assistance, and to William Morton and Mark Czarnecki for their careful editorial advice.

H. A.

The Northwest Territories after 1870

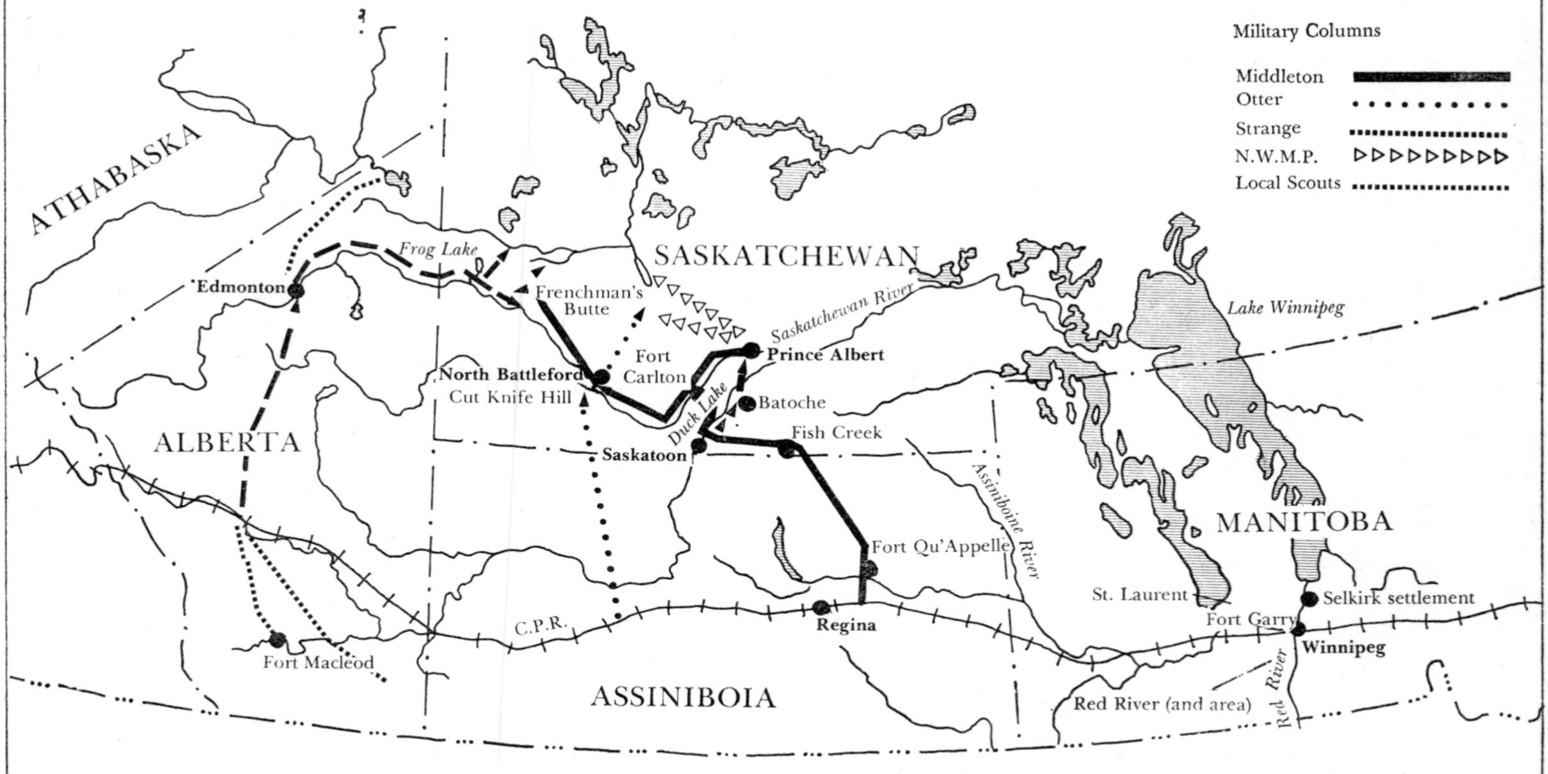

Military Columns

Middleton

Otter

Strange

N.W.M.P.

Local Scouts

ATHABASKA

Edmonton

Frog Lake

Frenchman's Butte

SASKATCHEWAN

Saskatchewan River

Lake Winnipeg

Prince Albert

North Battleford

Fort Carlton

Cut Knife Hill

Duck Lake

Batoche

Fish Creek

ALBERTA

Saskatoon

Assiniboine River

MANITOBA

Fort Qu'Appelle

St. Laurent

Selkirk settlement

Fort Garry

Winnipeg

C.P.R.

Regina

Fort Macleod

Red River

ASSINIBOIA

Red River (and area)

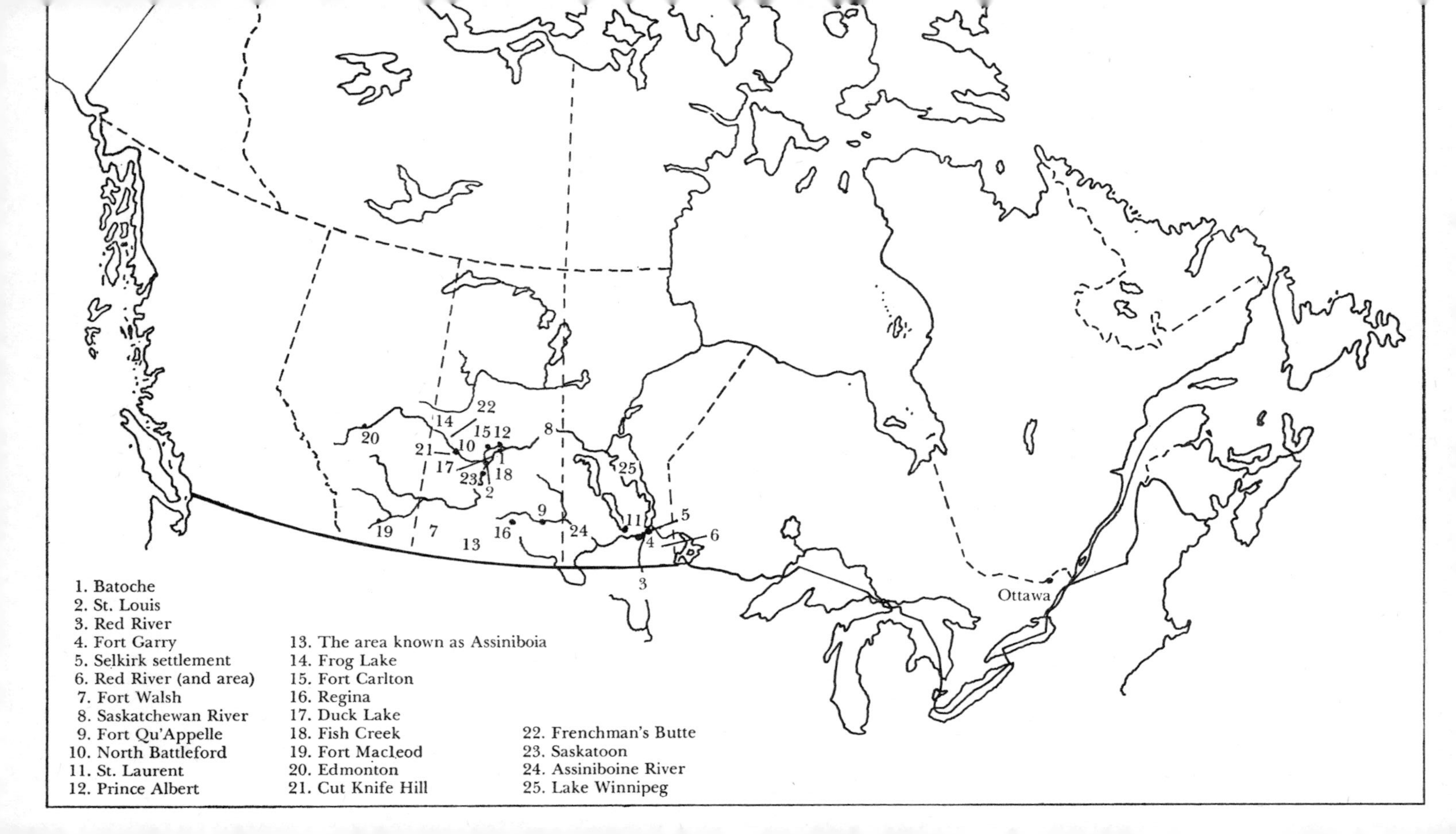
Ottawa
1. Batoche
2. St. Louis
3. Red River
4. Fort Garry
5. Selkirk settlement
6. Red River (and area)
7. Fort Walsh
8. Saskatchewan River
9. Fort Qu'Appelle
10. North Battleford
11. St. Laurent
12. Prince Albert
13. The area known as Assiniboia
14. Frog Lake
15. Fort Carlton
16. Regina
17. Duck Lake
18. Fish Creek
19. Fort Macleod
20. Edmonton
21. Cut Knife Hill
22. Frenchman's Butte
23. Saskatoon
24. Assiniboine River
25. Lake Winnipeg

Prison of Grass

One

The Indian Civilization

1 The Basis of Racism

In my halfbreed ghetto, finding a job was always difficult because the only employers were whites. It mattered little that I did not look truly Indian: all local employers knew whether I was half-breed or white. Seeking employment as a native was more than looking for a job, it was asking to be insulted. The boss did not have to insult me with his words; his actions and attitudes were enough to tell me his racist thoughts. As long as other jobs were available, a native would not apply for jobs he knew were for whites only. Even today Indians and Métis rarely apply for work as postmen, bus drivers, or for any position in which they would meet the public. Those jobs are taboo for natives because we live in a white racist society.

In my youth I therefore applied only for jobs that I knew had possibilities for halfbreeds, such as picking roots and rocks, haying, and unskilled labouring jobs in construction. The working conditions of these jobs were even more demoralizing than the ordeal of asking white bosses for such menial work. Furthermore, I knew that I would be paid lower wages than white workers, regardless of how hard I worked. When I settled with the boss for my wages at the end of the job, I was usually cheated out of several dollars. If I protested, he would threaten to call the police and have me thrown off his place. Since I knew how police regard halfbreeds and Indians and how they support white bosses, I would always leave immediately.

I was extremely fearful of white bosses – they terrified me. I always found them arrogant and cruel. Psychologically, their superiority practically crippled me. As soon as the boss gave me orders, I would become obedient and subservient, thankful for every small favour, no matter how insignificant. These work situations angered me deeply. When I discussed them with my mother – a deeply religious Catholic, who was illiterate but very wise in her own way – she argued that halfbreeds were hard workers only part of the time. She claimed that some had a habit of not being on time, and occasionally they went on a drunk and remained off work. Even though I didn't understand at the time why colonized native people behave the way they do, I felt instinctively that my mother's stereotype argument was false and I had little patience with it.

The hostility I nurtured during my ugly work experiences dominated my thoughts. I needed jobs to get money. The jobs degraded me and destroyed my sense of esteem and humanity, but I had to have money; therefore, there was no way of avoiding these nasty experiences with white employers. It was clear to me that white bosses were using these stereotypes of drunkenness and laziness as excuses to exploit halfbreeds. By classifying us as inferior workers, they could get their work done more cheaply. Native workers are invariably treated in this discriminatory way: branded with the same racial stereotypes – late for work, absent after payday, unreliable on the job – they are then forced to accept poorer wages. In my youth I never solved the puzzle of racism in employment, but today it is clear to me that racism is the product of economics.

The racism that native people encounter today had its origins in the rise of western imperialism during the 1600s:

> But modern society — Western civilization — began to take on its characteristic attributes when Columbus turned the eyes and interests of the world away from the Mediterranean toward the Atlantic. . . . The socio-economic matrix of racial antagonism involved the commercialization of human labour in the West Indies, the East Indies, and in America . . . Racial antagonism attained full maturity during the latter half of the nineteenth century, when the sun no longer set on British soil and the great nationalistic powers of Europe began to justify their economic designs upon weaker European peoples with subtle theories of racial superiority and masterhood.[1]

Businessmen of Europe realized that they would need a large supply of labour to obtain resources from the new continents. Natives furnished this large supply of cheap labour. Since labour was an important item of cost in the production of goods, European businessmen wanted to get the greatest amount of labour for the least possible pay, and the purpose of racism was to reduce native people to a subhuman level where they could be freely exploited. Racism therefore arose from economic factors inherent in capitalism.

In Canada, indentured or semi-slave labour had to be secured and made available for businessmen of the fur-trade industry. Racial stereotypes and prejudices then developed from the realization that Indians provided potentially cheap labour for trapping furs and for whatever other jobs had to be done. Not only that, but they were found to be the most efficient trappers and fur gatherers. So European scholars and clergymen began creating racial theories which showed that the native people of North America and other colonies were primitives, innately inferior and subhuman:

> Sepulveda [eminent Spanish theologian and university professor of the sixteenth century], then, may be thought of as among the

first great racists; his argument was, in effect, that the Indians were inferior to the Spaniards, therefore they should be exploited. . . .

Among the Spanish writers of the time [about 1535 onward] who were in rather complete accord with the drastic methods of human exploitation in the New World was Gonzolo Fernandez de Oviedo. . . . It was Oviedo's opinion, even after visiting America on a royal commission, that the Indians were not far removed from the state of wild animals, and that coercive measures were necessary if they were to be Christianized and taught the uses of systematic labor.[2]

These scholars stated that, because of their barbaric life style, natives were naturally inferior to white men. Churchmen provided great service in the development of racist ideologies: "A few of the Puritan clergy later asserted that the Indians were children of the devil who might profitably be wiped out and their lands appropriated."[3] Clergymen, particularly Anglican and Catholic clergymen, worked closely with the imperialist companies of Europe in the conquest and exploitation of native people; they were as important as the military in conquering the indigenous populations of the colonies:

With scriptural quotations to support his assertions, Gray [London preacher of the sixteenth century, scholar of St. John's College, Cambridge] proves that Englishmen have a solemn duty to seek out fresh lands to relieve the congestion at home. If these foreign countries are inhabited by savages, then, as the Israelites cast out the Canaanites, so Englishmen must take the land from the idolatrous heathen. But Gray suggests that it would be better if they could first convert the heathen and then peaceably move into the country. The sword is the last resort. . . . But the land of the heathen must be claimed *at any cost* for the children of God . . .[4] [Emphasis added] . . . During the spring of 1609 several preachers not directly connected with the Virginia Company lent the weight of their influence to the schemes for colonization. Most prominent of these was Richard Crakanthorpe, chaplain to Dr. Thomas Ravis, Bishop of London.[5]

These arguments created a new role for the missionaries; the conversion of heathens to Christianity not only saved their souls but also made them servile and obedient to their economic masters. In addition, university professors developed "scientific" theories that natives were stupid and bestial. These creators of racism argued that natives were mentally and morally inferior to Europeans and incapable of looking after themselves. Europeans refused to accept the fact that Indians had lived in Canada for thousands of years and did not need white masters to look after them. However, at the same time, it was stressed that natives were physically strong and therefore must have been intended for hard labour.

Establishing that native people were little more than stupid beasts of burden allowed easy and uninterrupted exploitation of them as workers, and also denied them all legal or human rights:

> When a philosophy for the dehumanizing of the exploited people has been developed with sufficient cogency, the ruling class is ready to make its grand statement, sometimes implicitly, and to act in accordance with it: The colored people have no rights which the master race is bound to respect. The exploiting class has an economic investment in this conviction and it will defend it with the same vigor as it would an attack upon private property in land and capital.[6]

Thus it became impossible to make appeals for humane and just treatment: the Indian stereotypes created by the exploiters had reduced native people in the eyes of the public to animal-like creatures. Racist schemes of inferiorization claimed that all native people were capable only of the lowest type of unskilled labouring jobs. Scholars did not develop theories that natives were capable of other work than labouring jobs. For example, racial theories did not say that Indians were inherently skilled as priests or merchants. Instead, the stereotypes claimed that natives were good only for work as miners, cotton-pickers, fur-trappers, and so on:

> . . . the Indians were represented as lazy, filthy pagans of bestial morals, no better than dogs, and fit only for slavery . . . The capitalist exploitation of the colored workers, it should be observed, consigns them to employments and treatment that are humanly degrading. In order to justify this treatment the exploiters must

> argue that the workers are innately degraded and degenerate, consequently they naturally merit their condition.[7]

In Canada, racism originated in the imperialist fur-trading industry, and over the centuries it has become deeply entrenched in Canadian society. As a result, assimilation of natives into mainstream society is today not a possibility, at least not in a capitalist society:

> Assimilation diminishes the exploitative possibilities. This social situation is not especially a derivative of human idiosyncrasy or wickedness, but rather it is a function of a peculiar type of economic order which, to repeat, has been developed in the west among Europeans. The exploitation of native peoples is not a sin, not essentially a problem of morals or of vice; it is a problem of production and of competition for markets. Here, then, are race relations. . . . They are labor-capital-profits relationships; therefore, race relations are proletarian-bourgeois relations and hence political-class relations.[8]

Once natives became integrated into Canadian society it would have been impossible to separate them from other people as a class of special workers. However, as long as Indians were isolated as a special group, they were easily exploited as trappers; isolation or segregation of native people was therefore essential for the fur industry.

The racism created during the centuries of the fur trade cannot be eradicated today. Although cheap Indian labour is unnecessary to the present Canadian economy, the early principles of racism remain as a dominant feature of the Canadian economic system. Canada has a long history of deeply entrenched racism because the fur trade, operating on the basis of racism, lasted well over 200 years. The Hudson's Bay Company, founded in 1670, also moulded certain Canadian social institutions within this racist framework. White supremacy, which had been propagated since the beginning of European imperialism, became woven into Canadian institutions such as the church, the schools, and the courts, and it has remained the working ideology of these institutions. In addition, native people cannot avoid seeing the cultural images and symbols of white supremacy, because they are everywhere in society, especially in movies, television, comic books, and textbooks. Since Indians and halfbreeds cannot live completely outside mainstream society, they are continually subjected to racial stereotypes through their encounters with police, welfare officials, and school authorities.

As soon as native children enter school they are surrounded with white-supremacist ideas and stories – every image glorifies white success. Because they are unable to resist it, they become conditioned to accept inferiority as a natural way of life. They soon recognize that all positions of authority – such as teacher, priest, judge, Indian agent – are held by whites. These people make all the rules and decisions that determine the fate of Métis and Indian people. An aggressive and sophisticated white-supremacist society intimidates colonized people, it makes them self-conscious and withdrawn. As native children grow up, these white-supremacist images become more alive, but natives are powerless to do anything about them. Consequently, the children internalize inferior images as a part of their true selves, often with strong feelings of shame. This partly explains why many native people attempt to hide from their Indianness, while others try to pretend that they are white, French, or Italian. White supremacy dictates that whiteness is beautiful, that mainstream life-styles are the most desirable, and that mainstream life is the only successful way of life. At the same time, white supremacy disfigures not only the native people, but the whole Canadian nation. Because of white supremacy, some natives attempt to abandon their culture and people. Many young persons abandon their parents and relatives and attempt to lose themselves in the mainstream.

When I left my ghetto as a young man, I made a complete break with my parents and home. To me, everything about them and the community seemed so definitely halfbreed, and therefore ugly and shameful. As a result, I attempted to dissociate myself from everything and everyone that appeared halfbreed. I wanted to be a successful white man in mainstream society. If I maintained a close identification and relationship with my parents, home, and community, they would anchor me to halfbreed society and prevent my success in the white world. I was fully aware of how whites mocked and condemned halfbreeds and their way of life. I wanted to escape from all that ugliness and mockery. Since my parents were precious to me, it was an agonizing experience, yet there was no choice if I wanted to succeed.

In a white-supremacist society, more opportunities and privileges exist for Indians and halfbreeds who "look white"; those who "look Indian" are doomed to stay at the bottom of society. They are forced into the extreme of racism, and they suffer most as a result. It was no accident that I managed to get a good education and a good job, since my appearance is predominantly white. Throughout my school years I was favoured, because I closely resembled white students. More privileges were extended to me than to other Métis children who looked more Indian. The white community responded to me in a less racist manner than it did to other halfbreeds. Through this kind of partiality I became aware of the possibility of acceptance in white society and the possibility of success in mainstream life. However, the question arises: What happens to the masses of Indians and halfbreeds who are forced into the deep crevices of the "caste" order because of their Indian appearance and lifestyle? There is no escape from such discrimination. It is understandable why intense racial feelings develop among these Indians and Métis, and it is not surprising that they are the strongest advocates of militancy and red nationalism.

Today, white supremacy is being exposed for what it is — a myth. The "scientific" theories that supported racism throughout the early centuries of imperialism have been shown to be usually erroneous. In school today, intelligence quotient tests and achievement tests that keep native students at the bottom of the class are being criticized as cultural and racial tests. The tragedy for Indians and halfbreeds is that for so long they have accepted these tests and theories as scientific fact. Even today, many native people still believe that they are inferior to whites and that they are not intelligent enough to become professional workers or to administer their own affairs. Many still regard themselves as awkward and incompetent, in comparison with whites. As a youngster at home in my ghetto, I saw this image very clearly. I tried to gain assurance from my mother that I was not stupid and not inferior to others. If I did not get these assurances, I would react bitterly against my Indian heritage. When

I walked through the snow I would look back at my tracks to see if I was pigeon-toed. Whenever I spoke to whites, I was extremely self-conscious about my halfbreed looks, manners, and speech. I was very sensitive about my inferiority because I knew that whites were looking at me through their racial stereotypes and I too began to see myself as a stupid, dirty breed, drunken and irresponsible. It made me feel stripped of all humanity and decency, and left me with nothing but my Indianness, which at the time I did not value. I hated talking to whites because it was such an agonizing experience – their attitudes and the tone of their conversation left no doubt about white supremacy. I would often cut the conversation short so that I could escape from these painful encounters. Not only did my sense of inferiority become inflamed, but I came to hate myself for the image I could see in their eyes. Everywhere white supremacy surrounded me. Even in solitary silence I felt the word "savage" deep in my soul.

2
The Communal Indian Society

The books I read at school said that my ancestors were cruel, sadistic savages who had not even reached the early stages of civilization, and I felt that I was constantly being reminded of the direct link between myself and my "barbarian" ancestors. My first reaction was to pretend that there was nothing Indian about me. I pretended that I knew nothing about early "savages", and I refused even to talk about native people, because of my great shame. Yet at home, among ourselves, our curiosity overcame our shame and we questioned each other. We speculated about Indians and their lives before the white man came to this country. Perhaps it was just to bolster our sagging self-esteem, but we were quite positive that they were not savages.

Perpetuating stories about "stone-age aborigines" made white men the great champions of progress, the great civilizers of the "barbarian" world. Since there were no written records left by Indians, the history of their civilization has had to depend on this interpretation. It is now becoming evident, however, that the white man's history of the Indians and Métis does not correspond to the facts.[1] An examination of 300 textbooks by white historians, currently being used in American classrooms, shows that:

> ... not one could be approved as a dependable source of knowledge about the history and culture of the Indian people of America. Most of the books were, in one way or another, derogatory to the native Americans. Most contained misinformation, distortions, or omissions of important history.[2]

Specific images of the Indians based wholly or in part on myth rather than on the objective reality of their society came to dominate the attitudes and beliefs of Europeans in the seventeenth and eighteenth centuries. Since these images were derogatory, it is understandable that subsequent writings on the subject were likewise derogatory. It is basic to Indian stereotyping that whites come to believe the images and myths portrayed by their own society as factual:

> . . . people, having no other views placed before them and being unable to investigate, to research, or to construct a theory of relations between advanced and backward peoples, have no other choice than to follow similar thought and to accept the actions of those governing the relations between European peoples and colonies by the patently false, but nevertheless dominating, ideas.[3]

The more theories of colonialism are examined, the more they are seen as mythical. Colonial myths are very powerful because they become an organic part of the thought processes of the people in the imperial nation and serve as their reality.

The particular interpretation or focus of white historians, diarists, and journalists depends also upon the particular circumstances of the period. For example, when it appeared that the Hudson's Bay Company might delay industrial expansion across Canada, writers were very critical of "the Bay" and gave explanations of how its officials severely exploited and abused Indians and Métis. However, as the Bay yielded its sovereignty and land, writers composed glowing reports about its generosity in its treatment of the native people. This same principle holds true for each historical period. Although we are taught that history is true and objective when based on primary sources, the observers' interpretations are bound to reflect the specific emphasis of the period and its unique circumstances. Furthermore, these capitalist historical writings represent only the forces contending for power and their power relationships. Consequently, the experiences and relationships of the "common" people are largely omitted from historical writing, because in capitalism the masses are not a ruling force.

Indian and Métis history suffers distortion in other ways as well. Early racial stereotyping develops a mentality that serves as a reference for most of a person's life. For instance, a textbook currently in use in a Saskatoon elementary school contains the following passage: "Their [the Indians'] ways of living are not at all as they used to be, and now, instead of going on the warpath and scalping their enemies, they are as peaceful as all other Canadians."[4] As a result of statements like this, many Indians in fact believe that their ancestors were totally savage and warlike. The truth is that scalping was done more frequently by whites than by Indians:

> White settlers early offered to pay bounties on dead Indians, and scalps were actual proof of the deed. Governor Kieft of New Netherland is usually credited with originating the idea of paying for Indian scalps, as they were more convenient to handle than whole heads, and they offered the same proof that an Indian had been killed. By liberal payment for scalps, the Dutch virtually cleared southern New York and New Jersey of Indians before the English supplanted them. By 1703 the colony of Massachusetts was paying the equivalent of about $60 for every Indian scalp. In the mid-eighteenth century, Pennsylvania fixed the bounty for a male Indian scalp at $134; a female's was worth only $50. Some White entrepreneurs simply hatcheted any old Indians that still survived in their towns. The French also used scalp-taking as an instrument of geo-politics. In the competition over the Canadian

> fur trade, they offered the Micmac Indians a bounty for every scalp they took from the Beothuk of Newfoundland.[5]

Writing about the Colorado River Indians in 1775, Father Font stated that "since the Indians are so free and live so like animals and without civilization they do not obey their leaders".[6] Other white writers were equally harsh in their descriptions of Indians. Frederick Olmstead, writing about the Indians of Texas in 1856, commented:

> Here . . . was nothing but the most miserable squalor, foul obscenity, and disgusting brutishness, if there be excepted the occasional evidence of a sly and impish keenness. We could not find even one man of dignity; the universal expression towards us was either a silly leer or a stupid indifference.[7]

Such harsh stereotyping persists to the present day with Canadian writers and historians. A booklet called *Batoche National Historic Site* describes the 1885 battle of Duck Lake in the following way: "The Métis and their Indian allies poured a murderous fire on the police and the volunteers and within forty minutes forced Crozier to make a difficult and costly withdrawal under fire." The story continues with the same racial stereotyping:

> A band of police on a lawful errand had been obstructed by armed rebels, loyal Canadian citizens had been killed and wounded by halfbreeds and Indians – these could be interpreted only as the acts of a savage and lawless mob threatening the West with murder and pillage.[8]

This booklet is issued under the authority of the federal Minister for Indian and Northern Affairs.

It is interesting to note also that white men insist that historical studies must be factual and objective. Everything that fails to meet this criterion is regarded as biased sloganeering or propaganda. Yet white men fail to recognize in their own writings racial stereotyping and a biased, inflammatory denigration of native people that has no relationship to authenticity and objectivity.

However, a few scientists have made helpful studies on early Indian societies before the European invasion, explaining how Indian society was governed according to tribal and clan organization. The basic unit was the clan, a kinship group claiming a common ancestor. Members of the clan were bound by strong bonds of solidarity and mutual assistance. Each clan had its own council, a democratic governing body composed of both men and women that selected and dismissed leaders. Most leaders held office only for a specific duty and length of time; for instance, a certain leader would be selected for a certain buffalo hunt because of his special skills as a hunter and organizer, and the people would respect his leadership and authority for this particular hunt. However, at the end of the hunt, he ceased to be a leader and thus had no further authority. These positions of leadership had no permanence or authority in any other capacity apart from the specified duty.

The next level of organization was the tribe, which was composed of several clans. The tribal council consisted of members from each individual clan. Each tribe had territory held in common by its members, consisting of settlements as well as hunting and fishing areas. A tribe had its own dialect or language, its own religious beliefs, rites of worship, and specific religious festivals during which dancing played an important part. The common land of each tribe was usually respected by neighbouring tribes.

The most important aspect of the tribal council was its governing functions. Councils met regularly and in public. Every man and woman had the right to attend council meetings and take part in the discussions: "The council sat in public session, attended by other members of the tribe, who had the right to join in the discussion. Among the Iroquois, all decisions were reached unanimously."[9] The council set policy with regard to the economic affairs of the tribe and established working relationships with neighbouring tribes. Since Indian society was based on consensus in public assemblies, single authoritarian rule played only a minor role:

> Tribes had little formal government. Most bands were autonomous under their own leaders or chiefs, who, by their courageous

> exploits, wisdom, or other abilities and qualities, had won the respect and support of followers. But they gave advice rather than orders; councils of leading men made decisions based on unanimous agreement.[10]

What little authority a tribal chief had was later amplified by the Europeans as an efficient means of controlling the Indians *en masse*. Eventually, chiefs supported by whites took power beyond that traditionally accorded to them by Indian government: furthermore, Europeans recognized chiefs in capacities not rightfully acknowledged within the Indian system. Unfortunately, many chiefs accepted this white flattery and tried to exercise a centralized and authoritarian rule over their native subjects, in imitation of white government. Some chiefs attempted a single, absolute rule, and, in cases where tribe members refused to obey them, often administered beatings to their own people. Naturally, these chiefs became hated rulers and the white authorities accordingly provided them with armed bodyguards.

Although Indian society did not have a highly developed system of government, it nevertheless had a social order, more organic than systematic, that dealt with organization and administration: "Most of the bands on the plains observed strict codes of rules that regulated behavior between people who were related to each other."[11] Order and discipline were maintained in various ways. In the first place, the individual had a strong sense of his or her responsibility to the clan and to the tribe. Also, public shaming and ostracism were effective in deterring unsanctioned behaviour.

Before the arrival of the horse in the eighteenth century, the base of the Indian economy was agriculture and hunting. In most cases, the women raised the crops, and the men hunted buffalo and other game on foot. The men devised various hunting schemes to capture the game, including driving buffalo into a pound or over a cliff. With the introduction of the horse about 1740, the economy, as well as the culture and the form of governing, changed substantially. The horse "increased mobility and hunting efficiency, brought new peoples onto the plains from its fringes, and led to a richer and more flamboyant culture than had existed before".[12] Because they were able to roam over larger distances and their chances for successful hunts were greater, the Indians began to place greater emphasis on hunting buffalo and less on their agriculture. As they became primarily nomadic, their culture also changed. The arrival of the gun shortly after the horse moved Indian society towards a single-crop economy based on the buffalo and a more flamboyant form of culture. The gun and the horse greatly increased intertribal trade, particularly in these two items. In the east, the rifle and the fur trade dislocated the ancient economy and turned Indians into trappers, which they had not been before. On the west coast, the fur trade and, later, the reduction of the native fishery destroyed the old manner of life for most natives.

Before the Europeans arrived, Indian society was governed without police, without kings and governors, without judges, and without a ruling class. Disputes were settled by the council, among the people concerned. Indian government was neither extensive nor complicated, and positions were created only to ensure effective administration for a given period of time. There were no poor and needy by comparison with other members, and likewise no wealthy and privileged; as a result, on the prairies there were no classes and no class antagonisms among the people. Members of the community were bound to give each other assistance, protection, and support, not only as part of their economics, but as part of their religion as well. Sharing was a natural characteristic of their way of life. Each member recognized his or her responsibility for contributing to the tribe's welfare when required, and individual profit-making was unknown. Everyone was equal in rights and benefits. Some native communities still function communally in this manner, particularly in poor areas. Very few members set themselves apart from the community and attempted to accumulate material wealth for themselves.

3
Fur-Traders Trespass

In 1670 a group of English nobles and adventurers who had never travelled to North America obtained a charter from the King of England that gave them nearly half the land in Canada. These new absentee landlords did not consult the Indians, the residents of the land, before taking it over. Their charter was in essence a gift of Indian land, resources, and people to a group of aristocrats, and the Hudson's Bay Company was to hold imperial authority over this vast territory and its people. It was granted monopoly control over the trade and commerce on all the seas, rivers, lakes, and land of the entire Northwest, and given full power to make laws and enforce them. It was empowered to employ an armed force, appoint commanders, erect forts, and keep control of Rupert's Land, as it was called, according to the company constitution, which was drawn up in England. The constitution was not responsible to the people of the colony and could be changed by the directors to suit their desires. As a result, the directors made laws that served only to consolidate their power and increase their profits. Intimidation was used regularly by the Hudson's Bay Company to instil fear in the native people and keep them in their place; terrorism during this era was notoriously cruel and brutal.

In its pursuit of furs, the Bay became the most destructive force working against the Indian people. Furs, particularly beaver, were in great demand from the beginning of the seventeenth century and brought high prices. English businessmen were anxious to develop this lucrative trade, and their greed for profits led them to the western prairies and into contact with the plains Indians. Before white men arrived, furs had been used by the Indians largely for domestic purposes, such as clothing. Killing animals solely for the sake of their skins became a business only after the arrival of the white man.

To encourage the Indians to trap furs, the Europeans had to offer trade goods that would appeal to them. Initially, some traders were successful in dealing away trinkets such as beads and mirrors. To the European, these were cheap goods with little market value, but the Indian desired them because he found them exotic and beautiful. Since he had no concept of property value, he did not assess the trinket in terms of its market value. However, the Indians prized the white man's manufactured goods much more, because they were of great practical use. Unfortunately, the Europeans quickly discovered the power alcohol had over the Indians. Initially used as an inducement to bring Indians to the forts, alcohol soon became a major trade item. But the white traders were anxious to create a solid market for their manufactured goods, and most of the trade in furs involved the exchange of axes, iron cooking kettles, clothing, and, of course, firearms. These new implements did not change the basic structure of the Indian economy, but simply made it more efficient and productive. For example, the traditional method of cooking was to heat stones and place them inside bark pots, which could not withstand direct heat; thus the iron kettle was a big improvement because it allowed Indians to choose cooking sites without regard to the availability of stones. However, the destructive function of the natives' use of European goods was that it created a dependence upon white traders. This, in turn, created a dependence upon the beaver, because its fur was necessary to obtain European goods.

For some time, however, the Indians of the West rejected trapping as a new occupation because they were too interested in buffalo hunting. Nevertheless, they had to depend on the whites for guns and ammunition, and inevitably they were drawn into fur-trapping and trading. Not until the second half of the eighteenth century did the plains Indians become seriously involved in this trade, which quickly formed a major part of their economy.

White traders encouraged natives to trap more and more furs. La Vérendrye urged them to hunt marten, lynx, and weasel, and in fact refused to trade guns, kettles, and tobacco for beaver, thus forcing Indians to hunt these other animals. He also persuaded women and children to trap the smaller animals:

> My object in saying this was to oblige them to hunt these smaller animals which they are not accustomed to do, and at the same time to get the women to take it up and also the children of from ten to twelve, who are quite capable of it.[1]

Many of these methods worked, and a greater breakdown of the traditional economy resulted, since the women had to abandon farming or other occupations in order to trap.

The Europeans were unprincipled traders, and the Indians would lose heavily if they were not cautious. Regular attempts were made by Indian councils to counteract harmful trading practices and to transact business properly. They complained that iron utensils were faulty: bottoms fell out of kettles as soon as water was poured into them. Many European goods disintegrated after a very short time. Food products were often spoiled, resulting in disease; guns would burst in the men's faces, injuring or killing them; and European clothes often caused smallpox and pulmonary ailments, as well as skin diseases.

At the same time, the Indians were unable to implement

policies that would stabilize their indigenous economy. They accepted the fact that some European goods, such as kettles, axes, and guns, had improved the technology of their economy, but trapping was inevitably harming their nation and their culture.

To improve their position in the Indian trade, independent traders, who were allowed by the British government to compete with the Hudson's Bay Company after 1768, established centres on the prairies so that they could intercept Indian trappers who were taking their furs to the Bay headquarters, and bargain with them. Later, the Hudson's Bay Company also adopted the policy of building prairie forts, since many plains Indians objected to making the long treks to the eastern markets. Indians did not seriously protest against the first trading posts built in the West. However, when they saw posts being established as warlike fortresses, they became concerned. They were sensitive to their dominion of the plains, and it began to look as if white traders were building a string of military bases in the Northwest. The numbers of competing white traders increased considerably after 1768. English, Scots, French, and Yankee traders were trading throughout Rupert's Land, attempting to make quick fortunes; canoe brigades with furs and supplies were a common sight on the waterways of the Northwest.

Not only did the Indians trap furs for the white traders, they also provided the traders with knowledge of animal habits, the weather, and plants that supplied food and medicine. In addition, Indians collected the furs, and prepared, stored, packed, and carried them for long distances over rugged country. Since they had an intimate knowledge of transportation and trapping routes, the Indians soon realized their importance to white fur-traders and, in an attempt to retain some economic bargaining power, they organized themselves in 1790 into trapping and guiding units. They had become particularly agitated over excessive exploitation and abuse during the canoe trips that transported European goods to the trading forts. On the basis of their special skills, they bargained with their employers for improved working conditions and wages. Their arguments were met with immediate hostility, and in several cases their lives were threatened by the trading company bosses. The result of this labour conflict was that many Indians were deprived of their guns, and the hardships on their trips became even greater.

The occupation of trapping led to serious changes in the native way of life. It meant that men had to spend most of their winters on trap-lines, which took them away from their homes and villages a great deal of the time. Consequently, their participation and influence in village and tribal government was considerably reduced. At the same time, Indians were denied any rights or participation in white administration: it was unthinkable for Hudson's Bay officials to allow Indians membership in Bay government. The fur trade also lessened the economic solidarity of the Indian nation. Instead of joining together on a tribal level for self-support, native workers allowed themselves to be forced into dependency on commercial trapping and on the Bay. As far as Indians were concerned, fur-trapping did not in the end provide as good a living as their indigenous economy of agriculture or buffalo-hunting, since the more they became involved in the fur trade, the less they could farm and hunt. Indian councils became concerned over the large number of their people exclusively dependent upon trapping.

There were other serious problems. Councils were particularly troubled over the degrading conditions resulting from the use of alcohol. This was a major issue at all tribal meetings. Natives throughout the land were worried about the demoralizing effects of the alcohol that was being freely supplied by white traders. There seemed to be an endless supply of this "firewater" – in one year alone the Hudson's Bay Company imported nearly 5,000 gallons of rum to be used in trade with Indian trappers. H. J. Moberly, a Hudson's Bay factor who wrote about his experiences, stated: "Carlton House had a number of Plains Crees who could buy all the rum they were able to pay for."[2] "Our goods, of course, consisted principally of rum, plentifully diluted. We selected our guard and the trade began."[3] Liquor was also commonly used as "treat", during which the trader would give the Indians free drink to get them intoxicated, so that they could cheat them of their furs; but, whether alcohol was used as a trade item or as treat, the results were the same. Indians were no worse drunkards than white men; the traders were simply nurturing and exploiting a normal human weakness for the sake of amassing a greater fortune:

> Our Indians are not of themselves addicted to drink but they are supplied with liquor . . . whiskey has destroyed a greater number of Indians than either war or disease . . . no barter took place between the Trader and the Indian without the first offering the other whiskey . . . the Trader, who looks at his own interest, is pitiless, and laughs at the misery and degradation of the Indian.[4]

The process of trading was always troublesome. Each sale meant a distressing argument if an Indian was to get a reasonable price for his furs. In return, white traders often wanted to give faulty goods, or goods that were relatively useless to the Indians. In some instances, when Indians argued against such shabby articles, they were beaten by company employees. Europeans also refused to pay fair prices to Indians for agricultural products, fish, and meat. "Short-changing" and "short-weighing" were common practices of Hudson's Bay officials, and it was standard policy to short-weigh every pound of powder sold to Indians. Although the trading prices were fixed, they were rarely followed. When policy said that one beaver skin should be taken, the Bay clerk frequently took it upon himself to demand two. Hudson's Bay officials themselves did not scruple to cheat their own employees as well as the Indians.

The profit motive played an important part in recruiting Indians to trap furs for the European merchants. Individualism was gradually infused into the Indian economy, and this played a major role in diminishing the practice of sharing. Profit changed the communal ideology of the Indians as more and more native people became involved in the competitive fur trade. Successful financial returns became more important than the methods used to acquire them. Consideration for other natives and for the nation as a whole decreased. As the supply of beaver dwindled, competition among trading companies increased, and this fostered hostilities among Indian tribes over trade practices, territory, and traditional rights.

In spite of the profit they gained from furs, most Indians and halfbreeds never became truly capitalistic in their way of life.

Although in their commercial activities they were engaged in free enterprise trade, they continued to live together in a communal society. Social relationships continued to exist essentially as they had before. Land and game remained under common ownership, as did hunting grounds, dwellings, and food stores. Only after 1885 when private ownership of property became the law in the Northwest was land no longer held in common. However, because Indians have been excluded from the mainstream of trade and commerce, capitalist ideology has not penetrated deeply into their social patterns, and many characteristics of early communal life still prevail.

4 Colonization and Missionaries

I grew up in the community of St. Louis, Saskatchewan, which, like Batoche, was founded by French halfbreeds who had fled from Red River in 1870 to escape the persecution of Ottawa's troops and the Ontario Orangemen. It is a town of approximately 300 people, situated on the banks of the South Saskatchewan River. Strung out along the south side of the river for nearly a mile is the main part of the town, centring on the Catholic cathedral and convent.

In World War II days, the town was easily identified as halfbreed, Catholic, and French: Halfbreed log shacks were scattered throughout the town; the huge cathedral with its towering steeple, magnificent rectory, and gowned nuns told of the Catholic influence; many of the townspeople spoke a French patois mixed with Cree and English. Although the majority of the population were Métis – French and Cree – not a single business was owned or operated by us. We remained the casual and unskilled labourers, the depressed and powerless people. The hotel, garage, store, lumberyard, and café were all run by white Frenchmen. A few Anglo-Saxons ran other small businesses and had importance and power in the community quite out of proportion to their small numbers. Dotted along the back roads were more halfbreed shacks, log and mud houses used as permanent dwellings throughout the year, built to accommodate large families and withstand the severe sub-zero Saskatchewan winters. They were typical houses of poor prairie people. On the north side of the river lived the English Protestant halfbreeds whose ancestors had migrated from Manitoba in the early 1870s via Prince Albert. The French and English halfbreeds on the two sides of the river got along well together.

Typical of most halfbreeds, our family lived in a state of deprivation and at times had to depend on welfare. In spring and fall we worked for white farmers and in summer we tended our gardens and small farms, picked berries, seneca root and rocks, cut brush, and grubbed trees*. In winter we cut and hauled cordwood and sold it to the white merchants in St. Louis for one dollar and fifty cents per cord. On Sundays we faithfully went to church to thank God for our "small blessings". We were always reminded to be eternally grateful to the Lord for giving us so much in life.

Our economic and political conditions were controlled by the local businessmen, government bureaucrats, and priests. Naturally, our social and religious life was under the domination of the parish priest, who ruled over his halfbreed flock like a king. In spite of our poverty, we always managed to fulfil our church obligations, and gave cordwood each year to pay for our pew. Although Father Charpentier was the parish priest for over 20 years, he rarely visited the homes of the halfbreeds except when someone had died or to remind us of our obligations. Yet we had to go to him to obtain the necessary dispensations so that we could work on Sundays. In our naïveté we regarded our priest as superior and invincible. This kind of ghetto mentality and sub-

*i.e., cleared farm land of tree stumps.

servience crushed any interest we might have had in politics, which might have led to control of our own affairs. We accepted the belief that we were incapable of administering our community and this religious domination controlled our daily lives, suffocating our social development. Throughout my childhood, I was conditioned to relate to these religious authorities according to the principles of colonialism and white supremacy.

History did not tell me that while my great grandfather was making a supreme sacrifice for his people, the parish priest, Father André – who had professed affection and loyalty to the same Métis people – was betraying them by giving information to the enemy. Together with Major Crozier of the North West Mounted Police (N.W.M.P.), he drew up a list of names of halfbreeds who were participating in the second Riel "rebellion" and had it broadcast to the halfbreed community. It offered "protection to all those who were forced to take part in the rebellion, on their surrendering themselves to the commanding officer at Carlton or Prince Albert".[1] Such is the work of missionaries. During the struggle of 1885, the priests revealed themselves as agents of colonization and traitors to the native people. While the Métis and Indians were killed or imprisoned, the priests were made heroes and given rewards.

The part played by the priests in the colonization of the native people was as destructive as that played by the soldier and the fur-trader. Missionaries were extremely effective in undermining the strength and spirit of the native society. Conversion to Christianity was a powerful force in the destruction of native culture and religion, and the imperialists fully understood how useful missionaries could be in subjugating colonized peoples:

> The stock companies, organized to make settlements in the New World, realized the value of the clergy's influence in the promotion of their enterprises and took steps to win the enthusiastic support of the preachers. Noteworthy in this endeavor was the Virginia Company of London, which, from its inception, made a consistent and systematic effort to utilize the clergy to produce a favourable public opinion. From all the evidence now available it appears that the Virginia Company achieved a remarkable success in gaining and keeping the aid of an able group of pulpit propagandists.[2]

Colonizing merchants and traders negotiated with Anglican and Catholic officials for the recruitment of missionaries for the colonies. This does not mean that the missionaries were aware of the specific function they served in the imperialist scheme. They were much more valuable in this service if they were naïvely dedicated to Christianizing the "heathens" and remained ignorant of their political function. Their Christianizing zeal gave them tremendous strength and courage to overpower the native religion: they had a total commitment to their mission and did not hesitate to sacrifice their lives in their pursuit of converts. Once missionaries succeeded in getting native people to internalize Christian beliefs, they had also partially destroyed the nation's traditional way of life and its vitality. However, some colonial rulers became impatient with the slowness of the priests' work and clashed with the missionaries and the church. The missionaries believed that God had commanded the clergy to save the souls of the heathen savages, so that conversion resulting in cultural genocide was regarded as a Christian service. By doing this, they served God, and the greater the sacrifice they made, the greater the glory to God. They also served as a powerful influence in spreading European culture and ideas of white supremacy. They maintained that Europeans had the right to rule over Indians because natives had only barbaric institutions; therefore, Indians should serve their natural masters and place themselves under the protection of the white man.

By the mid seventeenth century the Catholic and Anglican churches were seriously promoting colonization, with missionaries as their active agents. The Church of England envisioned a vast empire of millions of Anglican "savages" who would be hostile to Spain; meanwhile, the Catholic Church was rapidly expanding its empire in New France. Many shareholders in the early colonizing companies were clergymen:

> Moreover, among the shareholders themselves were many clergymen, some of them high in the church, who looked upon the Virginia Company as an enterprise especially ordained to carry out the divine plan.[3]

In this way, religion and commerce went hand in hand:

> . . . the full significance of the sermons on the subject has been overlooked. These sermons provide one of the best illustrations in the period of the essential harmony between religion and business enterprise.[4]

They firmly believed that, in His divine plan, God had reserved vast regions of the new world for white Christians.

In the early stages, Indians fought against Christianity because they understood that it was shattering the solidarity of their tribes, councils, and culture. However, missionaries did not give up easily: when verbal persuasion was ineffective, they did not hesitate to gain converts by more violent methods. For example, violent methods used by the Franciscan missionaries in the California area were the common practice, and not the exception. Jean de la Pérouse – an overseer of missions in the Spanish colonies of the eighteenth century – visiting the missions in the California region in 1786 – remarked:

> We saw men and women [in the missions] loaded with irons, others in the stocks, and at length the noise of the strokes of a whip struck our ears. . . . Corporal punishments are inflicted on the Indians of both sexes who neglect pious exercises . . .[5]

Missionaries came to the Canadian Northwest in the nineteenth century in the vanguard of industrialism. These missionaries penetrated native civilization to soften up the Indians and Métis for the railroad builders and land companies. In 1841 the Oblate priests reached the Northwest and, in spite of initial rejection, they set up missions among the Cree people at Ile à la Crosse, Frog Lake, and Lac la Biche. The Cree suspected that these inquisitive priests were trying to foster friction between themselves and their friends since they worked so closely with the Hudson's Bay Company, which gave the priests free transportation, canoes, interpreters, provisions, and houses inside the forts.

The Catholic priests were joined by Wesleyan, Presbyterian, and Anglican missionaries. James Nesbitt, a Presbyterian minister, established a mission at Prince Albert with the assistance of English halfbreeds. The Reverend George McDougall, a Wesleyan, was on the payroll of the Hudson's Bay Company as chairman of the Bay missions. His son, John, "carried on the work in his father's tradition serving the cause" of industrialism and Bay imperialism "in blistering sun or freezing blizzard". These missionaries constantly urged the federal government to establish a police force for the maintenance of imperial justice in the Northwest. It has been honestly stated that, "when the police came, their hands were ever present to help them" in suppressing the native people. During the struggle of 1885, the Reverend John McDougall and other missionaries took an active part in undercover work against the Indians and Métis, and their work as spies is well known among native people. In Third World liberation struggles, churches usually play an active role in fighting against the colonized people. These same churches and clergy have served colonialism and white supremacy in Canada for many centuries.

During the uprising of 1885 the Catholic priests who had been part of the Métis communities for many years did not hesitate to undermine the efforts of the Métis people. Because of the privileged position they enjoyed in the community, they had access to important information which they readily furnished to General Middleton. It is difficult to understand why the leaders of the Métis council allowed these priests to participate in such vital decision-making discussions with the Métis, and also allowed them to travel back and forth to the enemy forces. At times, the council restricted their activities, but it never imprisoned them. Of course, part of the answer is the Métis' great devotion to their religion and priests. They must have held a belief that priests were above the actions of betrayal. Trémaudan says the Oblate Missionaries of Mary Immaculate were tied to the partisan politics of Canada. Since the order was part of the ultramontane religious movement, they were indeed reactionary, and hence they supported the Conservative Party:

> At the same time, it [ultramontanism] feared the subversive effects of formal liberalism that it confounded with political liberalism. This may explain why certain leaders who supervised Western-Canadian clergymen demonstrated a zealous defence of the Government when they believed it threatened, and tacitly agreed to sacrifice a man's life.[6]

In summary, colonization and missionaries were not a pleasant or rewarding experience for native peoples. Herman Merivale, an English economist interested in imperialism, described in 1861 the treatment native people were receiving from the Christian civilizations, white colonists, and colonial governments, of which missionaries were active participants.

> I shall not detain you over the wretched details of the ferocity and treachery which have marked the conduct of civilized men, too often of civilized governments, in their relations with savages, either in past times, or during the present age.... You will there read of the barbarous and incessant warfare which has thinned the border tribes of South Africa; of the natives of Tasmania reduced to a few families by long maltreatment, and those few transported, six years ago, to the small island in the vicinity, almost as a measure of precaution, to save them from the settlers, who shot them down in the woods, or laid poisoned food within their reach; of the ancient race which inhabited Newfoundland reduced to a single pair, man and woman, and those two shot by a British colonist in 1823.[7]

5
Ossification of Native Society

After the political and economic subjugation of a native people comes the final stage of colonialism, the cultural takeover. Once prairie native society was arrested and ossified at the pre-industrial stage after 1885 by being prevented from developing along with the nation's advancing technology and economy, emphasis was placed on its archaic features. Traditional and ritualistic customs, black magic, and other superstitions were retained as long as they served to increase the colonizer's power over the native people. For instance, the position of chief, even though he was powerless, was kept for purely ornamental reasons. All real power and authority was removed from the chief's position and from the other institutions of native society and placed in the hands of white authorities. Consequently, decisions affecting native life were made by the white power structure.

After the Métis and Indians were confined to reserves, colonies, and ghettos during the latter part of the nineteenth century, they were geographically and culturally isolated from mainstream society. Under these conditions it was easy for white authorities to propagate suspicions and beliefs among native communities that served to ossify their culture. Each Indian reserve and halfbreed colony was encouraged to think that it was alone in its struggle, that problems were unique to each community and of their own creation. Primitive beliefs were reactivated so that all political thought and discussion would be smothered or excluded. Pow-wows and other rituals were allowed or discouraged according to the functions they originally performed in the native society. If they served the original political or religious purposes, they were discouraged because that tended to strengthen the native culture; if they were regarded by the whites as simply colourful, primitive performances, they were permitted and even encouraged. Because there was no basic economy and no work force in native communities, it was impossible for people to interact with one another or with outside workers on this basis. As a result of the witchcraft ideology and the absence of political power in the reserve, politics became irrelevant or non-existent. The cultural and political strength of the native community was destroyed once the meaningful components had been extracted. But the establishment of an archaic, caricature culture did not kill the native culture; on the contrary, it was forced to continue in agony in a limbo existence. The Indian and halfbreed culture that was once open and dynamic became closed and static.

Indians and Métis collaborate with their white oppressors by portraying archaic culture through such public spectacles as the Calgary Stampede. They present themselves as aboriginal people with a primitive culture, although they are performing in the twentieth-century space age. Teepees are exhibited, tomahawks and primitive tools displayed, as if they were current implements and customs in Indian society. They dress in traditional Indian garments, sit around and smoke the peace pipe. To make the display more authentic for whites, Indians live in the teepees during the exhibition. The Indian spectacle has no historical significance because the Calgary Stampede display is not an historical exhibition. Whites insist upon seeing Indians in this primitive way because it corresponds to their stereotypes.

This display is highly amusing to white people, especially to children, who, being easily impressed, come to regard Indians as quaint barbarians. It is a cruel mockery of the true native civilization and a grim misrepresentation of present native customs. The most pitiful part of these spectacles is the dancing, a humiliating experience for other native people because it has no cultural, religious, or artistic quality. These public performances are exclusively for the entertainment of whites. Officials of the Saskatoon Exhibition argued that its Indian show must be staged in this aboriginal manner and in no other way, claiming that the public would not pay to see an Indian show unless it was in this archaic style. These officials cater to the racist mentality of the Canadian people and even make a profit from it.

In the early stages of ossification, social institutions become mere caricatures patterned after the original fertile ones. For instance, the Indian councils used to have the full support of the people to govern their communities. However, the imperial rulers extracted the legitimacy and authority from such councils and left them as mere shells: their powers have been reduced to such matters as "the destruction of noxious weeds", and "the construction and maintenance of boundary fences".[1] Nevertheless, the form of the institution was allowed to remain. These caricature forms embodied a pseudo-respect, but they actually institutionalized contempt for the former traditions to the point of mockery and sadism. At the same time, Indians and half-breeds were allowed to indulge in all kinds of alien and sterile rituals, such as religious pilgrimages in which council members organized families into groups for long treks to Christian shrines. Since their political power had been reduced, their energy was directed towards trivial matters.

All activities of the native community were completely under the control of the colonizing officials, who made all the decisions affecting the daily operations of native people. Farming was an example of this extreme colonial control. The decision-making authority over these farming operations was complete, down to the most trivial detail. Marketing of grain and farm produce could not be carried on without the official permission of the white agent; natives could be imprisoned and deprived of their machinery and stock for breaking the smallest rules. Such were the farming "opportunities" allowed Indians on reserves. This grinding paternalism and prison-like authority has persisted to this day. Of course, each reserve has one or two "show farms" on which a couple of Indians are given special favours in order to develop "successful" farms. These are intended to give the impression that "every Indian could be a successful farmer, if he only tried", and the scheme is effective in degrading the reputations of all other Indians who are not successful farmers. Information showing the number of Indians who have been refused assistance is not made public. In any event, for a native person, farming has become an artificial operation since it was originally intended as "busy work" for the Indians who were forced onto reserves.

With the native population hidden from mainstream society, the philosophy was popularized that the natives would soon die out. The whites generally believed that Indians were horse-stealers and ritual sadists who burned missionaries at the stake, collected scalps, and ate human flesh:

> Coupled with his barbarous instincts . . . was his natural inclination to cruelty. It has been truly said that all savage races are like children, in that they have no adequate conception of suffering or pain suffered by others. They were entirely devoid of sympathy. The controlling instinct of the Indian was to kill.
>
> . . . He was animal in his instincts, and he neither knew nor cared about anything not connected with his material wants. . . . In conversation . . . all Indians were obscene to a degree unknown to any other people. They seemed to have no conception of vulgarity, obscenity, or decency.
>
> . . . All Indians are lazy and thievish, work being considered degrading . . . vindictiveness and ferocity . . . is a part of Indian nature.[2]

Newspaper reporters would casually refer to Indians as "idle and vicious aborigines".[3] Of course, it was easy for colonizers to standardize and propagate these distorted myths because they had control of the communications media. Perverted images were paraded before the public to help justify and legitimize the incarceration of the entire population of native people. There was nothing sacred in this historical process of colonization; the most intimate and sensitive aspects of native peoples' lives were debased in the most ruthless way. Mockery and ridicule were brutally employed and still are today. It is not uncommon to hear children cry in agony simply because they are Indians or halfbreeds — their misery is the direct result of colonization and white supremacy.

The fall that I was 18 I went to work for a farmer 15 miles from home. Not having any transportation, I was obliged to walk to his farm that day. On the highway I was lucky enough to be given a ride, or so I thought. A couple of Mounties in their car stopped and offered me a ride. It frightened me momentarily because I thought they were going to run me in. Mounties don't ordinarily give this kind of help, especially to Métis. I had heard many stories about how brutally the police treated Métis and how they pinned false charges on them. But a ride was very welcome at this point. As we started up, the driver asked if I was from St. Louis, and before I even had a chance to answer, the other cop remarked, "There's a lot of smoked meat around that town." I had heard that expression many times before and I knew what it meant. The comment really burned me but I was too scared to argue. As far as I was concerned the girls in St. Louis were very decent. The Mountie continued, "I hear that those halfbreed babes like to have their fun lying down." I tried to change the subject, but the police were interested in pursuing it to the end. The driver asked in a mocking manner, "Is it true they like it better from a white man?" I was getting really angry, while at the same time trying to explain that Métis girls are just as nice as white girls. They drove on with comments about "redskin hotboxes who didn't wear any pants at all", and kept calling me "chief" in a sneering manner. Although they seemed to have an obsessive interest in native girls, they were also implying that Métis girls were little more than sluts and too dirty for

Mounties. One asked, "Is it true that they'll go to bed with anyone for a beer?"

I was relieved when we reached the crossroads where I was to get off, but they drove on slowly and ignored my request to be let out. The driver said to his partner, "The chief probably has some little redskin heifer waiting for him in the bush." They joked together about "horny bucks" and "red peasoups always in heat". One wanted to bet me there wasn't a virgin in St. Louis. I began to think about jumping out since we weren't going very fast. They offered to let me out as soon as I would tell them the secret of "no knock-ups". At that point I said I was going to jump off, and they immediately burst out laughing. Between their fits of laughter they were half shouting, "Jump off, so that's it." They roared on about "jump on, jump off, breed games, up and down, in and out, and halfbreed fun". Finally they let me out and drove away in a thunder of laughter. I turned and ran down the road with their mockery ringing in my ears. Shame was burning in my mind like a hot iron. I ran as if I was trying to outrun the Mounties' image of the Métis. I ran till I was exhausted, swearing, spitting, and half crying. That is how the famous redcoats of law and order respect the native people and their society.

According to racial stereotypes, Indians and Métis are naturally shy and withdrawn; they are born that way. Incidents such as the one I have described apparently have nothing to do with it. This notion is pounded into the heads of native children by teachers, priests, white functionaries. Because the children are rarely free from this myth, they don't get opportunities to develop confident and assertive attitudes about themselves. It is a very effective way of preventing the development of bold and articulate leaders, and the absence of such native leaders over the last century shows the success of this inferiorization scheme.

Coupled with the destruction of self-esteem is the suppression and mockery of native languages. In racist institutions such as schools and churches, Indians are discouraged as much as possible from using their native tongues, and Indian names are anglicized and mocked. For example, an Indian child may be given an Indian name which, incorrectly translated, means Afraid-of-his-horses. The original meaning is impossible to get into a convenient English phrase, but it refers to a warrior fierce in battle who has many fast horses. The rough, incorrect translation made by white people is ridiculous and in some cases, as above, virtually the opposite of the original. However, whites take only the surface meaning of the anglicized version and mock the Indian as if he were, in fact, afraid of horses. This is a powerful means of degrading native people.

Of course, white men's names are never reinterpreted in the same way for the convenience of native speakers. Another example of how language is used to degrade the native people is provided by official government pronouncements regarding natives. As part of the program of national and cultural destruction, the government treats Indians and Métis as wards or children. Such attitudes, typical of the colonial mentality, were clearly revealed during the treaty negotiations and the relocation of Indians to reserves after 1885. In the negotiations of Treaty Six, Governor Morris addressed the masses of Indians saying, "Indian children of the Queen . . . I am glad to learn that they [Crees] are looking forward to having their children civilized."[4] The reason for this language is to convey the idea that natives are incapable of governing themselves, and that this justifies absolute government over them. In this way governments encourage their functionaries to look after the "children" in an authoritarian manner.

After reserves were established and Indians had developed a conscience of obedience, police were replaced by bureaucrats, priests, and teachers. The change to new wardens was made possible because Indians and Métis had internalized the myths of inferiority and become placid and subservient. The church was one of the most powerful and effective instruments in destroying native strength, and indoctrination leading to supplicant behaviour was done largely by the clergy. Church and school determine much of the ideology of the native communities by teaching native children to believe in white supremacy, and thus in their own inferiority; this paternalism is effective in keeping Indians and Métis in "child" roles and "in their place". Although these non-military authorities give the appearance of being liberal and democratic, their teaching and administration only continues the work of police.

The results of this mentality can be seen clearly in any reserve village whose population comprises both natives and whites. There are always two distinct communities. The native section has no gas or running water, no paved streets or sidewalks, only trails and dirt roads. Many of the houses are one- or two-room shacks. The differences are more than economic and cultural, they are vividly racial. According to the whites, the native section is a place of lazy, diseased, and evil people incapable of doing anything for themselves, a breeding-ground for violence. The whites claim that natives have no culture, no ethics, no sensibility to morality, and no appreciation of law and order. To these colonizers, Indians and Métis destroy and disfigure beauty. They speak of their native neighbours in bestial terms, complaining that "they breed like rabbits". They speak of the sinful and depraved behaviour of natives, of shacking-up, of common-law marriages, of sleeping around. The fact is that the native villagers are hungry – hungry for food, for houses, for clothes, for power, and for whatever the whites take for granted. They are crouching villagers, listening to the gossip of the shacks, listening to what the white man wants them to hear, think, and fear. Because the native villagers contain frustration, hostility, and envy, they are always on the defensive and rarely able to progress.

In contrast, the colonizers' section is clean and beautiful. It has electricity, plumbing, paved streets, and garbage collection. It has beautiful modern houses with central heating and all public utilities. It has white authorities who draw handsome salaries because of the native people. These colonizers are privileged because they belong to the power structure and they have physical comfort and luxury because they are white. They have opportunities and unlimited horizons because they are part of mainstream society. The law is on their side because they are administrators. They are able to talk about the native world in "rational and objective" terms because all the evidence is on their side.

Until fairly recently, the Indian agent managed the reserve people's personal business as official business, and had the right to open their personal mail. In this way, he emphasized that

Indians were not individuals in their own right, with their own personal, intimate existences, and that white agents had full power over them. The only other place where such extreme dehumanization exists is in prisons – perhaps there is a basis for claiming that Indians and Métis make ideal prisoners. By the same token, whites consider native people as objects and not as persons. This is reflected in phrases such as "our Indians", implying possession of objects, such as toys or pets. Indians and Métis are not allowed to take action on their own, action that would be completely independent from whites. To colonizers, natives are to be controlled; they are not human beings who can engage in normal social relationships and organizations. Natives have to be managed and programmed.

As colonized people in a white-supremacist society, Indians and Métis are dehumanized in every possible way. Indians are often denied their names and instead are given a treaty number; they then become officially known by this number. Native people are depersonalized to such an extent that their inner strength is pulverized and they are left without a vigorous will – as an ethnic group, natives have the highest per capita suicide rate in Canada. The purpose behind the dehumanization of Indians and Métis is to make them accept the denial of their human and civil rights.

Also injected into the view of native culture was the belief that Indians and Métis lack moral values. White-supremacy claims that natives have always been immoral and dishonest and that it is a losing battle to attempt to make them live up to decent moral standards. Many racist images are so distorted that they portray natives as little more than savages without intelligence or beauty. Because they are regarded in this way, natives themselves come to accept the cruelties of oppression as a necessary part of their colonized existence. In a dehumanized and racist society people lose sensitivity to moral and social issues. They have an awareness only of the trivialities and personal events in the ghetto, and not of the serious social, economic, and political issues. Furthermore, colonized people have difficulty uniting on human-rights concerns; for example, Indian and Métis people are frequently refused employment or decent housing because of their race, yet they do not protest seriously against this denial of civil rights. Instead, most of them simply accept this crime as a natural part of Canadian society.

Frustrated and confused by their state of powerlessness and oppression, native people sometimes turn to social behaviour consistent with racial stereotypes. Indians and Métis become subservient and grateful and therefore vulnerable to manipulation and exploitation by the authorities. In this way, native people weaken themselves politically. Some weaken themselves further by internalizing such racial images as the drunken, irresponsible, and shy native. Consequently, whites can claim that their stereotypes are correct, which, in turn, reinforces their racist attitudes. Not that this kind of confirmation is necessary to the racist mentality. Contradictions in racial stereotypes that debase Indians and Métis seem not to concern whites. Natives are portrayed as ignorant and gullible at the same time as they are considered sneaky and crafty cheaters. After all, according to white supremacy, to cheat a white man a native would have to be exceedingly clever. Even today, if something is missing in the classroom, the teacher usually questions Indian and Métis children first. This is racism in its everyday ugliness and oppressiveness.

To mainstream society native people all look alike and act alike. There is no individual appearance and behaviour. If an Indian or Métis is late for work, all native people are labelled as habitual late arrivers. Whites often complain, "They failed, just when so much was being done for them," even though only one native person failed. This allows whites to dispense with any obligation to improve their racist society. The white man rationalizes that he has done his best; if natives suffer hardship, it is their own fault. Colonization and racism not only harm native civilization but they harden the humanity of the entire Canadian society.

Canadian authorities and historians have nevertheless managed to perpetuate the illusion that Canada has never been a white-supremacist society, an illusion that Canadian people continue to believe. As a result, they have developed attitudes that harmonize well with apartheidism. Canadians have adjusted to their white supremacy; because they are unaware of their racism, they are self-righteous, arrogant, and free from any social conscience with regard to racism. In the past, unless a white was able to break free of his racism and search for the truth, the truth remained hidden.

The native people in a colony are not allowed a valid interpretation of their history, because the conquered do not write their own history. They must endure a history that shames them, destroys their confidence, and causes them to reject their heritage. Those in power command the present and shape the future by controlling the past, particularly for the natives. A fact of imperialism is that it systematically denies native people a dignified history. Whites claim that Métis and Indians have no history or national identity, or, if they do, then it is a disgraceful and pathetic one. When natives renounce their nationalism and deny their Indianness, it is a sure sign that colonizing schemes of inferiorization have been successful.

Two

Halfbreed Resistance to Imperialism

6
The Halfbreed Nation and the Civil War

Halfbreeds became a recognized separate racial group on the prairies during the last half of the eighteenth century. French, English, and Scottish fur-traders had mingled with the Indian population and from these relationships sprang a race of people distinct from both white and Indian society. In some cases, the fathers married the Indian women and established residence in Indian neighbourhoods. However, in these early relationships most fathers returned to white society, leaving the children to grow up in a native environment with their mothers. After 1760 the halfbreed communities began to evolve into a distinguishable society. To a large extent, the development of this Métis society coincides with the period of conflict between the Hudson's Bay Company and the North West Company (1768-

1821). The numerous trading posts established by these trading companies became centres of halfbreed population.

In the early days, halfbreeds followed a hunting and trapping way of life similar to that of the Indians. Gradually they settled down to a more sedentary life, while retaining some of their hunting ways. Many farmed the fertile land around the Red and Assiniboine rivers in Manitoba, which was also an important trading centre for the North West Company and the Hudson's Bay Company on the main path of company trade routes. Furs gathered by Indians and halfbreeds were brought to the Red River forts and exchanged for European goods, and Red River soon became the unofficial headquarters of the halfbreed population. Many descendants of the clerks in the forts were inclined to live close to the trading posts, and clerks were inclined to favour their offspring whenever jobs were available for native workers. But since many fort authorities held these people in contempt, racial bitterness prevailed.

The Red River area was the focal point of the struggle between the North West Company and the Hudson's Bay Company. Since all the trade of the North West Company was channelled through this site, the Hudson's Bay Company decided to block it by bringing in a large colony of Scottish immigrants to settle the area. The land grant for this settlement was "a free grant made by the Hudson's Bay Company to [Lord] Selkirk",[1] and the colony was intended to serve several purposes: the new settlers could act as militia for the Bay, private ownership of the land would interfere with the North West Company fur-traders, and the supply of pemmican for these traders would be checked. With this plan in mind, several hundred settlers were brought to Red River over a period of time beginning in 1812 under the direction of Lord Selkirk, a high official in the Hudson's Bay Company. To defend his settlement, Selkirk later recruited a regiment of Swiss troops and stationed them in Red River. The colony immediately struck at the heart of the North West Company's fur trade and it was virtually a declaration of war. Immediately upon their arrival, the settlers came into conflict with the Indians and halfbreeds because the Hudson's Bay Company took this land of 116,000 square miles as its exclusive property and denied others hunting and trapping rights.

In the decade preceding 1821, a war raged between these two fur-trading giants:

> Unhappily in the interval, the rivalries between the two camps on the Red River became inflamed to the point that, in order to unleash a bloody brawl, nothing other was needed than that one side should provoke the other sufficiently.
>
> While the soldiers Lord Selkirk thought would be useful in the Red River area were being mustered, he gave way to a bad impulse, and wrote to Governor Colin Robertson telling him that, come what may, he must expel the rival company. Robertson needed no instruction to act violently.
>
> This was in the spring of 1816. In the preceding year, four Hudson's Bay employees had been killed in a skirmish when the North West Company took Fort Douglas. Robertson wanted revenge.[2]

The result of Robertson's vengeance was the Seven Oaks Massacre, mistakenly attributed in the history books to Métis "savagery". The long struggle inevitably involved most of the natives in the Red River area. It was important to them insofar as it promoted the development of halfbreed nationalism, largely because the companies solicited halfbreed support for military purposes. These appeals gave the halfbreeds a strong awareness of their own power as a separate race and nation. The North West Company was more successful in obtaining halfbreed support since the Métis had legitimate grievances against the Bay colonists who had taken their lands.

After the union of the two companies in 1821, the Hudson's Bay Company immediately began its revenge against the halfbreeds and Indians. Bay governors imposed even more severe restrictions and oppressive conditions on the native population than formerly. The renewed monopoly market kept many natives in perpetual debt to the Bay, psychologically as well as economically. The Bay imposed this debt-dependency system deliberately on the native trappers:

> An important witness, Allan MacDonell, declared that the Company's system was designed to destroy any capability the Indian might possess of emancipating himself from the bondage of "an

avaricious group of trading monopolists". He described how Indians who attempted to work at another occupation than fur-hunting, were harassed by the company. The object, MacDonell said was to "prevent the Indians learning that there was another pursuit whereby they would become independent of the Company, and cease to be its hunters".[3]

Restrictive conditions were imposed on the native people; for instance, trading or selling of furs between native people was strictly forbidden and it was even against Bay law for a native to make a gift of fur to a friend:

The Hudson's Bay Company even prevented Indians from trading with Indians, or making presents of furs to one another, or wearing furs, "and tried to use missionaries to tell the Indians that the anger of God would follow wearing a foxskin".[4]

After 1821, it became standard practice for Hudson's Bay clerks to break into native trappers' homes with the assistance of Bay police and search for furs held for private use.[5] If any were found, they were seized immediately, without payment, and never returned. On one of these Bay searches, a trapper, after "having his goods seized, had his house burned to the ground and afterwards was conveyed prisoner to York Factory".[6] The Bay's policy extended to whites as well:

Armed constables received orders to search houses suspected of concealing furs bought from Indians. In the execution of their duty, these men committed many revolting acts . . . constables went so far as to burn the house and destroy the traps of two French Canadians at Lake Manitoba. One of the men was blind. For a like offence, a tinsmith of Italian origin was imprisoned and then deported.[7]

Now that the Bay had absolute power, it became increasingly tyrannical in its endeavour to make even greater profits:

[White] hunters could neither sell their pelts to foreigners nor take them out of the country to sell them. It was the Company that set the prices everywhere, and it goes without saying that the

> hunters' profits were slim. However, they were greater than those of the Indians, who were cheated unmercifully. For example, an Indian would receive only one shilling for a skin where a white would receive twenty shillings.[8]

A gun that sold in England for $4.50 was sold to Indians and halfbreeds for five silver fox skins, a value of $250; cotton checkered men's shirts were sold for seven beaver pelts, a profit of over 2,000 per cent. However, some historians argue that paying higher prices to natives for furs would not have encouraged them to trap more:

> A rise in prices would lead to the Indians bringing down less furs, not more . . . [because] the Indian did not react to the ordinary European notions of property, nor to the normal European economic motives.[9]

This is probably true: if the Indians had fully adopted the profit motive, they might have forced the company to pay higher prices; as it was, they had no ideological incentive to do so and were doubly vulnerable to exploitation. Bay traders also made great use of alcohol, particularly rum, to exploit natives even further, and, in spite of resistance by halfbreeds and Indians, Bay officials continued to give themselves greater powers for enforcing the law in the Northwest Territories.

As a result of the Bay's exploitative practices, native people became increasingly aware of their persecution and more united against it. Halfbreeds, who made up two-thirds of the population, began to demand that the Bay be accountable to them and that they have some voice in the administration of the Northwest. In 1845 halfbreed leaders demanded relaxed fur-trading policies, but company authorities refused to make any concessions. Four years later, native people felt that they were strong enough to take a stand against the Bay. When a young Métis was charged for trading without company permission, the halfbreeds organized a protest and demanded that the charges be dropped:

> The whole question was brought to a head in 1849, when Guillaume Sayer and three others were arrested and imprisoned for trafficking in furs. Although convicted . . . Sayer was merely dis-

> missed with an admonition, in view of the hostile manifestations of the Métis, three hundred of whom led by the fiery . . . Louis Riel père, and armed with rifles and buffalo guns, surrounded the Court House. The Métis hailed the decision as a virtual victory for their cause . . .[10]

At the same time, they issued a manifesto of civil rights demanding that free trade be allowed at Red River, that halfbreeds be represented on the local council, and that court proceedings against French halfbreeds be conducted in French. The power of the halfbreed nation became recognized for the first time in 1849, not only by themselves but by the Hudson's Bay Company as well.

Colonial struggles were taking place throughout western Canada in the 1860s. At the base of the trouble was the conflict between two different economic systems – the old economic system represented by the Hudson's Bay Company and the new industrial system. This new ruling class of British financiers and Canadian industrialists had consolidated its position in eastern Canada and was now extending its empire westward across the prairies. They wanted not only the land and the resources of the Northwest, but also a capitalist order that would consolidate and further their economic enterprises, so it was natural that they encountered opposition from the old order of the Hudson's Bay Company. The clash of these two economic systems fuelled the hostilities of 1869-70 in the Northwest, which resulted in Rupert's Land being brought under the constitutional authority of the government in Ottawa, the seat of the industrial empire.

Although native people were involved in this struggle and represented a major force against advancing imperialism, it was basically a civil war between two economic orders. The new capitalist order had to overthrow the political institutions of the old order before it could develop its new society. Up to 1869 the government and judicial system of the Northwest Territories was under the jurisdiction of the Hudson's Bay Company. The government bought the Rupert's Land charter in 1869 in the hope that it could simply transfer power from one set of rulers to another without consulting the people of the land or the Canadian factors of the Bay, the lower rank of rulers in the company. The most important proposed change was the surrender of the Hudson's Bay Company's constitutional authority over Rupert's Land, which would bring the entire Northwest under the jurisdiction of Ottawa. Since the top ruling class of the Bay had become members of the new industrialist class (certain wealthy shareholders of the Hudson's Bay Company, among them Donald A. Smith, had transferred some of their capital to the impending transcontinental railways), Ottawa expected a peaceful subjugation of the Bay empire and a willing surrender of the Northwest Territories. But Ottawa underestimated the strength of the factors within the Hudson's Bay Company. Because they had no share in the £300,000 paid by the government to the Bay and because their wealth and power was derived from the day-to-day fur-trading operations of the company, the factors opposed the transfer of Rupert's Land. According to most Canadian scholars and journalists, the resulting civil war was a rebellion by the Métis of Red River. Portraying it as a rebellion distorts the objective conditions and consequences of this struggle, justifies imperialist conquest, and at the same time falsifies the heritage of native people. The struggle of 1869 was not a rebellion because it was not an uprising against a constitutional government in existence at the time.

Ottawa took over Rupert's Land under the following conditions:

> The Hudson's Bay Company received £300,000 ($1,500,000) in cash. It also was allowed to retain the land — an area of 50,000 acres — around the various trading posts and, in addition, two sections in every township, making a reservation of one-twentieth of the entire region in the fertile belt from the Red River to the Rocky Mountains. For this cash payment and land grant the Company consented to surrender its trade monopoly and all its claims.[11]

However, in 1869 the Canadian government did not yet have constitutional authority to rule over the Northwest Territories, even though the Hudson's Bay Company had agreed to surrender the land. British investors and Ottawa industrialists and politicians such as John A. Macdonald, William McDougall, and Donald Smith stood for annexation of the Northwest Territories because they needed this vast area of land to expand their industrial empire. These people, many of them former directors of the Hudson's Bay Company, recognized where the new wealth and power resided. At the same time, they became a privileged group of investors in the Canadian Pacific Railway (C.P.R.), as well as influential members of the Macdonald government: "We have seen from Macdonald's own testimony how the Prime Minister recommended Mr. Smith for a place on the Board of Directors of the Canadian Pacific Railway."[12] The top directors simply transferred their wealth and power from feudalist to industrialist enterprises, and consequently they wanted the land for industrial and agricultural purposes, not for trapping.

Ottawa's plan to annex Rupert's Land gave no real power to the local residents, no guarantees to the natives of their civil rights or land titles, and was to be imposed on the populace by troops. The local people strongly objected to the arbitrary seizure of their land and homes and the fact that they had not been consulted on the transfer. There were cries of dictatorship and tyranny. The newly appointed governor, William McDougall, who expected personal wealth from the transfer, saw himself in the traditional role of a British governor, riding into a colony with all the pomp and ceremony of a nabob while the natives showed their humility and subservience. It must have been a shock to McDougall when he was met outside the colony by Ambroise Lépine, a native warrior with a gun in his hand and an order to stay out of Red River.

The opposing force of Hudson's Bay Company factors hid behind the native forces and concealed their official position. Some Canadian factors, particularly William Mactavish, who was also the governor of the local Council of Assiniboia, set up by the Hudson's Bay Company to administer what was later southern Manitoba, pretended support for the federal government, while in fact actively opposing Ottawa. Mactavish was still a major shareholder and an official in the reorganized company, but, because of the promises made in the transfer negotiations and the dual position of previous senior Bay shareholders such as Donald A. Smith, he could not openly advocate war against Ottawa. As a result, Mactavish had to play a cunning role, feigning support for Ottawa publicly and at the same time busily organizing resistance forces behind the scenes. W. B. O'Donoghue, one of the leaders in the civil war, claimed that:

> the insurrection was advised by Governor William MacTavish, who, with other officers of the Hudson's Bay Company, also aided and abetted it from its inception to the very hour it ceased to exist.[13]

To prevent Ottawa from taking over, Mactavish had to align himself with the halfbreeds, but he tried to push native resistance to the front so it would appear that they were the main agitators. In this way, he could easily deny association with the Métis if they failed; however, he was careful not to lend them extensive support so that if they were victorious he could quickly subjugate them. Mactavish therefore played a crafty war game in 1869-70:

> Mactavish suggested to Riel that he occupy the Fort . . . at the same time sending McDougall words of encouragement to the effect that Riel had told him nothing at all about his intention to seize the Fort.[14]

However, the Métis were suspicious of the Hudson's Bay officials and did not want to ally themselves completely with the Bay's struggles. Although they had common aims and there was some co-operation and communication between the two forces, each operated relatively independently. The native movement differed from the Hudson's Bay's actions because it involved masses of local people and was, therefore, a democratic political movement. When the Bay charter was sold to the federal government, they saw an opportunity to break free from Hudson's Bay rule and establish a democratic government in the Northwest.

Because these people had dwelt for some time on the fringe of white society, they had some skills in white government and politics and, together with the Indian nation, they represented a large political force: in 1869 the population of Red River included 10,000 halfbreeds, 6,000 of whom were French and 4,000 English and Scottish halfbreeds; there were also more than 1,000 Indians living in the surrounding neighbourhood of Red River. The white population at the time was only 1,500. By 1869, halfbreeds had become politically conscious and concerned about self-sufficiency: they felt that Red River people should have control over their own land and resources. They did not give serious support to the Council of Assiniboia because it was appointed by the Hudson's Bay, and, as the power of the local people developed, the council's power diminished. Worried about its declining position, the council attempted to assert its authority in October 1869 by calling in the Métis National Committee and asking for an explanation of its political activities. The Métis claimed that it had become necessary to organize themselves politically because there had been no recognized government in the Northwest since the Hudson's Bay had sold Rupert's Land in the summer of 1869. As a result, Governor Mactavish had "declared himself stripped of his authority. In this way the country found itself with no established authority other than that of the Métis."[15] The Métis National Committee organized the French halfbreeds for resistance against Ottawa and prevented McDougall, the newly appointed governor, from entering Assiniboia. The halfbreed people were not opposed to joining Confederation, providing they would be assured of title to their homes and land and given their democratic rights. They were, however, concerned about the Ottawa-Bay deal in this regard because negotiations had gone on for several years without a single consultation with local people, so they had decided to oppose all attempts by Ottawa to take over their country.

On December 6, 1869, the native people's militia took control of the entire area of Fort Garry, including the fort and Governor Mactavish's residence. Two days later, they issued a "Declaration of the People of Rupert's Land and the North West". It stated that:

1. When people have no government, they are free to adopt one form of government, in preference to another, to give or to refuse allegiance to what is proposed.
2. The Hudson's Bay Company having abandoned the people, without their consent, to a "foreign power", the people are free to establish a provisional government and "hold it to be the only and lawful authority now in existence in Rupert's Land and the

Northwest, which claims the obedience and respect of the people".
3. The provisional government would "enter into such negotiations with the Canadian Government as may be favourable for the good government and prosperity of this people".[16]

The main points were responsible local government, legal rights, and control of resources, including land. The objectives and actions of the halfbreeds showed that they were advancing on a systematic and responsible political course.

After McDougall had been prevented from entering Red River, he drew up a proclamation condemning the Métis and Mactavish; he slipped across the international boundary during the night of November 30 and nailed the document to a fence-post. As far as he was concerned he had taken possession of the Northwest on paper. McDougall then appointed Colonel J. S. Dennis, a government land surveyor in Red River, as lieutenant-governor and preserver of the peace in the vast expanse of the Northwest Territories. He authorized this "preserver of the peace" to attack Métis, to fire on them, to drive them by force from their homes and fortified places, and "to seize all the flocks, cattle, horses, sleighs and other Métis vehicles".[17] Under Dennis's implicit sanction, a small group of extremist Orangemen from Ontario engaged in clandestine and undemocratic activities against the Métis. They were interested in the colony partly because of the fortunes they expected to make when Ottawa took over. Their leading spokesman was the notorious Dr. J. C. Schultz, a physician from Kingston, Ontario. A principal agitator in this group was Thomas Scott, who tried to stage a *coup d'état* in order to get McDougall into the colony. They unexpectedly did a great deal to advance the struggle of the Red River people, most of whom despised the Orangemen and joined together against the common enemy. Because the Orangemen and their allies supported the federal government, the Northwest people began to consider carefully what kind of government existed in Ottawa and how it would operate in the Northwest. Following these incidents, the people under the direction of Louis Riel moved towards a provisional government on January 25, 1870, with John Bruce, a Scottish halfbreed, as president. Their purpose was to get a guarantee from Ottawa for the protection of their rights before administrative control of the Northwest was constitutionally transferred to Ottawa.

Most of Schultz's gang had been imprisoned by January, but were released once the provisional government was assured of support from the whole settlement. However, they continued to harass the Red River people – by attacking the French halfbreeds, they hoped to gain support from the English population of the settlement. On March 3, 1870, Thomas Scott was brought before the Council of War at Fort Garry. His history in Red River had been one of violence and crime: he had been found guilty of robbery and violent assault and had been sentenced to prison. As an Orangeman and passionate racist he had been involved in intrigues to foster hatred among the population of Red River, and he had instigated a plot for the murder of Riel. Scott had been imprisoned twice in Fort Garry under the authority of the provisional government, and had escaped once by overpowering and beating the guards, at the same time attempting to incite other inmates to do the same. This time, he was charged with having taken up arms against the government and with assaulting a guard. He was tried by a jury of seven men and was allowed to call witnesses and to defend himself. The jury, composed of local residents, found Scott guilty of his crimes and sentenced him to execution. Contrary to the propaganda of the federal government at the time, Louis Riel had nothing to do with his conviction; Riel gave evidence as a witness and in fact pleaded that leniency be shown to the accused. Although Scott's execution was a legal action of the provisional government, Ottawa used it as a pretext to generate a racist hatred against the Métis and the provisional government. Some historians still claim that Scott was harmless, but those alive at the time have unanimously condemned him:

> I now repeat, that Scott deserved his fate, and I defy any living man, who has positively known what sort of a desperate character Scott was, to conscientiously put forward the argument that his death was not a measure of public safety.[18]

An aspect of the civil war that greatly concerned Prime Minister John A. Macdonald and other ruling authorities was the possibility that the United States might annex the Northwest:

> Meanwhile, spurred by reports from Stutsman and scholarly analyses of them by Taylor, annexation fever was mounting daily in St. Paul and on the frontier, and Washington was eagerly watching developments.[19]

The American Congress had already discussed the question of whether this loosely held British territory should be annexed: "It was recalled that President Johnson publicly, in a message to Congress, had approved annexation of the British Northwest."[20] In 1869 the Minnesota state legislature had sent a resolution to the United States Senate in which it declared that it was anxious for the annexation of this Northwest colony. In actual fact, the provisional government officials were in close communication and on friendly terms with American authorities; they were giving serious attention to the question of joining the United States. Ottawa was in a difficult position. Although they ultimately wanted complete control of Red River, they were afraid to send in a military force because the provisional government could immediately appeal to America for support. Time was crucial; the United States was in an advantageous position close to the colony and able to send in supplies and troops easily. Ottawa therefore decided to withhold all serious action and resorted to a pretence of negotiations with the provisional government.

The emissaries from Ottawa who visited Red River during the winter of 1869-70, including Donald A. Smith, were surprised to find that the provisional government had the support of the people. John A. Macdonald and Donald Smith obviously thought of Northwest politics in terms of "money talks" because Smith took with him to Fort Garry money to buy off the provisional government leaders: "So Donald Smith intrigued, spent £500 bribing whom he could, and on January 18-19 spoke, together with Riel, to a two-day mass meeting of the settlers . . ."[21] After being in the colony for only a short time, Smith apparently decided against attempting to buy off halfbreed leaders once he realized that the Northwest people were deeply committed to their resistance.

The local people continued to grow stronger politically through the successes of their provisional government. In February 1870 the executive of the provisional government drew up a "List of Rights" for negotiation with the federal government. The main points may be summarized as follows:

> The Northwest would enter Confederation as a province with the same rights as the other provinces.
>
> This province would be governed by a lieutenant-governor, a senate, and a legislature that would be elected.
>
> There would be two representatives in the Senate in Ottawa, and four representatives in the House of Commons.
>
> This province would not be liable for any part of the public debt of the federal government.
>
> All properties, rights, and privileges presently held by the Northwest people would be respected by the federal government.
>
> There would be no direct taxation for the first five years.
>
> The local legislature would determine the qualifications of the Members of Parliament.
>
> The transfer of the Hudson's Bay to Canada would be withheld where it interfered with the people's rights.
>
> The local legislature would have full control over public lands of the Northwest.
>
> Indian treaties would be made between the federal government and the Indian tribes.
>
> The cost of all public buildings, bridges, roads, and public works would be paid by the federal government.

> Both French and English would be official languages.
>
> All debts contracted by the provisional government in consequence of the illegal measures adopted by federal officials to bring about a civil war would be paid by the Dominion treasury.[22]

Although this was not the final List of Rights that resulted from negotiations with Ottawa, it nevertheless contained the basic points for the province of Manitoba's entry into Confederation. By June 1870, Ottawa had agreed to most of the points in the list as the basic principles for the new government. According to the federal government's promises, the people of Red River seemed to have gained most of the conditions they had been fighting for. The Red River people were to be given self-government rather than colonial status and the provisional government was to remain in charge until the new governor arrived at Red River.

Unfortunately for the Red River people, another plan was unfolding in Ottawa and London. At the same time that federal officials were negotiating with provisional government delegates and making generous promises, they were organizing a military expedition to Red River. The imperial governments at Ottawa and London collaborated on this venture, London bearing the cost of 400 regular soldiers and Ottawa the remainder of the military costs. On July 15, the day Manitoba became a province, troops under Colonel G. J. Wolseley were already well on the way to Red River, ostensibly on a peace mission:

> Since Monseigneur Taché was worried about the military expedition under the command of Colonel Wolseley to secure the West, he was assured that this was merely a mission of peace, to prepare for the arrival of a new Lieutenant-Governor to whom Riel could confer his authority.[23]

The American government, though, much more wide awake than the Bishop of St. Boniface, was not taken in by the Canadian cabinet's protestations of good faith. It recognized that the alleged "peace mission" contained nothing of perceptible value, and it refused point-blank to allow the expedition to cross American territory on its way to Red River. Riel and the provisional government were equally aware of the situation:

> General Lindsay, commander of Her Majesty's forces in British North America, had told him [Riel] that he was only moving the troops from one point to another. Riel, who knew from reports provided by the Indians and from his own scouts what was going on, wrote that he did not want to reply — so much naïveté tired him. He knew that, while they were exchanging ideas, the troops were nearing the mouth of the Red River at Lake Winnipeg. Not only he, but other members of the Council were well aware of the situation.[24]

When Wolseley's forces finally arrived, Riel realized that resistance was futile. The democracy for which the people of the Northwest had struggled was shattered. Ottawa had already rejected several of the conditions previously agreed upon, and, with the campaign complete and Red River occupied by federal troops, Ottawa installed its dominion over Manitoba. The people's democratic government was crushed and the Hudson's Bay Company was revised from its earlier feudal operation and brought into line with capitalist development. A reign of terror against the halfbreeds followed in the wake of Colonel Wolseley and his troops. When they and the Orangemen had finished their violent destruction, the halfbreeds were landless and homeless:

> . . . they went up and down the country drunk with rage and alcohol. The Métis, not cautious enough to avoid them, were instantly insulted. A number of women and girls were molested. . . . On November 30 James Tanner, a Protestant halfbreed . . . was killed with the least plausible pretext while leaving a political meeting at which he had spoken.[25]

In spite of the racial tumult that followed, Louis Riel's popularity remained high enough in Red River that in the 1871 federal elections he was nominated for the district of St. Boniface. However, he allowed himself to be manipulated by Ottawa and Bishop Taché, and surrendered his nomination to Etienne

Cartier. After the death of Cartier the next year, Riel entered the election again. The federal government, fearful of Riel's victory, tried to bribe him: "During the campaign that preceded this election, Federal Government agents offered him [Riel] $35,000 to retire from the contest and leave the country."[26] Riel refused and was elected.

Apparently a Métis leader was politically dangerous, especially as a Member of Parliament. The execution of Thomas Scott, in which he had played no instrumental role, was now used against Riel. Ever since Scott's death, the Orangemen had been clamouring for justice, and a $5,000 reward had been offered for Riel's arrest. Despite this danger, Riel presented himself at the House of Commons in Ottawa and took the oath as a Member of Parliament. Riel's appearance in the House prompted a resolution to bar him on the grounds that he was "wanted for murder". Even though it was legally his seat by virtue of the people's democratic decision, the members of Parliament voted almost unanimously to deny Riel his seat. Racism was apparently stronger than justice in the Canadian House of Commons.

The vote scarred Canadian democracy and has doubtless caused some native persons to question its validity. This parliamentary decision leads one to wonder whether the electoral system will ever work for the Indians and Métis.

7
Subjugation of the Indians and Métis

In order to build the railroad across the prairies, Ottawa had to control land that belonged to natives. As long as the plains Indians remained strong, and capable of defending their rights and their lands, they presented, together with the Métis, a formidable opposition to the imperialist dreams of Ottawa and London. But the strength of the Métis and the Indians depended on an abundant supply of food on the prairies, and it was the buffalo that provided most of the people's needs. The skins were used for clothing, teepees, and bedding; cooking utensils and sleds were made from the bones. Very little of the animal was wasted. Of greatest importance, however, was the meat, which was the main source of native food. Since native people had based their economy on the buffalo hunt, as long as the buffalo was plentiful there was little reason for concern. But by the 1870s overhunting had so reduced the buffalo herds around Red River that the hunters were going as far as the Cypress Hills region of southern Saskatchewan for the pemmican on which the fur-traders, as well as the hunters, depended.

It is well known that the United States, its army, and its government deliberately exterminated the buffalo in order to exterminate the Indians who lived on them. This may have been one of the reasons why many Canadian herds migrated to the grazing lands south of the border. However, the Canadian government was following a policy similar to that of the American government, but with less violence and devastation. It is possible that the Mounted Police were herding the buffalo across the international boundary where they knew the buffalo would be slaughtered. Certainly the increasing export of buffalo hides to the northern United States accelerated the destruction of the Canadian herds. By 1885, when the railroad was completed across Canada, the buffalo was virtually extinct and the Indians and Métis who had depended on it were starving. The sudden and systematic slaughter of the buffalo certainly helped to serve Ottawa's plan. Also, the confinement of the Indians and Métis to reserves and rural ghettos immediately after the slaughter makes it hard to believe that the fact of millions of dead buffalo on the prairies was coincidental. Too many pieces of the imperial plan fitted together too neatly. The truth about the historical situation in the United States very probably applied to Canada as well:

> But the overwhelming force and fire-power brought against the tribes, together with the systematic slaughter of the buffalo herds, the Indians' source of food and the basis of their way of life, finally ended their ability to resist. With their power broken, and their food supply gone, they were gradually confined by the American government on reservations.[1]

After the slaughter of the buffalo, the Indians and halfbreeds were virtually prisoners and beggars, dependent upon the charity and patronage of their white colonizer. Not only were the native people denied their land and economy, but they were also denied the right to participate in the mainstream agricultural and industrial activity of Canada; even construction work on the railroad was denied them. Instead, cheap "coolie" labour was imported, while native people by the thousands were confined to rural "prisons". The death of the buffalo meant the death of the native people's freedom and independence on the prairies.

With the end of the buffalo came the end of the unofficial command the Métis held over the hunting territory. Their administration and policy-making was now restricted to their local communities. The political sovereignty over the plains that they took for granted because of the buffalo economy had now been eliminated by Ottawa authorities.

To complete its expansion plan, Ottawa needed the vast Northwest lands, not only for the C.P.R. but also as an agricultural area for immigrants. Since a market was needed for manufactured goods, European settlers were needed to perform the function of consumers. Once the buffalo were gone, the native people were reduced to complete dependency on whites, and the treaties served to justify the seizure of Indian lands. It was government policy to locate reserves on rocky, sandy, and hilly land. Because halfbreeds were not considered aboriginal people, they were not placed on reserves but were confined on farm colonies and rural ghettos. Some halfbreeds were left with no alternative but to become squatters on road allowances.*

Very few halfbreeds took up homesteads, because the intention behind such land settlement plans was to exclude most of the indigenous people who had aboriginal claims. In the first place, the halfbreeds did not have the required down-payment, small as it was. But, more important, the halfbreeds had lived in the Northwest Territories long before the government surveyed the land and implemented its homestead policies. Halfbreeds had moved into the Saskatchewan area shortly after the Red River struggle in 1870. They selected sites along the river which they divided into river lots. They built homes and developed their farms. As far as they were concerned, this land belonged to them.

*The narrow strips of land between the road itself and the private property on either side.

Nevertheless, the requirements to qualify for a homestead were restrictive, in the sense that certain bureaucratic and legal matters were involved. Also, homestead regulations demanded that a set number of acres had to be cleared, broken, and cultivated within three years. This regulation alone made it almost prohibitive for halfbreeds to own homesteads, because they lacked the machinery and tools to fulfil such development requirements. Halfbreeds were allowed to buy their river lots *after* April 1885.

Superintendent Pearce of the Department of the Interior stated on December 14, 1885, that:

> every Dominion Lands Act which has been in force has contained a provision making it an illegal proceeding to settle on land subsequent to survey without first obtaining entry thereto . . .[2]

Many Métis families settled on the South Saskatchewan River in the 1870s and had unofficially divided their land into river lots. Therefore they were residents or squatters before any survey was made. There was considerable delay in granting entries to the halfbreeds because of the problems surrounding One Arrow's Indian Reserve, which was near Batoche. Pearce stated:

> . . . it was not till November, 1884, that entries could be granted them. When the plan was sent to the agent in March, 1884, so much time had elapsed after the survey had been done on the ground that it was feared complication might arise, and, as the result proved, disputes over certain of the claims had arisen: therefore, I, at that date, verbally instructed Mr. Duck not to grant entry until he had gone through the entire parish, and obtained the evidence necessary to adjust such disputes. So much time had been occupied in obtaining the requisite evidence, as has been explained, that the parties were not notified till late in the following February, or early in March [1885].[3]

Entries were only applications for grants of land and not patents. Therefore it was impossible for the halfbreeds of Batoche to obtain titles to their land before the uprising took place.

Treaties and reserves are common to all native people in colonies around the Third World because they serve the purposes of colonization more efficiently than other forms of imperial conquest. Treaties legitimized the imprisonment of native people under white agents backed by police and soldiers. In return, natives received almost nothing for their land and resources except promises as empty as the treaties themselves. Negotiations satisfactory to two parties are not possible when power is unequally distributed between them. Ottawa officials were bargaining from a position of state power, backed by the Mounted Police and the combined military force of Canada and England. They were familiar with the English language and legal contracts based on English law. The Indians, on the other hand, were powerless: they did not speak English, they were seriously divided, and they were economically dependent; they were on bended knee in supplication to the white negotiators. All this was called treaty negotiation. To most Indians who were forced to attend these spectacles it was an agonizing experience of final surrender to the colonizer. Politically, they were unable to disagree with the terms that white officials dictated to them, but they were not fooled by beautiful speeches about the greatness of reserves or by promises of government charity and protection.

Chief Big Bear* stated that, before he signed the treaty, he had been promised by government officials as much land as he wanted, and wherever he wished to choose it. Without these conditions Big Bear claimed that he would never have signed the treaty.[4] And in the treaty negotiations he took it for granted that these promises were being included as part of the treaty terms. However, the white authorities were still resorting to the old fur-trading practice of bribes. At negotiation proceedings, Colonel Irvine of the N.W.M.P. called Big Bear into his office and gave him a present of $100 and a good horse. This was unprincipled bargaining in many ways. First, it was a bribe to get the Chief to agree to the treaty, which automatically suggests that it was a poor deal for the Indians. Second, it was an exposé of the kind of policies and principles employed by the federal government in dealing with Indians. Also, it showed the mentality of government authorities, in that everything and everybody could be

*A Cree Indian who was Chief of Fort Pitt, N.W.T., in 1882-5 and a rebel leader against General Middleton.

"bought" for a price. On the other hand, Big Bear was also at fault for accepting a horse and $100 as a bribe for selling the aboriginal land and resources of his people. All in all, the Indian people were the losers. This is only one of the many deceitful practices that were used by white agents in negotiating with Indians for their land. While such bribes took place behind closed doors, Governor Alexander Morris was addressing crowds of Indians with flowery speeches behind an armed guard of Mounted Police. The following statements are typical of Morris's speeches:

> I see the Queen's Councillor taking the Indian by the hand saying we are brothers, we will lift you up, we will teach you, if you will learn, the cunning of the white man. All along the road I see Indians gathering. I see gardens growing and houses building; I see them receiving money from the Queen's Commissioners to purchase clothing for their children. . . .
>
> They [Crees] read my face and through that my heart and said my words were true – and they took my hand on behalf of the Queen.
>
> . . . since I was a young man my heart was warm to the Indians and I have taken a great interest in them.[5]

A few years later, the editor of the Saskatchewan *Herald* complained that the government Morris represented was restricting the Indians' hunting-grounds and treating them as wards and incapable children. He claimed that the mortality rate of Indians was deplorable.[6] Governor Morris's warm heart and great interest in the Indians seems to have turned cold and disinterested as soon as the Indians signed their land over. There are two distinct levels of operation in a colonial society: one is the level of rhetoric, ideals, and promises; the second is the level of the actual operation of the system, the daily struggle for existence. In most cases these two levels remain separate and bear little relationship to each other. It is common for government officials who have power over the indigenous people to hold elaborate conferences in luxurious hotels and discuss "Indian problems" with the native élite. At such conferences, great promises are made to improve the conditions of the native people. Noble resolutions are passed for important changes and for social action that will result in considerable benefits to the rank-and-file natives. This is the level of promises and rhetoric. At the same time, the Indian and Métis masses in their ghettos are being humiliated, by having to ask for a few extra dollars of welfare, simply to exist. They know nothing of the conferences or of the great promises that will never be kept.

The colonizer attributes the failure of his promised programs to faulty communications. The rhetoric and promised action never get translated into real benefits for the people at the local level. The colonizer cannot understand the needs, frustrations, and insecurities of the colonized because he has never been locked as a life-member into a reserve or colony, or processed by the ghetto. On the other hand, the native has never had the freedom of the bureaucrat, who has various alternatives in occupational opportunities, or experienced power over others. These two levels are separated by a structure of power. The colonizer will never allow his power to diminish. At the same time, the colonized acknowledges and submits to the authority of the colonizer. The colonizer cannot give any of his power permanently to the colonized, because such gifts can be taken back by the colonizer whenever he wishes. The native would have to seize power, hold on to it, and not share it again with the oppressor. As a result, the oppressor continues to operate at his comfortable level of rhetoric and promises while the native is locked into a daily struggle for existence, uninformed about or at least indifferent to the colonizer's rhetorical promises of improvement.

This dual level of operation was particularly obvious at the time of the treaty negotiations, when the white man made lavish promises to induce the Indians to surrender their land. But the reality of these negotiations was that the Indians lost their land and their rights with very little compensation except for small plots of land known as reserves. A modern example of this principle is Sunday morning Mass. The priest sermonizes extensively on brotherhood and love of mankind; but this same priest later in the week segregates the native people from the whites in the community theatre. Only the white people are allowed to sit in the main-floor front seats, while the Indians and Métis are personally commanded by this Father to sit in the back rows, or upstairs, in inferior seating accommodation.

There were many isolated Indian resistance battles during the period of relocation to reserves. However, Indians were unable to mobilize a major united resistance because of their weakened economic and political position. In 1873, Ottawa established a permanent occupation force of Mounted Police in the Northwest that could immediately crush any people's movement that might arise or threaten the Ottawa régime and served as a constant reminder of Ottawa's absolute power. As a further injustice, the government also took back reserve land from the Indians and then sold it to land speculators:

> Mr. Oliver, the Minister [of Indian Affairs] in charge, heard some plain truths about his administration. The Opposition members severely criticized the notorious deal by which the Department assisted a group of speculators to get the rich lands of the St. Peter's reserve [in Manitoba] from the Indians for a very inadequate price. . . . Mr. Armstrong [a member of the opposition] . . . said this was not an isolated case. The Laurier Government had sold *700,000* acres of Indian land [to speculators], much of it for *ten and fifteen cents an acre.*[7] [Emphasis added]

Treaties made Indian subjugation look honourable, or at least legal. There was little doubt about the underlying purpose of treaties. Treaty Six states that "all Indians . . . do hereby cede, release, surrender, and yield up to the government . . . forever, all their rights, titles and privileges whatsoever to the lands included."[8] The tract of land referred to embraced an area of 121,000 square miles. In case the first clause failed to make it clear, another clause was added to the surrender: "And also all their rights, titles and privileges whatsoever to all other lands wherever situated in the Northwest Territories."* Indians had no say in choosing the site for their reserve: ". . . the superintendent of Indian Affairs shall delegate and send a suitable person to determine and set apart the land for each reserve." This is one policy the government carried out faithfully; in re-

*The same clauses appear in Treaties 3, 4, 5 and 7.

turn for their land, Indians received very little. Terms of the treaty state that "Indians extinguish all claims heretofore", and the government "makes them a present of twelve dollars for each man, woman and child". Thus Indians sold all their rights, titles, and privileges to their aboriginal land for twelve dollars in cash, an annual treaty payment of *five* dollars, and confinement to a stony compound.

Treaty money of five dollars a year certainly looks like conscience money; however, it has a deeper purpose than that. This "charity" has a tremendous influence in creating and retaining within native people a psychological dependency, which, in turn, encourages attitudes of subservience and gratitude. These factors are essential in maintaining effective control over colonized people. By the same treaty, Indians also surrendered their hunting and fishing rights: ". . . Indians shall have the right to pursue their avocations of hunting and fishing throughout the tract surrendered ... subject to such regulations as ... made by her government ..."[9] The federal government therefore has constitutional authority to make regulations prohibiting Indians from hunting and fishing at any time. One clause in the treaty states that "the Government will pay a sum of fifteen hundred dollars per annum per reserve for the purchase of ammunition and twine", but it has rarely been honoured. Some Indians are trying to claim this sum of money today.

Indians must adhere to certain conditions set down in the treaty. In addition to total surrender of their land, titles, and rights, Indians have duties whereby

> They promise and engage that they will in all respects obey and abide by the law, and they will maintain peace and good order . . . they will aid and assist the officers of Her Majesty in bringing justice and punishment to any Indian offending against the stipulations of this treaty or infringing the laws in force in the country so ceded.[10]

Not only were they forced to obey the oppressive laws of their colonizer, but they were required to act as stool pigeons against their people. A tragic consequence of the treaties was that Indians later accepted them as a kind of legal Bible which they felt gave them special right and privileges. This attitude persists with most Indians today. Not only do the treaties represent cruel thefts of aboriginal rights, but they are also contracts of continuing oppression. When Indians hold the treaties as sacred testaments, the process of colonization is indeed complete. Indians possess a certain political awareness today but they still cling to the illusion, dating from the time of the treaties, that they have "citizen plus" status. Indians were not citizens, were judged incapable of participation in society as civilized people, and were denied even the basic right of voting in elections. In fact, they became citizens only in 1961. This is unmistakable evidence as to how the Canadian people and their government regarded the Indians in terms of political civilization. Stanley's statement, which is contradictory in itself, nevertheless is probably typical of the Canadian mentality towards Indians:

> On the whole, Canada has followed the tradition of the Imperial Government in its relations with native tribes, and has endeavoured to deal fairly with her aboriginal wards.[11]

More than four centuries after white men brought "democratic civilization" to North America, the Canadian Indian was still being denied his democratic voting right, and he was being treated as an "aboriginal ward" as recently as 1961. There are few white-supremacy countries that surpass Canada's shameful record in political discrimination. This shows the deep state of colonization of the Canadian Indians who accepted this denial of rights for 400 years.

It is not surprising, therefore, that many Indians held off as long as they could from entering their concentration camps:

> Little Pine and his band . . . having nothing to depend on . . . are selling their horses to buy food, and as they cannot last long, they will soon become so reduced in circumstances as to be glad to fulfill their part of the conditions . . . and settle on the reserve.[12]

Some preferred to die fighting for their independence rather than die on the reserve later from starvation. Chief Yellow Calf and 75 members of his tribe in the Fort Qu'Appelle area refused to go to their reserve and decided to fight it out with their colonizers. Their resistance against the police lasted for two months, but when additional police and troopers were brought in from Regina they were finally crushed and put on their reserve at gunpoint. Indians could see that the economic conditions on reserves would mean a slow death; in some cases, death did not come slowly: "A Cree Indian . . . says that his mother, brother and children died of starvation and that his wife, weary of the suffering she was enduring shot herself."[13]

By 1880 most of the native people had been herded into reserves and colonies where oppression, misery, and death plagued them. A priest of the North Battleford area wrote about the conditions of the Indians in 1883:

> . . . the cakes made with some bad flour did not satisfy the appetite of the Indians. I saw the gaunt children, dying of hunger come to my place. Although it was 30 to 40 below zero, their bodies were scarcely covered with torn rags.[14]

Later, this same priest illustrated the "protection" Indians received when they held their tribal meetings: "All families had gone to join bands . . . for a religious meeting at the edge of Battle River. . . . Later 30 policemen arrived. Later another 30 . . . and again some."[15] There seemed to be an endless supply of Mounted Police at native settlements, but although the federal government could provide scores of Mounties it could not provide funds or food for the starving Indians. The Canadian government's subjugation policy was just as devastating as the extermination method employed in the United States according to this same North Battleford priest:

> . . . the Dominion Government intends to carry out a starvation policy with the Indians, then we will be no better than our cousins across the line whom we condemn so lustily for their extermination policy.[16]

The colonial administration of the federal government divided each plains Indian tribe into several small bands and then appointed a chief for each band. Consistent with colonization principles, Indians Affairs agents made a practice of sowing dissension by exaggerating band and tribal differences so that native people were led to believe that neighbouring Indians and Métis were mean, cruel, and unfriendly. This systematic colonization makes colonized people suspicious of their neighbours, while the colonizers appear peaceful and civilized. The colonizer encourages the different colonial groups to distrust each other and thus keeps them divided and isolated, weaker and easier to control. Since colonizers hold all the power and influence, they are able to manipulate the kind and degree of hostility that will exist in the native community.

For the Indians, reserve life meant the end of basic freedoms such as speech, assembly, franchise, and civil rights. They were not even allowed to leave their reserve without written permission from the government agent, who could grant or deny a pass on the basis of personal whim. The pass permitted the Indian to go only to the place specified on the pass and he had to return to his reserve at the time stated by the agent. This official had the right to ask any question about the Indian's leave and any unco-operativeness meant that the Indian was automatically denied future passes. It is not difficult to imagine how this would be abused, particularly with regard to women. Indians obtained no relief from their chief, even when they elected him themselves, since the pressures exerted on them to elect subservient "Uncle Tomahawk" chiefs were enormous. These chiefs represented the ideology and policies of the Indian Affairs Branch and tended to be conservative and obedient servants to the Indian agents, helping to impose upon their people ideas and programs that would keep them in a colonized state.

8

Causes of the 1885 Struggle

The term "Riel Rebellion" for the hostilities of 1885 is not only misleading but incorrect because it implies that Louis Riel alone was responsible for the hostilities. The truth is that he entered only the later stages of a long struggle involving many groups in the Northwest. The war of 1885 was the culmination of a complex struggle that had arisen over the previous two decades between the people of the Northwest and the industrial rulers of Ottawa. Western protests were made by local merchants, farmers, settlers, workers, Indians, and Métis, and their demands essentially centred around the need for a responsible government to make economic and land reforms. The hostilities of 1885 proved to be an important turning-point in the social and political development of Canada. The new rulers established capitalism in the Northwest, and the way was clear for modern agriculture and industrialism to expand through the private enterprise system.

Although responsible government had been granted to the small province of Manitoba in 1870, including the authority necessary for provincial administration, the federal government had not imposed its constitutional authority on the remainder of the Northwest: "The Territories in 1870 were wholly without government of any form. The institutions of law and order, as understood in civilized communities, were non-existent."[1] Nominal control remained solely in the hands of the lieutenant-governor of Manitoba until 1873, when the governor general of Canada appointed a council to help him. The council and the new lieutenant-governor, Alexander Morris, urged the government to create a police force, the N.W.M.P., which they did in 1873. Control of Indian Affairs and of the N.W.M.P. was retained by Ottawa at this time, and has never been relinquished. Finally, the Northwest Territories Act of 1875 reorganized the Northwest Council and named a lieutenant-governor exclusively for the Northwest Territories, whose population of about 20,000 at that time included 13,000 Indians, 5,000 Métis, and 2,000 whites. The appointed council of five members and a lieutenant-governor had the power to pass ordinances relating to taxation for local purposes, public health, highways, and the administration of justice; however, they did not have a judicial system or a police force of their own capable of carrying out these functions. Ottawa reserved the right to disallow any ordinances passed by the Northwest Council. This pseudo-federal administration was imposed on the Northwest people without their participation and had no connection to their local political development, but, since federal troops did not move beyond Manitoba after the civil war, the Northwest people were able to establish a certain degree of local autonomy. As early as 1873 there was already considerable regional interest and involvement in local political affairs. Unlike the Indians, some Métis were still relatively independent within their communities, and their native councils acted as their local government. At St. Laurent, Saskatchewan, for instance, the Métis population of approximately 800 people became highly organized and very involved in local politics. By 1875 the Métis of St. Laurent had established their own local government, including a five-member council and a president.

Apart from the injustices suffered by the Indians and Métis, discontent among all people in the Northwest, both native and white, began in the early 1880s, mainly centring around economic issues. The cost of machinery was 40 per cent higher on the prairies than in the East. Local wholesale merchants charged a high price for all goods, regardless of whether they were imported or not, while farmers received low prices for their products. Freighting companies, like the Hudson's Bay, imposed excessively high transportation rates. Many farmers who were forced to live on credit were charged high interest and fell increasingly into debt. By 1884 the economic crisis was at its worst: the Northwest land boom had collapsed, C.P.R. construction had almost come to a standstill because the federal treasury was empty, and immigration to the prairies slowed to a trickle as prices for western goods dropped seriously. Moreover, the increasingly authoritarian leadership of Lieutenant-Governor Dewdney discouraged local participation in the political and economic concerns of the community. The people felt themselves to be voiceless victims in a corrupt system; discontent accelerated, with the centre of agitation at Prince Albert, where many land investors had lost large sums of money in 1882 when the C.P.R. route was diverted from Prince Albert to Regina. Throughout the Northwest, the generous grants of land given to the C.P.R. by the federal government angered the people. For example, in one transaction, 17,000,000 acres were given to the C.P.R. even though some of the woodlots in that area had been promised to settlers. These injustices were perpetrated without warning or consultation with residents of the area, leaving many embittered and hostile.

Supporting the Northwest struggle were many different groups. Farmers and Métis felt a bond of mutual oppression and wanted a redress of their shared grievances. Following the recession in the West in 1882, white settlers began to petition for better conditions, but, although they presented their demands to the Macdonald administration on frequent occasions, their requests were ignored each time and they became increasingly aggravated. People at a mass meeting in Prince Albert dealing with the sale of local land to the C.P.R. stated:

> Another sale is shortly to be held, when we may expect just such another outburst of popular feeling. In some parts the settlers threaten bloodshed rather than ejectment and should it come to this, the Dominion Government will be powerless to enforce the law as neither Mounted Police nor Canadian Volunteers will be willing to engage in the work of driving Canadians from their rightful homes in order that the land grabbers may have quiet possession thereof.[2]

A typical conflict arose over the construction of a telegraph line between Humboldt and Prince Albert. A small group of local businessmen favoured by Ottawa received the contract. When the official town committee selected a route contrary to the one chosen by these businessmen and had the poles moved to another location, a member of the group became exceedingly angry. He charged the men who removed the poles with unlawfully and maliciously removing property of the Dominion government. But, when the six defendants appeared in court, they were accompanied by 300 local supporters, many of them armed. The case was immediately adjourned by the presiding judge and the town remained in a state of near-riot for 10 days. On November 15, 1883, when the six accused reappeared in court, the judge quietly dismissed charges because police reinforcements had not arrived to quell the disturbances. Feelings of resentment towards these prominent businessmen and the Hudson's Bay Company had been festering for some time: a militant mood was revealed as early as April, when "rumours were heard of a bizarre plot to seize the Dominion Lands Office in Prince Albert, and hold Governor Dewdney as a hostage until every settler got his patent".[3]

White settlers became insistent in their demands for responsible government throughout the Northwest Territories, not just in the Saskatchewan area. Settlers throughout the Northwest made four basic demands of the Ottawa authorities: first, lower the tariff rates; second, cancel the C.P.R. monopoly at once; third, give provincial status to the Northwest; and, finally, construct the railway to the Hudson Bay. In Manitoba general labour strikes and expressions of protest warned of serious trouble. However, the major weakness of the Northwest people's confrontation was a lack of effective leadership above the local level that could provide systematic organization of the various groups into one integrated force. Emerging from the local white population and shaping the direction of the agitation was William Henry Jackson, a white farmer who was a liberal militant and an effective spokesman. He became one of the major leaders of the white settlers and worked closely with the native people's movement. Together with Charles Adams, president of the English Halfbreeds Association, Thomas Scott, a white farmer, and others, Jackson helped organize the Settlers' and Farmers' Unions throughout the Northwest. Operating at the local level, these groups arranged for the election of delegates to a central committee, which became the governing body of confrontation activities.

In the spring of 1884, a delegation of three including Gabriel Dumont was sent to fetch Riel from the United States, where he had lived in exile since 1873. Macdonald now had in Riel the ideal scapegoat on whom to lay personal blame for the agitation: if shooting began, the Métis would be the victims and Riel was a made-to-order scapegoat.[4] Propaganda was circulated that described Riel as an advocate of hostilities and a leader of the "poor ignorant" Métis who would do what he commanded. Finally, Macdonald began to show a personal interest in the western political scene, although he still pleaded ignorance of Métis grievances: "A month after Louis's arrival Sir John sent a couple of observers to Saskatchewan and informed the Governor General of Canada that he was watching the situation."[5]

The Prime Minister had taken steps to make sure that his opinions of the Northwest troubles would be circulated to the local people by assuming financial control of the Prince Albert *Times* newspaper. On July 18, 1884, he wrote to Lieutenant-Governor Dewdney: "I forget whether I told you that I had arranged to secure the Prince Albert paper, so if any little patronage can be sent them from below, it will be appreciated."[6] Thus, in control of the only Prince Albert communications medium, the Macdonald régime began its task of putting out propaganda against the white settlers' movement. Exaggerations of potential Indian and Métis uprisings were headlined and used to justify the recruiting of police in the area. The presence of a greater number of soldiers and police intimidated the people and threatened the militant leaders.

By the summer of 1884, the Métis and Indians were becoming isolated from the white people's organizations and forces. The leaders realized that some sort of scheme seemed to be working against the whole Northwest people's movement, but they became more determined to resist whatever action Ottawa might launch. A manifesto was issued through the central committee's secretary, William Jackson, on July 28, 1884, which outlined their intentions and actions, and pointed out the need to keep all groups working together:

> To the Citizens of Prince Albert:
>
> Gentlemen:
>
> We are starting a movement in this settlement with a view to attaining Provincial Legislatures for the North-West Territories and, if possible, the control of our own resources, that we may build our railroads and other works to serve our own interests rather than those of the Eastern provinces. We are preparing a statement of our case to send to Ottawa as a matter of form. We state the various evils which are caused by the present system of legislation showing:
>
> 1. That they are caused by the facts that the Ottawa legislators are responsible to Eastern constituents, not to us, and are therefore impelled to legislate with a view to Eastern interests rather than our own; that they are not actually resident in the country and therefore not acquainted with the facts that would enable them to form a correct opinion as to what measures are suitable to North-West interests, consequently liable to pass legislation adverse to North-West interests even when not favorable to their own; lastly that they have not the greater part of their immediate private interests involved in the interest of the said Territories, and are therefore liable to have their judgement warped by such private interests.
>
> 2. That the legislation passed by such legislators has already produced great depression in agricultural, commercial, and mechanical circles, and will continue to increase that depression unless the system is revised; that is to say, unless our legislators are chosen by and responsible to ourselves actually resident in the

country and having the bulk of their private interests involved in the interests of the country.

We give the complete list of our grievances, but instead of asking the redress of each of them separately, we ask the remedy to the root of the evil, i.e., Provincial Legislatures with full control over our own resources and internal administration, and power to send a just number of representatives to the Federal Legislature whatever and wherever that may ultimately lie. Possibly we may settle up with the East and form a separate federation of our own in direct connection with the Crown.

Louis Riel of Manitoba fame has united the halfbreed element solidly in our favour. Hitherto, it has been used . . . [by] whatever party happened to be in power in the East, but Riel has warned them against the danger of being separated from the whites by party proposals.[7]

Throughout the summer of 1884, Settlers' and Farmers' Unions organized and agitated for their cause. Representatives from Qu'Appelle and Assiniboia visited Ottawa to make their demands heard, and the people of the Northwest were clearly prepared politically for organized confrontation with the federal government. They talked as well of secession from Canada and possible annexation to the United States. There was certainly a large number of people in the Northwest Territories who were prepared for annexation, and all that summer more people joined them.

It was a political necessity for Macdonald's government to hold onto the Northwest, since western settlement and the trans-Canada C.P.R. were part of the Conservative Party's promise. The federal government also knew that they had to crush the secession movement and the Northwest agitational forces in order not to lose this valuable land and its resources. The plan constructed by the federal authorities was that they would make certain concessions to the white residents of the Northwest, while at the same time allowing the Métis and Indian situation to aggravate itself to the point of desperation and hostility. In this way, Ottawa could justify troop movements to the Northwest by saying that savages had created an uprising and were massacring innocent settlers. Military occupation of the troubled Northwest in the eyes of the whites of eastern Canada would be not only an urgent necessity but an act of justice on behalf of all Canadians, and Macdonald would be hailed as a hero.

At the Northwest Farmers' Union convention held in Winnipeg in early January 1885, a declaration of rights was drawn up. Basically, it condemned the "oppressive duty on agricultural implements, the monopolistic operation of the C.P.R., and the vexatious methods in the administration of public lands". The members denounced the federal government for its deceitful practices in luring immigrants to the West as "the promised land" when in fact they experienced only hardships and failure. The farmers complained that the price of grain was so low it did not allow even a subsistence living. They claimed that agriculture had been in "a fair state" a few years earlier, but that lately the lands were deserted and overgrown with weeds and the buildings were fast decaying. Their declaration demanded the right to autonomous local government, provincial control of railways and public lands, the removal of custom duties on farm machinery and building materials, representation in the Dominion cabinet, and the construction of a Hudson Bay railway. They wanted greater authority for the Northwest Territories Council; they insisted that council members should be elected by local residents rather than appointed by friends of John A. Macdonald, and they demanded lower tariffs, systematic marketing of their goods, better homestead laws, and local control over large land companies. In short, they wanted an end to the corruption of the Northwest administration. These requests were ignored by the Macdonald government.

Although the white farmers and settlers were experiencing serious problems, the Indians and Métis were suffering even greater economic difficulties in the early 1880s. Chiefs complained that many of the great promises made by Ottawa during treaty negotiations had not been kept. Councillor Fine Day of Battleford Reserve stated that "most Indians had come into reserves by 1882, but it was very much against their wishes. It was either come in, or starve to death."[8] He claimed that his people were trying to make a living by cutting cordwood, but they received so little pay for their wood that it barely kept them from starvation: "The Government's policy could be summed up in six words: feed one day, starve the next."[9]

> From the Touchwood Hills, the Interpreter reported a similar state of starvation: "I beg to inform you that the Indians around here are starving very badly . . . I fear that many of these people will not see spring."[10]

Indian Affairs officials apparently felt that once the Indians were placed on reserves they would become totally conquered people who could be treated as subservient children. Some of the worst Indian Affairs officials were those at Frog Lake. The Hudson's Bay factor there stated: "They ill-treated these poor people in a most brutal manner. They kicked them, beat them, and cursed them in a most revolting fashion. Two stood out as particularly miserable beasts."[11] The local minister held a similar opinion of these officials: ". . . in numerous instances, the way they treated the natives could not but produce harmful effects. Certain men treated the Indians like dogs."[12] The fort officials also exploited their positions:

> At the beginning of winter, the Government agents halved the Indians' rations and sold the excess for their own profit. The Indians could not complain of this shameful practice because all the Government representatives did the same thing, right from the Governor of the Territories down to the sub-agents on the Reserves.[13]

By the spring of 1884, the economic conditions of the Indians were so serious that Chief Poundmaker called an assembly of Indians of the Northwest. He claimed that Indians realized they had made a serious mistake in agreeing to treaties with the federal government. Superintendent Crozier of the Mounted Police attempted to arrest the Indian chiefs for assembling, but they were so desperate that they defied Crozier's authority.

The Métis, likewise, were close to starvation, since their means of livelihood had practically disappeared, and in 1878 they began petitioning the federal government for assistance. As Riel had stated, these lands belonged to them once through original title, twice for having defended them at the cost of their blood, and thrice for having cultivated and inhabitated them. The Métis had requested assistance in obtaining seed grain and farm implements, but, instead, they were asked by the federal government to pay two dollars per acre for their own farms which they had improved and developed. Between 1878 and 1884, the Métis submitted 84 petitions to Ottawa requesting better conditions and better services. Not one was answered. According to an Ontario newspaper: "The Half-Breeds of the plains have not been dealt with by the present government. On the contrary, steps were expressly taken in the direction of delay."[14] Not even Mounted Police requests for assistance to the halfbreeds stirred the government. Sergeant Kennan explained the serious economic conditions and the need for government action in a letter to Superintendent Crozier in September 1884:

> The crops here are almost a total failure and everything indicates that the halfbreeds are going to be in very straitened conditions before the end of the coming winter which of course will make them more discontented and will probably drive them to an outbreak and I believe that trouble is almost certain before the winter passes unless the government extends some aid to the halfbreeds during the coming winter.[15]

Such concern was unusual, coming from the Mounted Police. According to popular explanation, the Mounted Police force was established to prevent whiskey traders from buying Indian furs, which the Hudson's Bay Company claimed as its exclusive right. However, it is not just a coincidence that the Mounted Police were established during the development of Indian reserves to ensure the "success" of the treaty negotiations with the Indians and "help" relocate Indians and halfbreeds to their reserves and colonies. The Mounted Police had the responsibility of patrolling the reserves and Métis communities but proved instead to be a source of oppression and agitation, much disliked by the native people. Councillor Fine Day claimed that the Indians suffered brutality under the Mounties, who frequently paraded through native settlements in order to intimidate the people and remind the natives that they had to "stay in their place". When the Hudson's Bay factor at Fort Carlton complained to the Mounties that the halfbreeds were becoming lawless and threatening a rebellion, 50 Mounties marched into the Métis community of Batoche and threatened the entire population. They attempted to arrest Gabriel Dumont, Chief of the

Batoche Halfbreed Council, and at the same time terrorized the people. This display of force successfully intimidated most of the natives, as it was intended to.

The Indians, who had lived in the area for thousands of years without police, saw no reason for the establishment of a force in the Northwest since there was no serious disorder or lawlessness in the country. To the native people, this military force was similar to the federal troops who had invaded Fort Garry in 1870. The Mounties were not ambassadors of goodwill or uniformed men sent to protect Indians; they were the colonizer's occupational forces and hence the oppressors of Indians and Métis. The volumes written about how helpful and understanding the Mounties are towards native people are sweetheart myths written by "WASP"s* who have never experienced insults, beatings, and bullets from a Mountie.

The attempt to arrest Dumont was particularly resented by the Métis, since the Batoche Halfbreed Council was a representative body elected by the local people of Batoche, St. Laurent, and St. Louis, which they felt should be respected. The council had 15 members, a president, and a constitution:

> The inhabitants of St. Laurent held a public assembly to draw up laws and regulations for the peace and tranquility of their community. In the absence of any form of government among them to administer justice and to judge the differences that may arise among them, they have thought it necessary to choose from among their number a Chief and Councillors invested with power to judge differences and to decide questions and matters affecting the public interest.
>
> The Chief with the members of his Council is elected for one year and during their term of power, the president and the members of Council are empowered to judge all cases that shall be brought before them. The Chief, by the advice of his Council, can convoke the general assemblies of the public, in order to submit for their decision matters of higher consequence, concerning which they would hesitate to pass orders without knowing the opinion of the majority of the public.[16]

*White Anglo-Saxon Protestants.

Since most Métis people were directly involved in the difficult political issues of their community, they had a fairly good understanding of the struggles they encountered in making a living and dealing with the federal government. A specific issue that had generated considerable anxiety among the Batoche Métis was the land claim of the Prince Albert Colonization Land Company. A confrontation with this company was developing because attempts were being made to seize a vast tract of land in St. Louis on which several halfbreed families had settled. The Métis had decided that they would make a stand on this issue. This became a serious confrontation. The Prince Albert Colonization Land Company was composed of cabinet ministers' relatives and top government officials. At the same time, the halfbreeds made a stand on this land deal, "to protect it with guns, if necessary". It remained largely as a stand-off until after the halfbreeds' defeat at the Battle of Batoche. In the confusion that followed, it is likely that most halfbreed families lost their land, as some of the men were sentenced to penitentiary terms.

Another source of agitation in the Northwest was Governor Dewdney, a corrupt and arrogant man who encouraged similar attitudes among his subordinates. Besides cheating the Indians of their rations, Dewdney and his government generally held these people in contempt and were likewise corrupt and dictatorial in their dealings with white people. He neglected his duties as governor and spent his time dealing in lands, mines, and timber. Although Dewdney had been approached by the people of the Northwest concerning their grievances, he did little to alleviate their suffering: his response was a message to Macdonald suggesting that more troops should be sent west if the agitation continued. The governor also retained a great deal of personal power over the people within his jurisdiction. Individuals were unable to keep liquor in their homes unless Dewdney personally granted them this privilege and he reserved the right to revoke these permits at any time if he was dissatisfied with the permit-holder's behaviour. Because the Northwest Territories Council was subservient to him, Dewdney made himself virtually an absolute ruler in the Northwest.

Contrary to the traditional interpretation, Louis Riel was not the main source of agitation in the Northwest struggle of 1885.

The Batoche halfbreeds had a local government whose council members and president were democratically elected. Under these circumstances it was not possible for Riel or anyone else to come to Batoche and take over individual control of the people and their government. The decision to invite Riel to Saskatchewan was taken after the matter had been discussed by people in several districts, both native and white. The invitation specified what Riel would have to do and his main function was to aid the people of the Northwest in their constitutional struggle. He was responsible to the people and therefore took direction from them: "That there is anything in Mr. Riel's ability as a leader to cause alarm is not believed by those who have had the opportunity of judging him . . . his own statements are so pacific in nature that no one could be surprised to hear of his volunteering for missionary work."[17] Riel was working for the Northwest people's movement, not leading it. He was not in a position to command the forces of confrontation, and he tried to persuade the Métis people to avoid violence and separation from the white people's forces. As William Jackson stated in his formal statement to the citizens of Prince Albert:

> . . . in regard to his public attitude it is better to accept his services *as long as he works for us. . . .* As long as both elements work on the square, doing justice to each other, there will be no clash, but a marked advance toward our end, i.e., justice in the North-West.[18] [Emphasis added]

9 Ottawa Invades the Northwest

The federal cabinet was watching developments in the Northwest very carefully. They needed to bring the entire Northwest under their command, but the Mounted Police had neither popular support nor sufficient staff to command the Northwest Territories. In addition, the depressed economy had to be revived so that immigrants would move to the prairies and buy land. Above all, the construction of the C.P.R. had to be reactivated.

In order to attract new financing for the C.P.R. a new plan would soon have to be devised and implemented for improving the economy. The Canadian people had earlier called a halt to the millions of dollars of public tax money being given to the

C.P.R. and Macdonald was under pressure to restore public faith in the railroad. British financiers had also postponed investing in the C.P.R. until economic conditions in the Northwest improved. A comprehensive plan was needed to aid the economy, but this was impossible as long as Ottawa did not have control over how the Northwest was to be governed and administered. Although a military invasion was a drastic measure, it was the simplest and most efficient method of achieving this control; the main problem was to make it appear to be necessary for the sake of law and order in the Northwest, so that Macdonald could escape political censure from the Liberals in the East. To justify a military invasion, the Macdonald government obviously allowed the Indian and Métis problems to become aggravated and possibly even encouraged them so that conditions would result in violence.

Ottawa had been recruiting soldiers and policemen a full year before March 1885. The Prince Albert *Times* reported in March 1884 that a circular was published calling for 5,000 recruits to do army service. In April 1884, 200 additional police had been recruited. In the following month,* the Prince Albert *Times* reported that 20 additional police and 150 militia were sent to Fort Carlton:

> Such a movement was calculated to have the twofold harmful effect of showing the Métis that Ottawa intended repressive measures instead of the just settlement of their difficulties on the one hand, and of providing more profits for North-West business interests on the other.[1]

Throughout the entire year a build-up of troops and police took place. By the spring of 1885 western Canada looked like a military camp; the police force at Battleford had been doubled, while that of the Prince Albert area had been tripled. Superintendent Crozier of the Mounted Police regularly requested additional police, and the federal government leased Fort Carlton from the Hudson's Bay Company in 1884, for one year, for use as a police fort.

*Before Macdonald took control of the paper.

The expansion of the army, Mounted Police, and militia indicated that a military invasion of the Northwest was imminent. The central committee of the Settlers' and Farmers' Union suspected that the Macdonald government might try to provoke an incident justifying an invasion of the Northwest, and Jackson urged his people to refrain from forcibly taking charge of their own affairs. It soon became evident that Ottawa had chosen the halfbreeds as scapegoats: Governor Dewdney had requested protection in case of a halfbreed attack; local authorities, trying to present the Northwest people's struggle as a strictly racist uprising of Indians and halfbreeds, were sending propaganda in their communications to Ottawa that reached the eastern news media and was read by whites throughout the nation; furthermore, the Prince Albert *Times,* under Macdonald's control, intensified its racial stories and was partly successful in alienating some white support from the Indians and Métis.

The Ottawa régime apparently had considerable help in its intelligence work and subversive activities from a halfbreed named Charles Nolin. Serving as a provocateur for the federal government in 1885, Nolin assisted in bringing about the initial armed clash between halfbreeds and Mounted Police which made possible Ottawa's military conquest and occupation of the Northwest Territories. Nolin's history of political activities goes back to the Red River war in 1869. In Manitoba he was active in the halfbreed struggle and in the provisional government. After Manitoba became a province, Nolin was appointed minister of agriculture, thus occupying a position of considerable significance. Howard claims that:

> Nolin was a prosperous, cautious and ostentatiously pious man . . . a Mountie who had kept him under surveillance regarded [him] as "the most intelligent and most dangerous" of the malcontents. Unlike the other leaders of the Red River movement in 1870 he had quickly made his peace with the Manitoba government and had been briefly a member of the Provincial Cabinet. . . .
>
> In the early stages of the Saskatchewan agitation Nolin had been especially valuable to the Métis because of his education, his skill in drafting communications to Ottawa, and his political prestige; but Riel had good reason to distrust him.[2]

The main reason for this distrust was that Nolin was in continuous communication with all the priests in the Batoche area. The Métis council knew that the priests and particularly Father André communicated frequently with Macdonald and his government, but the Métis were sufficiently devout and faithful to their clergy that they did not suspect their irregular activities, at least not in the beginning.

Nolin worked in close co-operation with the priests from the beginning of the agitation, a fact that suggests that he was working for the government. There is no other explanation for the co-operation between these two diverse factions, since Nolin advocated violence and the priests advocated non-violence. It is a recognized fact that the priests were communicating with and aiding the government:

> After resorting to all possible ways of undermining the insurrectionist movement, these Missionaries [Fathers André and Fourmond] did not hesitate to fill the role of informers for General Middleton, commander of the Federal troops — and furnish him with complete information that their privileged situation among the rebels gave them access to.[3]

As early as 1884, Father André sent communications to Macdonald describing the situation in the Northwest and offering advice as to what should be done. Possibly Nolin received his instructions from Ottawa through the priests.

However, as political circumstances turned for the worse, council members looked more seriously at the priests' mysterious activities. Certain members decided to take action: "From Council Members we learned that Dumont finally became exasperated by the intrigues of Father Végreville who did everything to disrupt the movement."[4] The council held Végreville for a short time, but finally "freed him on condition that he cease his activities".[5] Végreville's secret nightly rendezvous with Nolin had to stop:

> When Charles Nolin, flanked by Federal policemen who guarded him all the time, made nightly visits to the St. Laurent presbytery, the Council wanted to know why. It sent Napoléon Nault and Patrice Fleury to find Father Fourmond to have him explain the nature of his interviews with Charles Nolin.

> Father Végreville accompanied Father Fourmond. No sooner were they seated in the Council house than Riel asked Father Fourmond the reasons for Charles Nolin's comings and goings. Father Fourmond, not a patient man, lost his temper and spoke sharply to Riel.[6]

Howard explains in his book that a system of communications was operating between Father André and John A. Macdonald. Shortly after Riel arrived in Batoche in 1884, Macdonald informed André that he was watching the Métis situation through intelligence surveillance. According to Howard, "They [the government] could count upon Father André to keep them informed of developments."[7] The Métis people were aware of André's work as an informer to the government, but they disapproved of it: "The secrecy of his [André's] operations among the people also was condemned . . . since André was regularly reporting to the Governor . . . the priests had become informers."[8] Even after Nolin fled to Prince Albert and to the police on March 26, "Father André maintained constant contact with Charles Nolin after his defection."[9] As a result, Nolin had relatively easy access to private communications with John A. Macdonald and other officials from the time of his arrival in Saskatchewan until after the Métis were suppressed.

All the time that Nolin resided in the Batoche community he was intimately involved in the Métis struggle. He served on the council and was one of the main leaders. In the provisional government, Nolin was the commissioner. However, he had a very special function within the halfbreed community of Batoche: the treacherous activities of a provocateur. In this capacity, his main function was to get the Métis to take up arms against the government. In this onerous task of a call to arms Nolin had to agitate towards a confrontation incident that would bring police action against the Métis in the guise of maintaining law and order. Nolin had to develop the agitation to the point where the Mounties and Governor Dewdney would believe that a halfbreed uprising was inevitable. In this task, of course, Nolin had the help of John A. Macdonald, who simply by his inaction deliberately allowed the halfbreed agitation to accelerate. The name of "Old Tomorrow" had more meaning than simply a procrastinator; its meaning was more closely related to a schemer, at least in this particular case:

> The Ottawa authorities ignored it [the petition] as they had all other petitions; they were either filed away somewhere or tossed into the waste paper basket.
>
> . . . The meetings continued with more petitions being signed and sent to Ottawa. This lasted all winter. No replies were ever received from Ottawa.[10]

Macdonald was in close communication with the developments in the Northwest from many sources: Governor Dewdney, Crozier, André, Nolin, etc.; therefore, he was fully aware of the effects and implications of his silence and inaction on the Métis petitions. Also, he knew precisely the political developments and moods that were emerging from his deliberate "do-nothing" policies. Doubtless this would assist Nolin greatly in rousing the halfbreeds to take up arms. Nevertheless, Nolin was not leaving things to chance. He was busily engaged in agitating armed insurrection.

According to Trémaudan, the Métis people whom his committee interviewed in the early 1900s, and who had witnessed the rebellion, claimed that Nolin was the strongest advocate of armed rebellion:

> According to the unanimous testimony of all those we interviewed at Batoche, Charles Nolin was primarily responsible for the taking-up-of-arms. Everyone accused him of being the author of all the wrong they had endured. It was he who first spoke of shedding blood in September 1884 and again on February 24, 1885, and sometime afterwards again . . . he had boasted of having 800 men with whom to seize Fort Carlton.[11]

The Mounted Police were very concerned about Nolin's urging violence and resorting to armed struggle. Sergeant Kennan reported this to his superior:

> Charles Nolin, another member and one of the most unreasonable, proposed that the Halfbreeds make certain demands on the government and if not complied with, they take up arms at once

> and commence killing every whiteman they can find and incite Indians to do the same.[12]

He constantly spoke in favour of stirring up the Indians so that the Ottawa government could justify the movement of troops into the area. Historians, journalists, and reporters claim that Nolin broke with the Métis over the issue of taking up arms against the government. According to most writers, this break is supposed to have happened on March 6. This date is given because it is the date Nolin claims he turned against Riel, according to his evidence in the trial. If this was true it would mean that Nolin had opposed the Métis council for the last 20 days that he was associated with them. But, in fact, he did not; he was one of the active supporters of violence. Found among the Batoche documents in May 1885 was a letter written by Riel's council to the English halfbreeds. It is dated March 21, 1885, and it reads as follows:

> To the English Halfbreeds of Red Deer Hills
>
> Dear Brothers in Jesus Christ – The Ottawa Government has been maliciously ignoring the rights of the original halfbreeds during fifteen years. . . . Justice commands us to take up arms.
> (Signed) Charles Nolin[13]
> [and 16 other Métis
> including Riel]

This is consistent with Trémaudan's explanation. He claims that the Métis did not resort to arms until March 18 when Lawrence Clarke, a Hudson's Bay factor who had just returned from Winnipeg, told the Métis what he considered official information, stating that:

> . . . 500 policemen are on the way here to keep them [Riel's council] quiet. In answer to your requests, they have chains for Riel and bullets for the members of his Council. You will soon have news of them. I met them at Humboldt.[14]

This information shocked the Métis. They had not actually expected police and bullets as a response to their petitions. As a result of this information a meeting was called the next day that was attended by both French and English halfbreeds. The question of armed resistance was the only issue discussed. Finally, it was decided unanimously to resist the federal government's police. Charles Nolin was one of the most ardent advocates of armed resistance. In his main provocateur task of getting the halfbreeds to take up arms, Nolin was now successful. However, it was precisely at this point that Riel became suspicious of Nolin and his intrigues with the priests and government. Possibly Nolin had become somewhat arrogant, overconfident, and jubilant of his success and allowed himself pleasantries that exposed him as a conspirator. In any case, the Métis council arrested Nolin as a traitor of the Métis people, and not because he failed to take up arms. He was court-martialed by the council and condemned to death. According to Howard, "the people were again summoned to the church and Nolin was taken there under guard; no one apparently protested against the severity of the council's action [against Nolin]."[15] However, the priests intervened on behalf of Nolin and convinced the council members that Nolin's secret action had not harmed the Métis people and that he was truly dedicated to the honourable cause of the Métis people. Doubtless Riel and the council were convinced, because Nolin was allowed to go free and to continue to participate in the movement.

Nevertheless, Riel was not entirely satisfied about Nolin's suspicious activities in relation to the priests. To Riel, these were subversive activities that were opposing his efforts of constitutional agitation and leading instead to violent warfare. The discovery of the intrigues and their possible continuance bothered Riel so much that he wanted to return to the United States. However, on March 19 a provisional government was formed. Pierre Parenteau was elected president; Charles Nolin, commissioner; Gabriel Dumont, adjutant-general; Baptiste Boyer, Donald Ross, Damase Carrière, Ambroise Jobin, Norbert Delorme, Moïse Ouellette, Baptiste Parenteau, David Tourond, Pierre Gariépy, Maxime Lépine, Albert Monkman, and Baptiste Boucher, members of the council; and Philip Garnot, secretary. Although "provisional government" was a common term among the Métis, it had originally meant only an organized hunting party on a particular buffalo hunt. Used by historians, provisional government has a constitutional meaning. Nevertheless, this provisional government meant that the Métis had accommodated one of Nolin's tasks, as a provocateur. A formally organized government had arisen among the Métis. And what was important was that Riel had been kept in the leadership.

The most difficult and dangerous tasks that Nolin faced as a provocateur were to rouse the halfbreeds to an unlawful confrontation incident that would force the police to act, to maintain law and order; and, secondly, to have the Métis council expand its confrontations so that Ottawa authorities would sincerely believe that a halfbreed uprising was inevitable. On March 4 Nolin was caught behind schedule with his plans for a systematic development whereby all hostile parties would come together at the right time for the explosion. To his surprise, Nolin was informed by Riel that the Métis were taking up arms. For one thing, the Mounted Police were not yet properly mobilized. Commissioner Irvine of the N.W.M.P. was not leaving Regina with his 108-member force until March 18, and he would take approximately seven days to make the journey. Although Superintendent Crozier at Fort Carlton had approximately 100 police and another 50 volunteers, that was inadequate to deal with the armed Métis warriors. Primarily for this reason Nolin was able to convince the Métis council that a novena, nine days of special prayer, should be held. Beginning on March 10, the novena would end on March 19. These nine days would permit Nolin to get all the essential information out to government authorities, through the priests; it would also allow him time to accelerate the confrontation activities and heighten the mood of militance, defiance, and hostility. Osler says that Nolin was stunned when he heard Riel talk of taking up arms, capturing hostages and acts of guerilla war:

> Momentarily, Charles Nolin was stunned by the impact of these words. He, himself was essentially a schemer; the thought of rushing headlong towards total commitment appalled him. Then a possible means of causing delay suggested itself to him. . . . Then why not ask the priests to organize a novena to him?[16]

During the next few days Nolin helped push circumstances

towards open hostilities. With Maxime Lépine they delivered a message to Superintendent Crozier demanding that he

> give up completely the situation which the Canadian Government have placed you in, at Carlton and Battleford, together with all Government properties. In case of acceptance, you and your men will be set free, on your parole of honor to keep the peace.[17]

Of course, this ultimatum to Crozier was intended to aggravate the already tense situation and challenge Crozier and his excited recruits. A hostile confrontation was beginning to take shape as expected and the jigsaw pieces were fitting together as planned, though somewhat precariously. Howard, discussing the situation on the eve of hostilities, stated:

> But just to be safe he [Macdonald] would anticipate the wishes of Parliament and would increase immediately the strength of the Mounted Police. Superintendent L. N. F. Crozier in charge of the northern detachment at Battleford had warned that unless the Métis were placated soon more police would be needed.
>
> This was precisely what Sir John had been warned by Father André not to do, but obviously it held much more appeal for him than the wearisome sifting of petitions and a genuine effort to meet the terms of the distant colonists. So in September [1884] he shoved aside the letters from the Northwest and wrote a confidential note to Donald A. Smith of the Hudson's Bay Company.
>
> Would the Company lend the Government its buildings at Fort Carlton, about twenty miles west of Batoche, to be used as emergency quarters for additional Mounties? I write you privately, Sir John said, "because it is not well that any intelligence should go to the Northwest of our intention to increase the force, in advance."[18]

Part of this increased police force for which Macdonald had planned was Commissioner Irvine's 108-man troop that bypassed Fort Carlton and went directly to Prince Albert, arriving on March 24. This was two days before Superintendent Crozier and his policemen made their attack on the Métis at Duck Lake. Why did Irvine and his men go directly to Prince Albert and then wait there for two days, when the situation at Batoche,

Duck Lake, and Fort Carlton was in a state of crisis? Did Macdonald not want such a huge force of Mounted Police and militia stationed at one location? Would Ottawa's intentions become too obvious? Would such a large force overpower and totally crush the unorganized Métis in its first encounter, and thus end forevermore the halfbreed uprising? Did Nolin blunder in his secret communications? There were spies operating on both sides, therefore each knew the fighting strength of the other.

For the next few days Mounted Police and their spies made scouting trips around Duck Lake and Batoche; in turn, Dumont and his warriors kept a close survey on the developments around Fort Carlton and Duck Lake. The economic situation of the Métis and Indians by the end of March was desperate; some were starving. A Toronto newspaper stated the situation clearly:

> The whole trouble has manifestly been provoked by a wanton disregard of the rights and wishes of these people [Métis] in the first instance, and then by neglect and indifference on the part of the First Minister and his subordinates which were positively criminal.[19]

The hungry Métis were not about to perish silently while the neighbouring stores held an abundance of food and goods. The double-barrelled agitation of the Métis people, caused first by Macdonald's total neglect and second by Nolin's agitation for hostilities, was about to reach the point of igniting. On March 25 Gabriel Dumont and a small group of Métis journeyed to Duck Lake and seized goods from the Stobart and Eden store. The circumstances surrounding the ransacking of the store seem to have been prearranged. Hillyard Mitchell, one of the merchants who was also a spy for the Mounted Police, was absent. According to Trémaudan:

> He [Mitchell] had launched so many threats just a few days before he had cleared out . . . only one clerk was there, Magnus Burnstein, who hastened to give him [Dumont] the store keys. Dumont helped himself to some merchandise and left the next day with ten men.[20]

Also, the stores had been recently stocked with a supply of guns and ammunition. Yet these merchants and Mounted Police at Carlton knew precisely the recent militant activities of the Métis, and their call to arms only a few days previously. They were fully acquainted with the Métis' militant mood and state of desperation. The goods at the store were readily available to the Métis. Why was there no police protection? Crozier's spies knew what was going on in the Métis community. Likewise, Nolin, being on the council, was aware of the raiding plan. It is interesting to note that Nolin did not take an active part in this confrontation incident. This would keep him clean for his evidence against Riel in the trial.

As soon as the first shots were fired in the Duck Lake battle, Nolin fled to Prince Albert as fast as possible.

> He took his sister-in-law's wagon and fled, protesting that he must not be delayed, that he was going to seek God's help for the wounded. In Prince Albert he sought police protection and from that moment became an informer on those whom he had encouraged to rebel.[21]

For the next several months Nolin was well protected, because he was valuable as the main witness for the prosecution at Riel's trial. The federal government and the media promoted Nolin as a great patriot, a highly respected man, and a special favourite among the Catholic priests. Therefore, his evidence was readily accepted as being credible. He was generously rewarded by the Ottawa régime with a grant of money and the important position of magistrate in the Northwest Territories. His signature appeared at the bottom of numerous declarations against his former colleagues and leaders.

While preparing for the invasion, the Macdonald cabinet carefully isolated the Indians and Métis from the white people. Some time before the battle at Duck Lake, federal authorities made concessions to the white people's forces of the Northwest without surrendering any of their political power. A very effective way of dividing the Northwest forces, these concessions disrupted and gradually immobilized the white people's movement. Ottawa agreed to reduce freight rates, allow elected representatives on the Northwest Council, improve the granting of land and homesteads, and make other minor changes demanded by the white settlers. They were enough to confuse and dissipate the militancy of the Settlers' and Farmers' Unions to the extent that they were forced to stop and discuss the validity of the proposals. Some people felt they had won adequate reforms and that there was no need for further agitation or action, so they removed themselves from the struggle. This was the first major victory for Ottawa and it would allow the government a full and final triumph against the remaining forces.

On March 21, 1885, five days before the Duck Lake battle, John A. Macdonald publicly announced to Canadian citizens that halfbreeds had taken up arms. In fact, before the Duck Lake battle, the Métis had not been engaged in any armed hostilities whatsoever. Major-General Sir Frederick Middleton, commander of the invasion forces, began to move his troops west as early as March 23. This action was ordered by the Prime Minister without the consent of Parliament: when questioned about it in the House, Macdonald expressly denied doing it. He was later forced to admit that he had misled the House of Commons.[22] When the news of Middleton's advance came east many more soldiers volunteered to go west and suppress the uprising.* On March 25, the 90th Regiment of the Winnipeg Rifles marched off to Qu'Appelle in the Northwest Territories. Between March 23 and 25, an additional force of Mounted Police reached Prince Albert. All these military moves took place before the battle of Duck Lake on March 26, and Commissioner Irvine with his 100 police arrived at Fort Carlton while Major Crozier was at Duck Lake attacking the halfbreeds. Some of the local men joined the government forces only to divert suspicion from themselves as members of the early protesting forces: ". . . more than one of them kept up communication with the enemy [the halfbreeds] and betrayed the secrets of the garrison".[23] The majority of the troops came from Manitoba and eastern Canada.

Although the enemy was approaching, the Métis people refused to desert their homes and flee, but decided instead to de-

*This word is used here and elsewhere, despite the colonialist connotations. In truth this was a resistance action, but the term is clumsy.

fend themselves the best they could. They knew the countryside well and were skilled in riding, shooting, and ambushing; in short, they were excellent guerilla fighters. When Superintendent Crozier's forces attacked the Métis community of Duck Lake on March 26, he was well aware that he would encounter resistance – but his men advanced in a reckless and naïve manner. A military force composed of 177 men, several horses, sleighs, ammunition, shields, and a cannon made slow and easy targets for the Métis hunters. Gabriel Dumont and 27 other halfbreed guerillas had stationed themselves on a small wooded hill near their homes. In the battle, which lasted only 45 minutes, the police were completely routed and forced to retreat. Dumont with 15 Métis pursued the police, attempting to surround them in hand-to-hand combat. Riel, who had just arrived on the scene, pleaded with Dumont for the lives of the enemy. Dumont granted his request because of his affection and respect for Riel. The Mounties left behind 10 dead and one wounded; five halfbreeds lost their lives. The hurried retreat of Crozier and his men left the halfbreeds with a large supply of abandoned guns, ammunition, and horses, which aided them in the future confrontations.

To give further credibility to the idea that Indians and halfbreeds had gone on the warpath, the police burned down most of the fort and its supplies at Fort Carlton that night and then implied that the natives had done it.[24] The police fled to Prince Albert, and when Dumont heard of their flight he decided to attack them that night. He knew they would have to pass through a certain pine grove, which provided an excellent location for an ambush, but Riel was again able to persuade him to spare the enemy. The next day the Canadian nation was amazed to hear the news that Crozier and his troops had been defeated by the western rabble. Ottawa was easily able to convince them that "a savage and lawless mob was threatening the West with murder and pillage".[25] More soldiers volunteered at several eastern cities: according to official reports, men rallied to the cause and enlisted in the forces by the thousand.

Crozier's demand for immediate reinforcements in the Northwest was underlined by the bodies of 10 policemen, who probably never knew the real purpose behind their journey to

Duck Lake. The situation was clarified by the events of the next few days. The Macdonald cabinet had arranged to transport by rail soldiers, provisions, and equipment needed for the Northwest invasion. It was an excellent opportunity for the C.P.R. to prove itself and restore public confidence in its operations. A top C.P.R. official was conveniently in Ottawa at the time of the crisis: "Van Horne with his experience of moving troops over the Chicago and Alton during the American Civil War and with his knowledge of what could be done in an emergency *happened* to be in Ottawa [Emphasis added]."[26] The C.P.R. management was to prove its capability beyond a doubt by their efforts in the Northwest hostilities:

> . . . in 1885 Riel's forces were dispersed and Riel captured at Batoche on May twelfth, the national importance of the Canadian Pacific Railway and the efficiency of its management were triumphantly vindicated.[27]

However, Middleton's troops did not encounter any fighting until a month after their departure. Since the Métis were fighting only to protect their homes, they stayed near their community and did not venture into battle. Because there were no battles to engage the soldiers, General Middleton was accused of bungling the job, but it is difficult to be a brilliant commander if there is no enemy to fight.

After a month of wandering on the plains without encountering any enemy, Ottawa's troops began to converge on Batoche with their cannon and Gatling gun. It was only a matter of time before enemy forces would be firing on the Métis community. Gabriel Dumont, who was realistic about the enemy, insisted that the halfbreeds should go out and harass the troops as they moved across the prairies rather than waiting for them to arrive in their communities, but Riel objected and the plan was dropped. As the enemy neared Batoche, it was finally agreed that Dumont and his men should attack Middleton's forces at Fish Creek, several miles from Batoche. At 4:00 a.m. on April 24, Dumont positioned 130 men in a deep ravine near Fish Creek where Middleton's soldiers had camped. As soon as they were within range, the native guerillas opened fire from behind bushes and boulders, moving quickly after each shot and keeping up a continuous fire. The 1,000 soldiers were caught by surprise and scattered in all directions. However, they soon opened fire with their cannon and Gatling gun. Although the natives had only muzzle-loaders that fired either ball or shot, they held the enemy in check until late afternoon, when their ammunition began to run low. Dumont then decided to set the grass on fire to disorganize the enemy and force them to retreat. The strong wind and damp grass combined to create a thick smoke that engulfed and confused the troops. At the same time, the native guerillas closed in, singing and yelling and firing the last of their ammunition:

> The Federal soldiers, finding themselves out-manoeuvred, took to their heels and fled, leaving behind a mass of equipment. Even the Major left his box and two bottles of whiskey "with which we drank his health," added Dumont.[28]

Seven enemy soldiers were killed in the battle and 40 more were wounded; the halfbreeds lost four men and two wounded. Middleton, a soldier in the old British tradition, had shown himself incapable of dealing with guerilla warfare. At daybreak on April 25 the victorious Métis returned to Batoche, jubilant in their victory – a small band of native warriors had defeated a force of 1,000 soldiers armed with the latest weaponry.

In addition to the troops, Ottawa sent a ship to control the Saskatchewan waterways. The Hudson's Bay steamer *Northcote* was used to bring in supplies and reinforcements via the South Saskatchewan River. "[Middleton] began to transform the *Northcote* into a gunboat. On the bridge, he erected a wooden barricade with sacks of oats capable of resisting the heaviest fire of the Métis who had no artillery."[29] This clumsy vessel was a sitting duck for guerilla fighters. Halfbreed warriors waited for the vessel to sail past Gabriel's Ferry Crossing and lowered a huge ferry cable as the boat passed. Dumont's intention was to have the cable snag the *Northcote* and then fire on the 35 "marines" in the boat. However, the cable wasn't lowered quickly enough and it only sheared off the smokestack, which set the boat on fire. Native snipers on the bank fired on the men who came on deck to put it out, and four were killed. The smouldering boat, with its crew, supplies, and the troops hidden below decks, drifted helplessly down the river. Three miles downstream the *Northcote* stuck on a sandbar where it remained, useless, until the fighting was over.

After the easy victory over Middleton's army, Dumont wanted to take several native warriors and systematically harass the enemy. It seemed inevitable that the Métis would soon have to fight on their doorstep unless they met the enemy outside their own communities. Eight thousand Canadian troops covered the Northwest Territories from Winnipeg to Fort Macleod, Alberta — an area of more than a million square miles of land occupied by fewer than 45,000 people. There was one soldier or policeman equipped with the latest weapons for every five persons in the Northwest, including women and children.

Middleton knew that Batoche was short of supplies because he was being kept informed by the priests, so he surrounded the town and the battle began on May 8, 1885. It lasted for three days, and on the fourth day Middleton closed in for the final victory. Instead of offering terms, as he might have done knowing that the Métis were almost out of ammunition, he pounded the town with rifle, machine-gun, and cannon fire. The troops sprayed the Métis homes with bullets, although they knew that only women and children were in the houses:

> On the fourth day, the 12th of May, around 2 o'clock in the afternoon, on definite information furnished by those who betrayed us, that we had no more ammunition, the troops advanced and our men came out of their trenches; it was then were killed: José Ouellet, 93 years of age; José Vandal, who had both arms broken first and was finished off with a bayonet, 75 years; Donald Ross, first fatally wounded and speared with a bayonet, also very old; Isidore Boyer, also an old man; Michel Trottier, André Batoche, Calixte Tourond, Elzéar Tourond, John Swan and Damase Carrière, who first had his leg broken and whom the English then dragged with a rope around his neck tied to the tail of a horse.[30]

Riel decided to surrender, but Gabriel Dumont kept on fighting. According to Trémaudan, Dumont would not surrender to "those demented killers". He would prefer to die fighting right there and he was going to urge others to do the same. He returned to the front line and captured blankets and food from the enemy, which he gave to the terrified women and children. In a second daring raid, he seized supplies of meat and flour which he again gave away. In his final meeting with Riel, Dumont boasted that the Ottawa régime would never capture him or lead him around because this was his country. Dumont made a decision then that he would never be a prisoner under the Macdonald régime or live as a second-class citizen in Canada. He was saddened by the sight of his people after the battle and exclaimed, "It is painful to see these wretched human beings crouching in the hay like animals."[31] The atrocities committed against native people by the troops were observed, described, and recorded by easterners.

> What a distressing picture is offered by these halfbreed families; cruelly plundered and stripped by the volunteers. The soldiers only came out of the houses of the halfbreeds after having broken whatever they could not carry away; stoves, clocks, bedsteads, tables, etc., were all mercilessly destroyed by these raving maniacs [soldiers]. Poor mothers of families who had only one bed and one blanket were brutally deprived of the articles. The soldiers being unable to carry off the bed, took hold of the blanket, and splitting with their knives the ticking, which contained the feathers, enjoyed the sport of throwing them to the wind. . . . the soldiers have robbed and destroyed everything they could lay their hands on in that region, leaving the residents in the most destitute conditions.[32]
>
> At Clarke's crossing on the 8th of May, soldiers pillaged the houses of the halfbreeds and destroyed a quantity of articles belonging to them . . . they demolished Madame Tourand's house at Fish Bay, broke her furniture and broke up the clock and bedsteads and strewed the floor with the rest of the furniture, and then set fire to the house.[33]

After the battle of Batoche, several native heroes were judicially murdered, imprisoned, or exiled, while Middleton and his soldiers received medals, pensions, and gifts of cash and land. For this brutal campaign against the Northwest people the soldiers were made heroes: Middleton was given a reward of $20,000, a pension for life, and a knighthood. The 5,300 regular soldiers were offered land grants of 329 acres each for their services or cash, if they preferred. Most of them took cash. If they had taken land it would have amounted to nearly two million acres, which, at two dollars per acre, represented nearly four million dollars. By offering them land, the federal government intended these soldiers to remain in the Northwest as a permanent occupation force. One of the reasons the Macdonald régime claimed it had been forced to suppress the halfbreeds was their agitation over land claims, yet the Métis had only asked for a title to 160 acres per family – less than one-half of what Ottawa later offered to each soldier.

If the struggles of the Indians in the 1885 uprising had been co-ordinated with the halfbreed movement, in all likelihood their combined forces would have defeated Middleton's raw recruits and untrained militia. For one thing, the Indians were a very determined people, largely because of their desperate conditions on the reserves. In the early 1880s the Indians on the reserves probably experienced greater oppression and poverty than any other group in the Northwest. As we have seen, the Indian Affairs officials apparently felt that once the Indians were placed on reserves they could be treated as children; but they could not be conquered that easily.

However, the Indians were not formally organized for a systematic struggle against the federal government. The Indians at Frog Lake knew very little about the halfbreeds' struggle at Batoche. They "were alerted to what was happening in the South Saskatchewan by the Mounted Police"[34] and not by the halfbreeds. Apparently the Mounted Police had an inkling of the Indians' hostility towards them because almost immediately after the Duck Lake battle they fled from Frog Lake. Trémaudan argues:

> If, instead of running away they remained at their station and organized with the whites of the neighborhood, they would have

had all the resources necessary to hold the Indians and prevent the massacre.[35]

Chief Big Bear of Frog Lake and his tribe had reasons for hostility towards government agents and other authorities, including the priests:

> Tom Quinn, the Frog Lake government agent, was no exception. To the best of his ability, he exploited Big Bear and his band, adding to his avarice a contemptuous attitude towards the natives. He drank rather freely, and when he was drunk he liked to stage a "power play". In the middle of winter, he denied rations to the Indians unless they cut cordwood. . . . The real reason for this inhuman act was that Tom Quinn and Delaney, the agricultural instructor wanted to clear the land that they coveted as future "homesteads" after the Indians had left for their reserve.[36]

It is easy to understand how hostility could have developed among the Indians who were being continuously humiliated and brutalized by their oppressors in return for barely enough rations for survival. There was no redress for these grievances. The Indians were probably watching for the opportunity to make a thrust for freedom, and the Duck Lake victory on March 26 sparked this thrust. It seems obvious that the Indians chose their victims according to their oppressiveness. Their war was against those white men who held them in subjugation, and not against white people in general. They knew precisely who were their colonizers. It was not an accident that they disposed of Quinn, the Indian agent, and Delaney, the farm instructor, and the two priests. This was not an act of revenge; it was a struggle against colonization, a historical development. A few days after the massacre at Frog Lake, the Mounted Police at North Battleford fled from their fort, leaving behind a supply of food and ammunition. From these forts the Indians took the provisions that rightfully belonged to them and distributed them among the tribe. Also, they now had a supply of ammunition for new battles.

By the end of April 1885, the Indians and halfbreeds had scored several significant victories over their white colonizers. They had captured three forts – Pitt, Carlton, and North

Battleford. Also, they had defeated Middleton and the Mounted Police at the battles of Duck Lake and Fish Creek. Then, on May 2, Chief Poundmaker and his warriors were to prove to Colonel Otter and his 325 troops in the battle at Cut Knife Hill how powerful a fight for freedom can be. They led Otter's soldiers into a trap at the crest of the hill and then completely surrounded them at the base among the shrubbery and rocks. Stanley explains that "from their concealed position [the Indians] poured a rapid cross-fire upon the soldiers as they lay exposed upon the hill".[37] If it had not been for Poundmaker's compassion, the Indians would have wiped out Colonel Otter's entire force. Morton claims: ". . . largely thanks to Poundmaker, Otter had escaped the annihilation or capture which might conceivably have been his fate".[38]

In the following weeks, Middleton was able to direct all his military forces against Chief Poundmaker, Chief Big Bear, and their warriors. Poundmaker was arrested on May 26.

On May 28, Chief Big Bear engaged Colonel Strange and his troops at Frenchman's Butte. When Strange discovered that he was surrounded on three sides by guerilla fighters hidden among the shrubbery, and unable to make any headway in the battle, he decided to retreat. With his nearly 200 soldiers, the Colonel fled through the only opening to safety. Even though internal dissension weakened Big Bear's force, federal troops that chased him for several weeks did not succeed in capturing him. Big Bear surrendered on July 2. From the trials that followed this conquest, eight Indians were judicially murdered, and 20 were given jail sentences of from two to 20 years. Big Bear and Poundmaker were sentenced to three years each. Every member of the Indian nation heard the death-rattle of the eight heroes who died at the end of the colonizer's rope and they went quietly back to their compounds, obediently submitting themselves to their oppressors. The eight men who sacrificed their lives at the end of the rope were the champions of freedom and democracy. They were incomparable heroes, as shown by their last moments:

> They marched to the place of execution with a firm step, imitating the funeral march of the soldiers who accompanied them. We

went to the scaffold with them, where one told me, "Father . . . we are anxious to die singing. I pray you to allow us to sing in our style." . . . Whilst the ropes were being placed around their necks they sang together. Having observed in the midst of the crowd some relations and friends, they shouted farewell, advising them to forgive their enemies.[39]

10 Courtroom: The Mask of Conquest

Seven years as a political prisoner in a colonial jail is what my great grandfather, Maxime Lépine, got for fighting the cause of native freedom and justice. He was completely cut off from his family, friends, and relatives, and the seven years must have seemed to him like an eternity. For women and children to make a 600-mile journey from Batoche to Winnipeg in a Red River cart across prairie trails was nearly impossible. My grandmother made the trip only once – to see her father treated like an animal in a cage was too depressing to experience a second time.

In my childhood, I often stayed with my grandparents on the old scrip farm* of Maxime Lépine at Batoche. I did not realize

*Farm given to a Métis family by Ottawa in recognition of aboriginal claims.

at the time that I was tramping in the footprints of a noble guerilla warrior. Maxime's spirit was not there, not felt at all. Of the many games we halfbreed kids invented, not one was related to the struggle of 1885. This history was hidden from us because our grandparents and parents were defeated generations. We were a new generation, starting our lives of defeat, without hope, ashamed of ourselves as halfbreeds. Although our forefathers – Régnier, Boucher, Fiddler, McDougall, Parenteau, Ouellette, Short, Adams – had fought gloriously against the Ottawa régime, we were still the wretched of the earth. How much easier and happier it would have been to start knowing the glory of our forefathers and their accomplishments. The truth would have given us all strength and pride, but instead we followed in the debased path cut out for us by the white image-makers.

As I look back, I feel ashamed for not having inquired about my great grandfather and his distinction. Together with Gabriel Dumont, Maxime was a leader among the native people of the prairies. In the uprising, he fought in the front line of action and led attacks into the enemy camp. Not only did he prove himself a brilliant guerilla fighter, but he valiantly withstood atrocities as a political prisoner. When captured at Batoche, Lépine refused to answer questions, even though the soldiers threatened to use "persuading tactics" on him. A true warrior, he was committed to the cause and would have died for it, if necessary. The violence continued for my great grandfather throughout the long hot summer of 1885 in the Regina jail. Leg irons and chains were used to lash together 25 Indian and halfbreed prisoners, until all were brought to trial in August, three months after their capture. The trial was a complete travesty of justice. The defendants did not speak English, and many of the legal terms employed were difficult to translate into French and impossible to translate into Cree. They were charged with treason and told by the presiding judge:

> You have the option of being tried before a stipendiary magistrate and a justice of the peace, with the intervention of a jury of six, or before a stipendiary magistrate in a summary way without the intervention of a jury. Which do you elect?[1]

It would have been difficult enough to understand what was going on even if they had known English; as it was, their lawyers had to answer for them and plead their cases virtually ignorant of their clients' wishes.

These lawyers followed the lead of Riel's advocates and chose not to argue the innocence of their clients. Lépine and his compatriots were forced to plead guilty, and thus the entire issue for which they had struggled so valiantly was made irrelevant. The intent of the lawyers, among whom was the Macdonald sympathizer Henry Clarke, was to prove irresponsibility by describing them as:

> . . . poor miserable unprotected creatures who had no representative in Parliament, nobody to speak for them, nobody to advance their interests, nobody to lay their claims before the Throne. . . . We are dealing with men of the territories.[2]

It was probably just as well that Lépine did not understand these insults. He was an intelligent man, a capable and enlightened politician who had assisted in drafting the numerous petitions the halfbreeds had submitted to the Conservative government in Ottawa. While the defence lawyers were attempting to get the sympathy of the judges, they remained completely insensitive to the shame and dishonour they were heaping upon the prisoners:

> Some of them are little removed from the Indians . . . consider the creature yonder with one eye, his hair and face indicating one degree above an ordinary born idiot. . . . Look at some of them tottering on the brink of the grave . . . trembling there before you, not understanding a word that is said.[3]

For all this, they should have been profoundly grateful, according to their lawyers:

> Now let them understand . . . when a halfbreed comes before a British court he will find a British advocate to stand up and defend his rights, to defend his interest, to defend his life with as much energy, with as much vigor and with as much determination as he would that of a white man.[4]

My great grandfather and 10 other patriots did not have to wait long to appreciate British justice: within the hour they were sentenced to the penitentiary of Manitoba for a period of seven years. The suffering and torture during his imprisonment took its toll and, two years after his release, Lépine was dead. The Canadian government had its own peculiar way of exterminating the Indian and halfbreed people, less dramatic and violent than the American way, but equally effective.

William Henry Jackson and Thomas Scott were also brought to trial. Jackson insisted that he was as much involved in the resistance as Riel and should be tried on the same charges. However, after a trial which was only a "formality",[5] he was declared insane. The federal government wanted Jackson out of the way to avoid a public trial that might reveal the truth about the economic and political issues behind the white people's participation in the struggle. Ottawa therefore placed the entire blame for the rebellion on Riel and silenced Jackson, one of the main leaders of the agitation. The evidence and testimony produced to prove his insanity were, to say the least, very inadequate. Two months after Jackson was committed to a mental institution, he "miraculously" escaped. The probable reason behind the arranged escape was that, if Jackson was kept in the mental institution, doctors would soon arrive at the conclusion that he was sane. This would result in a public trial that would reveal the whole sordid story of 1885.

Thomas Scott was charged with complicity in the rebellion. There appeared to be no real case against him, yet he was forced to go through the procedure of a formal public trial. The reasons for prolonging the trial were purely political; because Quebec was demanding equal punishment of the "white rebels", it was necessary to put a white man on trial. The Conservative government probably hoped that by trying Scott the French Canadians would be satisfied that justice had been served, regardless of race. Although no convincing evidence was presented by the witnesses against Scott, Judge Richardson stubbornly refused to grant a dismissal. Scott's lawyer was Henry Clarke. Since the same men were witnesses for both the prosecution and the defence, the trial turned into little more than a farcical debate, and the actual outcome of the trial was never in question.

In my research on the history of Louis Riel's trial, I found certain contradictions among historians. More important, August Trémaudan's interpretation differed considerably from other histories. The explanation is that much of Trémaudan's work is based on documents and personal testimonies of Métis persons who were involved in the uprisings of 1869-70 and 1885. Trémaudan made a statement in his preface that suggested that the standard history books on the Métis were misleading, if not deliberately incorrect: "The point was established that [our] truth was entirely different from what was being told as the truth, either in public opinion or published books."[6] As a result, in examining the standard historical sources, I assessed them critically, particularly the primary sources, such as sessional papers. One set of documents that seemed to stand out as seriously inaccurate and contradictory was the documents that were reported to have been found in the rebels' council room in Batoche on May 12, 1885, which were supposed to be Riel's papers and the orders-in-council of the Métis council.

There are documents that show that the halfbreeds were organized into companies. Each company supposedly consisted of ten men with a captain at the head. Such a paramilitary arrangement was the standard organization for every buffalo hunt. Therefore, these lists would simply be old buffalo lists. In the guerilla war of 1885 in which the Métis fought, it was a case of spontaneous and intuitive action as a response to an advancing enemy. It was a matter of finding enough men who would volunteer to fight. Any one of those who volunteered at the beginning, and who may have become frightened once the firing got heavy, was free to return home or hide wherever he could until the battle was over. No one was punished or held as a prisoner for lack of willingness to participate. They were normal human beings, with feelings of bravery, fear, anger, loyalty, and so on, and they performed the best they could under the distressing circumstances. To claim that warriors were billeted in barracks and had official guards and rules is deliberate falsification. The idea behind these documents is to give the impression that the Métis were organized into a strict military formation capable of controlling the entire Northwest. These are the only documents that show the halfbreeds as being systematically organized in a sophisticated way. The Métis were not any more formally organized in 1885 than previously. Battle reports by Métis leaders also indicate that they fought as individual guerilla warriors and not in organized companies under specific leaders. Other suspicious documents are the lists of soldiers and captains, who required passes that were supposedly granted only on approval of the council and that had to be signed by the secretary, Philip Garnot. This contradicts the way in which the Métis lived, worked, and fought. There was no possible way such rules could be enforced, because they were living in their own homes.

Again, in the Batoche documents there are serious discrepancies with regard to "Rules for Kitchen Service".

> Rules which the cooks are to follow strictly:
> They must 1st have breakfast ready for 7 o'clock.
> do 2nd do dinner do 12 do
> do 3rd do supper do 6 do
> do 4th keep the kitchen perfectly clean.[7]

The halfbreed fighters ate when and where they could, and whatever food was available. Gabriel Dumont's account of the halfbreeds' arrangement for obtaining food and eating is much more likely to be the truth.

> Eight miles from Batoche, at the farm of Roger Goulet, who had fled, I had two of his cows slaughtered for food. We were scarcely through supper when two Métis . . . came to warn us that the mounted police were coming . . . we had left nothing at all, unless it be the bull I had killed at Calixte Tourond's, and a few chickens which we had eaten and which came from Isaac Tourond's hen house.[8]

Since these men were usually engaged in activities close to the homes of relatives and friends, it is highly unlikely that they met regularly for meals in a designated mess hall.

There are several reasons for believing that these documents of the "insurgents" could be false or contrived. Many of the statements and the topics in the documents are conspicuously incongruous with the reality of the halfbreed situation. Some contradictions are noted:

1. The meetings were run according to formal parliamentary procedure with movers and seconders of motions and minutes being kept. Halfbreeds did not conduct meetings in such a manner.

2. The motions deal with irrelevant and trivial matters at a time when the people were engaged in a serious struggle for their lives.

3. The movers and seconders of motions are always given as "Mr." and not by the first name. Halfbreed people do not address each other as "Mister", especially when they are old acquaintances.

4. These orders-in-council concern ordinary, routine matters that people would handle without calling a meeting. They involve the sharing and communal aspect that did not require consultation or meetings.

5. These Métis men knew they were involved in a guerilla war, and that documents such as minutes of meetings were a danger to security.

6. Words used in these orders-in-council are not common words among French-Canadian Métis; for example, "soldiers", "to the bearer", "cavalrymen".

On March 24 a motion was apparently passed that said

> . . . that no soldier be permitted to go out without a pass or without the consent of his captain and the captain himself should come and ask permission of the Council; and that the captains should replace those soldiers who are without arms.[9]

In the first place, this order implied that the Métis were living according to military and barrack rules. In fact, their council chamber consisted of the log shack of G. Delorme. There was no such thing as a designated barrack room or guard room where soldiers slept and ate.

The capture of the documents is said to have occurred on May 12, at Batoche. Initially, the documents were not thought to be very important. Middleton did not mention their capture in his official reports, nor was there word about them in the eastern newspapers until some time afterwards. Middleton later made statements to the press about the documents that did not correspond to the contents of the documents that were produced at Riel's trial. In a Montreal newspaper, Middleton mentions the capture of the documents only in a postscript:

> I find from the papers captured at Batoche yesterday that the number of rebels at Fish Creek was 280 under Gabriel Dumont, that they intended to let me enter the ravine or crest and then destroy us taking me prisoner and holding me as a hostage to assist them in making terms with the Government in Ottawa.[10]

It was claimed that Riel had refused to speak to any reporters, but it was Middleton who refused Riel permission to speak to reporters. Yet Middleton released supposed press interviews between himself and Riel. The impression then, as now, was that Riel fomented rebellion, but the truth was that he had been invited by people of good standing all around Prince Albert to return as a leader in a legitimate struggle for western rights. "Riel was moderate in his views . . . there was little spark in his manner and none in his words."[11] He did not know that the Batoche documents had been "doctored" to give the impression that he was the sole leader in the rebellion, as well as a religious heretic. The situation must have been confusing to Riel, since he and his lawyers were not allowed to examine these documents that were being used as evidence against him. The Crown prosecutors knew that, if Riel had been able to view the documents, he would have known immediately that they were contrived, and that he could have called witnesses to substantiate this.

Another source for checking on the credibility of the Batoche documents is Father Végreville's diary which he kept during the months of April and May 1885. Since he was intimately involved in community activities of the Métis people at Batoche, he was a first-hand witness of the daily affairs. In his journal, Father Végreville describes in some detail the events that were taking place, affecting himself and the local Métis people. Since this journal has been held to give the true historical facts of the battle of Batoche, it may be used as a basis of comparison. Father Végreville's journal reveals some serious differences from the Batoche documents. In the first place, there is nothing in Végreville's journal to even suggest that the Métis council held formal meetings every day. In contrast, the Batoche papers show that on one day, April 17, the Métis council held six formal meetings. Végreville's writings suggest that council meetings were indeed very informal, being held whenever a serious matter arose, or when all council members happened to meet by accident. These meetings would be held at the most convenient place at the time.

But, most important, there is nothing to suggest that the council had an official secretary or that there was any recording of minutes of meetings. Father Végreville's diary covers the period in which Philip Garnot was supposed to have been secretary to Riel. Végreville mentions Garnot only once, May 21, nine days after the defeat of the Métis at Batoche. Végreville was present at some of the council meetings, and he appeared to be intimately informed on a great many of the affairs of the Métis council. In his diary, the priest wrote about issues that were of prime concern to himself and to the church. But he also discussed the social and political issues that were being discussed by most people who were involved in these intense hostilities. Therefore, in contrasting Végreville's diary with the orders-in-council found at Batoche, vast differences show up in terms of the priorities Métis people dealt with. For example, in the Batoche documents, at a meeting on April 17 it was "Proposed by Mr. Lépine, seconded by Mr. Jobin that a bull be loaned and placed in the hands of Mr. Joseph Pilon." Another document stated that "an order-in-council is passed to make six or eight oars for the ferry." In contrast, Végreville reports for the same day:

> The Reverend Mothers cross [the river], camp at X. Boucher. Riel complains of the Fathers and Sisters who want to live so comfortably and of the Sisters who were the cause of his sister's death. Brother Piquet follows the Reverend Mothers all the time. An English Canadian [soldier] appears on the left shore and announces that tomorrow at noon four hundred Canadian soldiers will arrive.[12]

In every way these daily records differ. It is more than a different point of view, or a different interpretation, or different priorities. The Métis council members and the priests were in constant contact with each other, although somewhat restrained; they knew what was taking place throughout the community. Végreville's diary shows that his discussion with the council was highly informal, lengthy, and rambling. Judging by the priest's journal, the significant decisions were those that stated: "I am condemned by 9 counsellors to be held as an arrested prisoner in my residence on my word of honour."[13] However, there is no recording of this decision in the orders-in-council of the Batoche papers. This is true for the numerous decisions recorded in Végreville's diary; yet none appear in the Batoche papers. Another major fact that makes the Riel orders-in-council appear contrived is that the names of the council members differ from Father Végreville's sixteen council members whom he listed on April 17. According to the Batoche documents, the Métis council held six meetings in a single day, April 17, and they fail to record the names of nine members noted in Végreville's diary. Instead, five different Métis are listed as members of the council. This is a serious difference because surely the council members were the same for that one day. An important name, that of Charles Nolin, was omitted from the Batoche documents. This supports the theory that Nolin was a subversive, and that it was essential to keep his name off documents that would likely appear in court and implicate him. If these documents were contrived after the fall of Batoche, it would have been a simple matter to omit Nolin's name.

Another interesting point of comparison between these two reports concerns Philip Garnot. In the Batoche documents, the name of Philip Garnot, as secretary, appears at the end of every order-in-council. In Father Végreville's diary, there is only one mention of Garnot, and that is on May 21, nine days after the fighting ceased. Végreville states only that "Garnot received $25.00 of wages". Important unanswered questions are: For what services, and from whom? The mystery question about the Batoche documents is: How was the government or the prosecution able to make additions to these documents without being discovered? The answer is not difficult once the full circumstances are understood. The government obtained the services of Philip Garnot, the secretary of the Métis council. Garnot, a French Canadian, had lived in the Batoche area for several years and had known all the Métis people. Thus, he was able to incorporate the names of actual Batoche residents into the documents and add other information that would appear factual. In this way, the prosecution hoped to authenticate the added documents. Garnot showed by the testimony he gave at Riel's trial that he was willing to betray the Métis people. He testified to Riel's supposed religious heresies and personal command of the rebellion. Since Garnot had been convicted of treason and had received a sentence of seven years in the penitentiary, he was vulnerable to government offers in return for "co-operation". He was likely offered a partial or complete reprieve if he would draw up these orders-in-council and other documents. Although Garnot stated on his homestead claim that he had served two years in the Manitoba penitentiary, there are no official records to substantiate this. It is known that he was back in Batoche after just one year.

Garnot's possible complicity has been commented on by Mr. Isidore Ledoux of Leask, Saskatchewan, who knew Garnot personally. He stated in August 1973 (at the age of 100) that Garnot had been involved in activities that exploited the Métis people. Concerning the theory that Garnot forged documents, Ledoux stated emphatically that Garnot was capable of such an act. To Ledoux, Garnot was the type of person who would sell out the Métis people for personal gain, and particularly for his freedom from prison. Therefore, it seems quite likely that Garnot compiled documents that were used in the preparation of the case against Louis Riel whose trial bore little, if any, relationship to the real circumstances.

There are many unanswered questions about Philip Garnot as Riel's secretary. For one thing, Garnot claimed that he was forced to support Riel, as this exchange shows:

Prosecutor: Are you one of those who followed him, "Riel"?
Garnot: No, I followed him, but against my will.
P.: What do you mean?

G.: When a man has a stronger force than I have, I have to follow him, he came to me with an armed force and I had to go.

P.: Do you say you were forced to follow him by violence. Is that what you mean?

G.: I don't mean to say I was forced exactly by violence. He came with armed men and I saw there was no use resisting.[14]

It is strange indeed that a person involved in such a critical situation would write so extensively and profusely. All in all, there appears to be little doubt that the federal government and other ruling authorities were involved in "doctoring" documents and preserving only those official papers that would support and advance their aims. Referring to the events of 1870, G. Myers stated that John Schultz – the infamous agitator who later became lieutenant-governor of Manitoba – claimed that official papers were destroyed. "It was the general belief that the papers of the Provisional or Rebel Government had been destroyed by the Hudson's Bay Company."[15]

Louis Riel had been captured on May 15, and he was put on trial for treason in Regina at the end of July. Both Indians and Métis suffered permanent degradation during the showcase trial of Riel, which was given great prominence and dragged out for three main reasons. First and most important, it diverted attention from the actual economic and political issues that forced the Northwest people into confrontation with Ottawa. Second, by blaming a single individual for the "rebellion", the federal government was able to obscure the fact that the struggle was one between the ruling industrial class in Ottawa and the settlers, farmers, natives, and workers of the Northwest. Third, it further justified the large-scale military occupation of the Northwest by publicly making Riel appear as a dangerous leader, capable of mobilizing a continental native force. But when Riel was eventually found guilty and sentenced to hang, Macdonald was in a difficult political situation. He and his Conservative government were dependent on Quebec support in order to remain in office, because Ontario people split their vote between Liberals and Conservatives, whereas Quebec people usually voted Conservative. Many people in Ontario were dissatisfied with Macdonald's high-tariff policy and wanted a return to free trade, an alternative offered by the Liberal Party. Consequently, Macdonald was obliged to cater to the Quebec voters. Quite naturally, the Québécois sympathized with Riel and the Métis, who were French-speaking and Catholic like themselves, and after the 1885 rebellion they began to protest against the Conservative government's brutal suppression of the Métis.

Macdonald realized that he would have to take drastic action if he wished to retain his political strength in Quebec. Two alternatives were possible: release Riel and grant a general amnesty, which would draw the wrath of the Ontario voters, or hang Riel and alienate Quebec support. Since Ontario and, more specifically, the Orangemen were screaming for the blood of Thomas Scott's "murderer", the first alternative had to be rejected. The second course could be carried out only by making special appeals to the Québécois in order to alienate their sympathies from the Métis. Hence, it became important to exaggerate Riel's anti-church ideas. The priests in the Northwest had already willingly provided the court with the evidence needed for such a plan, and the focus of the much-publicized trial had been to emphasize that Riel had renounced his faith, founded a new cult, installed himself in the confessional, and compelled the Métis to abandon their Catholic faith.

Each of these accusations implied a direct attack on the authority of the Catholic Church and hostility to the Catholic faith on the part of Riel. The government hoped that many French Canadians, being staunch Catholics, would turn against Riel for perpetrating such anti-church actions when this evidence was made public. The plan was not highly successful. There were several reasons for this, the most important being the widely known fact that the Métis were orthodox in their religious practices and would have refused to follow Riel in attacking the faith. Nevertheless, some of the Québécois turned against Riel as a result of the trial. Some of the evidence against Riel was biased, being given by priests who had extensive personal, as well as vested clerical interests in destroying a Métis leadership that challenged their position. Besides providing the government with prejudicial and false evidence concerning Riel's actions, these same priests wrote a "collective manifesto" to the people of Quebec stating that Riel was not worthy of the sympathies of a Catholic people because of his inexcusable transgressions against the church. The only time Riel went against church tradition was when he advised his men to confess to God or to one another just as the first Christians had done. This, however, he suggested only when the priests refused to perform any religious services for the Métis. Riel aimed and struggled for a society in which true Christian principles would prevail. He was deeply religious, but he was also a great humanitarian. He realized that the church and its clergy had perverted Christianity and turned it into an oppressive tool serving the interests of a white colonizing class. Since the church was no longer serving the people, particularly the Métis, he believed it had to be changed.

Although Louis Riel was an American citizen, he was charged with treason – a violation of allegiance to the sovereign. Doubtless, the federal government deliberately chose treason over any other possible charges they could have laid. Treason had the implications and conditions that the Macdonald régime needed to stabilize and entrench itself in its newly conquered territory. Howard explains this importance:

> Treason, as distinct from another crime, is an offence against the current political régime of the state and the régime therefore becomes an intensely interested party to the proceeding – not as agent for the social community, as in an offence against the moral order such as murder, but in its own right. Acquittal of a treason defendant is an implicit repudiation of the policies of the ruling régime.[16]

Howard claims also: "There can be little question that the circumstances of Louis Riel's trial were immoral. Whether the trial itself was also illegal has been debated ever since it was held."[17] The trial was held within the mechanics and rules of the judicial system, at least as far as was obvious to the public. However, beyond that it seems to have unfolded according to intrigues and conspiracies, collaborations and collusions among the power politicians and the capitalists with their vested interests. It is exceedingly difficult to obtain evidence on conspiracies or collusive arrangements between individuals and groups among the ruling-class establishment; such people do not need to conspire, since they hold the ruling power and control the institutions and agencies that govern the masses. However, there is one significant document that found its way into the archives, among the Macdonald papers. It is a "private and confidential" letter written to Macdonald by Henry J. Clarke, attorney-general in the first government of Manitoba.[18] Clarke was a prominent lawyer in the Northwest Territories, where he defended some of the Métis prisoners. In addition, he was a member of the Conservative Party and a very close personal friend of Macdonald's.

In this letter Clarke reveals certain intrigues behind the uprisings in 1869-70 and in 1885. The general tone of the letter is one of a yeoman who has done his services but has failed to receive his rewards. Clarke insists that it is now time for him to be given his reward, a judgeship. He is now 53 years old and has been a long-time fellow-worker with Sir John in the Conservative Party. Speaking about the trials in 1885, Clarke reveals some astonishing facts. He refers to "the French Halfbreeds (*who had been forced to plead guilty*) [Emphasis added]".[19] This statement by a defence lawyer makes it clear that the French halfbreeds did not receive a just and fair trial. It might be closer to the truth to say that several halfbreeds were sent to prison by a kangaroo court. Further, Clarke states:

> I think you can without much difficulty guess who is the author of the depositions of Pères André, Fourmond, Coucheau, Chas. Nolin and others — all of which have been or ought to have been of great use to the government, placing as they do all the responsibility of the Rebellion on Riel and others, and all condemning him without stint.[20]

Three of these people — Nolin, André, and Fourmond — became "professional witnesses"; they gave evidence at all other halfbreed trials. In fact, the prosecution in Riel's trial based nearly all of its arguments on the evidence of these three witnesses; whereas the three defence lawyers did not cross-examine these witnesses beyond a few simple, friendly questions. Therefore, it may be said that Clarke in his letter revealed how the court proceedings took place in a seemingly honest and just way, while in fact the real trial took place behind the scenes. Clarke is proud of his collusive efforts in this showcase trial. After all, the trial resulted in success for Macdonald, his Conservative Party, and the industrial class. Clarke was part of that success. And for his efforts Clarke was now demanding his just reward. It was not a question of ethics, or morality.

On the second page of the letter, Macdonald is reminded of Clarke's significant role in the rebellion:

> I know every man of any importance in any way mixed up with the Rebellion, every man who took an open or *secret part* in *goading* the ignorant Half breeds into rebellion, the personal object of every man of any importance in getting up the Rebellion.[21] [Emphasis added]

Again Clarke reveals that secret conspiracies were involved in the rebellion; but, even more important, secret conspiracies were employed to goad the ignorant halfbreeds into rebellion. He does not tell if these secret operations were carried on by halfbreeds or by whites, or by both. From my studies of Charles Nolin, Philip Garnot, and the priests André, Végreville, Moulin, and Fourmond, these men were definitely members of the secret group. But there may be others; possibly government officials, cabinet ministers, or C.P.R. officials. Clarke substantiates the theory that the halfbreeds were agitated or provoked into hostilities; he uses the work "goad". There seems to be no doubt that Nolin was employed to provoke hostilities. Further on, Clarke reveals the inner operations of the uprising of 1885:

> As to the last Rebellion [1885] I can get such a true and unvarnished history of the whole affair as will take all the patriotism and romance away from what was in reality only a vulgar speculation on the part . . . of those who urged or pushed the unfortunate Halfbreeds to desperation and bloodshed.[22]

Two of the people from whom he might have gotten this true and unvarnished history were Philip Garnot and Monkman, whom he had at his office for two weeks after their release from prison – one year after their sentencing, although they were both given seven-year sentences. Clarke may not clarify the puzzles and mysteries of the secret conspiracies and provocations, but at least he makes it known that such intrigues and plots were unfolding in the shadow of the Gatling gun, the soldiers, and the hangings.

Clarke is prepared to perform one more yeoman service for John A. Macdonald, but it is the typical intrigue of partisan patronage, using the Métis people for his advantage: a Riel story that would cause the Québécois to condemn Riel and support Macdonald. He proposes:

> Now by setting about this matter at once for there is no time to be lost, I could within a few weeks have the proofs all ready for publication in time to be used in the Quebec campaign. But before I move in the matter I will make my conditions in a business like way, and must be satisfied with the arrangement. No more telegraphed promises.[23]

Clarke feels that it is time that he stated things frankly to Sir John about patronage appointments:

> Dubuc is on the bench, who was twice a grit and always false to the Conservative party, and Royal, who ought to be in the Penitentiary for robbing the Indians, who fought against us in 1872, for [Donald] Smith against Morris, is trusted as far as you can trust him and I have always been overlooked.[24]
>
> . . . In the first place I want an outline of what you think would best meet the present requirements in Ontario and Quebec. I shall consider it as a professional secret, will note it and return it to you if you so desire it. Next I will want sufficient money, say about $1000. If I do not use it all I will return the balance. Next, *no one* must know my business in the North West, I am there on Halfbreed business. . . . And as soon as I get my mission accomplished I shall go straight down to Ottawa, submit the results to you and the Minister of Justice if you wish, and if you are satisfied with what I bring to you I shall want to be provided for at once. I believe I can fill a place on the Bench in the N.W. to the satisfaction of all parties there, or you can give me a place in B.C. or if you would like to have me in Commons, representing

> Saskatchewan as the representative of the N.W. till the elections take place next year, and I will go in and fight for you in the House with all the vim I can command for a year or two and then retire me to some quiet place.[25]

Louis Riel's showcase trial was really a matter of going through the motions for the sake of the news media and the national public. It seems apparent that the major decisions on the trial had been predetermined. It might be difficult to prove absolutely that there was collusion; however, Henry Clarke's letter and the statements of witnesses from Trémaudan's historical committee give some insight into the schemes of the ruling forces used in this case. The Crown had declarations from many Métis persons supporting the charges against Riel. However, Trémaudan claims that the persons whose names appeared on those declarations were questioned personally by the historical committee. Every single one of them denied that they had given such a declaration, or signed one:

> Why did they [priests] get together with Nolin to prepare a series of sworn declarations which bore the signatures of certain Métis who still swear that they had never even heard of what they were supposed to have signed?[26]

Riel's three lawyers proved to be more of a hindrance to him than a help. They fought their case almost exclusively on the basis of Riel's alleged insanity. They quarrelled frequently with their client, and prevented him from cross-examining the witnesses, particularly Charles Nolin. Once the four medical doctors had pronounced Riel sane, then the defence lawyers' case became almost useless. Although the decision that Riel was sane did not benefit him legally, it gave him great personal comfort. Also, it gave the public an opportunity to see the greatness of this man, his sensitivity and courage:

> I will now cease to be called a fool, and for me it is a great advantage. . . . If I am going to be executed, I would not be executed as an insane man; it will be great consolation for my mother; for my wife, for my children, for my brother, for my countrymen.[27]

Riel was a leader in ideas who wanted to guide his people through a struggle in order to create a better society where love and freedom would prevail. Riel was inspired by a revolutionary vision of the world, but he was not insane.

In view of what is known about the 1885 uprising, it is possible that the defence lawyers were "planted", to prevent efficient lawyers from acting for Riel. According to Trémaudan, the Crown presented everything and anything that could possibly be raised against Riel:

> Witnesses for the Crown argued that Riel was sane and imputed to Riel the crime of high treason. Twenty-seven witnesses were heard. From the first it was evident that the Crown prosecutors were doing their utmost to extract from witnesses admissions that Riel was an old offender and that the 1885 rebellion was but a continuation of the 1869-70 insurrection and that Riel was motivated solely by greed.
>
> The prosecution did everything to distract attention from the true cause of the rebellion. It goes without saying that the "murder" of Scott was introduced repeatedly. Indeed, it was the only crime introduced against the prisoner. . . . They strove to make him personally responsible for all the blood spilled during the rebellions. They practically accused him of having ordered the massacre of Fathers Fafard and Marchand and the other unfortunate victims of Frog Lake. They painted him as a common felon, an avaricious Judas, a bloody monster, who could not but forfeit the general sympathy of Canadian citizens.[28]

In spite of the glaringly unjust proceedings taking place in full view for all to see, Riel still believed that he would get justice through the court. Among the most important possible witnesses in the trial were the several Métis prisoners who were in jail only a few yards away from the courtroom. Why were they not asked to testify? Not even the defence lawyers called these prisoners. This alone is reason to suspect that the defence lawyers were not making serious attempts to get justice for Riel. Certainly, the halfbreed prisoners knew they had nothing to hope for; they were being realistic in their estimation of British justice. Thus, they were willing to state the truth in the courtroom for all of Canada to hear. But this is exactly what the courtroom did not want. Not one of the 30 Métis prisoners was called to the witness stand. Trémaudan argues that this is convincing proof that the truth was not wanted. That was the kind of evidence and procedures on which Louis Riel was convicted and murdered. Being a pacifist, Riel believed that justice could be achieved through peaceful methods. And when he surrendered he thought he would receive justice through the courts. In the most profound way Riel opposed violence and bloodshed: during both the civil war of 1870 and the resistance of 1885 Riel never carried a gun, nor did he advocate violence. This was Riel's chief weakness as a leader. He was amazingly naïve about the willingness of the members of the ruling class to use force to achieve their ends.

Even when he saw the mobilization of large forces of Mounted Police in Prince Albert in the fall of 1884, Riel did not suspect that Ottawa would attack the halfbreeds. He failed to see that the federal government might use his constitutional agitation as an excuse for this massive police recruitment; whereas, a newspaper reporter in Toronto could see it:

> He [Macdonald] admitted in the House of Commons that he knew that the Métis of the Saskatchewan were discontented — so discontented that it was deemed advisable to send a hundred of Mounted Police to garrison the fort at Carlton, but that he did nothing to remove the cause of such complaints as were well founded. . . .
>
> . . . The whole trouble has manifestly been provoked by a wanton disregard of the rights and wishes of these people in the first instance, and then by the neglect and indifference on the part of the First Minister and his subordinates which were positively criminal.[29]

Likewise, Riel did not think that the eastern newspapers would purposely distort news against the Métis. But they were quick to make Riel out as an unpopular rebel leader.

"The news from the Northwest is a little disquieting," Macdonald told Lord Lansdowne in a letter dated July 17, 1884.[30] Riel, at the request of a delegation of French and English Métis from Assiniboia, had arrived in the area of Prince Albert, where the Métis discontent was at its peak. The information sent to Macdonald was that Riel's arrival had created something of a panic.

Although Riel recognized the danger of American support, he did not realize that the American Gatling gun would help the Canadians to deliver the fatal blow to the Métis nation. In a letter addressed to the editor of the *Pioneer Press* of St. Paul, Riel wrote:

> Sir: Is it true that American arms and American citizens are to be used against the Halfbreeds? The Canadian Government are trying to crush us with tyrannical acts. What have the Halfbreeds done to provoke American hostility?[31]

Riel finally came to a realistic understanding of Dewdney's underhanded efforts in crushing the Métis nation, but it was too late. Riel's perceptions were reported in a newspaper in April 1885:

> Riel says Mr. Dewdney must have misled the Government, in which case he is responsible for all this trouble. He says the Dominion surveyors had no sooner ceased to harass the Halfbreed settlers by threatening to deprive them of portions of their farms than timber inspectors began to persecute them, fining settlers for taking timber off lands which they had been cultivating for years, though patents had for some reason or other been withheld. . . . He [Riel] asserts that war is being forced upon them, and that they are being hunted to death, although Parliament at Ottawa knows that they have been wronged.[32]

Before concluding the discussion on Riel's trial, the question of government bribes and Riel sell-outs needs to be considered. The issue of Riel as a sell-out has been disputed almost as extensively as the issue of his supposed insanity. More than one attempt was made by federal government authorities to bribe Riel. The first attempt is clearly explained in a Toronto newspaper. Archbishop Taché stated that he went in December 1871 to Ottawa where he had several private conversations with Macdonald on the matter of bribing Riel:

> It was on the 7th of December, about noon, in his office. I do not remember who began, but he insisted that I should advise Riel to leave the country for a while, and added these words, so far as I can recollect them. "If you can succeed in keeping him out of the

way for a while I will make his case mine, and I will carry the point." I made to Sir John the same observations which I had already made to Sir George about the necessity of giving some money to Riel if he were asked to leave the country. It was agreed by Sir John that they would do something about that matter — that he would consult with Sir George Cartier and give me an answer afterwards. I got an answer dated 27th Dec., 1871, from Sir John, which I produce under direction of the Committee, as follows.—

Sir John Macdonald to Archbishop Taché
(Private and strictly confidential.)
Ottawa, 27th Dec., 1871.

Mr Dear Lord Archbishop — I have been able to make the arrangement for the individual that we have talked about. I now send you a sight draft on the Bank of Montreal for $1,000: I need not press upon Your Grace the importance of the money being paid to him periodically — say monthly or quarterly, and not in a lump, otherwise the money would be wasted, and our embarrassment begin again. The payment should spread over a year. Believe me, Your Grace's

Very obedient servant,
(Signed) John A. Macdonald.

[to] His Grace, the Archbishop of St. Boniface, Manitoba.

The Archbishop went on: — I understood the words in Sir John's letter "and our embarrassment begins again," to refer to the possibility of Riel's coming back again before the Ontario elections and the embarrassment caused thereby to the Government.

Riel and Lépine at first refused to leave the country, but afterwards they consented on these conditions: — First, that I (Archbishop Taché) would give them a letter, under my own signature, stating that it was at my request that they determined to leave; secondly, that they would be furnished sufficient means to travel and something to be given to their families during their absence. I said I had $1,000 at my disposal, and as it had been given only for one that I would add something from my own pocket to help them. Riel said, "No, I will not consent that you spend one cent in this business. You have done too much already both for myself and my family. Besides we leave at the request of members of the Ottawa Cabinet, and it is but fair they should pay the expenses. We have enough of the trouble and risk for ourselves, and I wish it to be understood that all expenses are to be paid by the Canadian Government, because I consider that we are going away on their behalf, and we would consider ourselves as under pay in their service, otherwise we would not accept one cent from them." I asked him how much he thought they would require for travelling expenses. He said he thought they could not leave without $1,600 each, and that a certain additional amount £8 or £10 sterling a month should be paid to the family of each. I objected at first to the amount, and they answered: – "We see now and then the public accounts of Canada, and we know that the officials do not travel with small amounts. For instance the Canadian officials who came to the Boundary Line in 1869 have expended many times that amount." I told him that having but $1,000 in my hands I would see what could be done for the balance before giving my answer. It was then that I saw Lieut.-Governor Archibald on the subject of money. There were many conversations between us on the subject. The Lieut.-Governor called on Mr. Smith, and in my presence asked if he could furnish the funds, which of course he said would be reimbursed by the Canadian Government. I named at first £800 sterling to the Governor as the sum required by Riel and Lépine for themselves and their families. The Governor asked Mr. Smith to lend £800 sterling. I mentioned that I had $1,000 at my disposal without mentioning the source, and thus the sum to be furnished by Mr. Smith was reduced to £600. I understood that the advance was asked of and made by Mr. Smith in his capacity as agent for the Company, who were bankers for the Territory. Mr. Smith said he could, and did in fact furnish £600 sterling. It was handed to me, and I added to the amount, out of the $1,000 before mentioned, a little over $200 to make up $1,600 apiece for Riel and Lépine, which I gave them in accordance with their demand to enable them to go and live outside the Territory. The remainder of the $1,000 I kept in the bank of the Company, to be used as required for the support of their families, and it was so used."

A few days afterwards, in February, 1872, Riel and Lépine received the money and left the country.

It was several months after that when Riel and Lépine were living in the United States upon money furnished by Sir John Macdonald, that the latter worthy made his hypocritical lament at Peterborough. "God knows how I wish we could catch him!"[33]

This evidence is absolutely conclusive. There is no escape from the fact that while Sir John Macdonald was crying in the name of his Maker for Riel's capture he was treasonably paying out public money to facilitate his escape.

According to Trémaudan, during the political campaign that preceded the election of 1875: "Federal government agents offered him [Riel] $35,000 to retire from the contest and leave the country. He rejected the proposal with understandable indignation."[34] Later, he was elected to the House of Commons. However, Macdonald was able to get revenge on Riel for refusing to take the money and get out of the country and out of the government's way. What could be worse for the Prime Minister and his western ambitions? "Sir John Macdonald conferred with Henry J. Clarke C.R., the Queen's Procurator in Winnipeg, who placed before the Provincial Grand Jury a warrant for Riel's arrest."[35] However, the federal cabinet tried again to bribe Riel in 1884. They continued to work through the Catholic priests. In the troubles of 1869 it was Bishop Taché; in 1884 it was Father André. Trémaudan explains it this way:

> Riel had visited Father André at the priest's request. Listen to the witness who accompanied Riel to Father André's house, the man who was there at the interview. . . . Riel told me that Father André asked him to ask me to accompany him. I did so. Once there, after a minute or two in conversation, Father André and Riel spoke directly to one another:
>
> André: Did the Federal Government ever pay you for your services in Manitoba 1869-70?
>
> Riel: My sole recompense was five years in exile and a price of 5,000 piastres on my head.
>
> André: But you know that the Government owes you a huge sum. What would you say if I got it for you?[36]

Riel then discussed this matter with the Métis council, asking for advice on whether he should accept such an offer; and if he did, how could the money best be used for the Métis people?

> For a long time, the assembled Councillors debated the amount to ask. Charles Nolin opined that $100,000 would be proper. However, it was finally decided to accept $35,000, approximately what was needed to buy printing materials and equipment.[37]

However, nothing more was ever heard from Father André on the deal. But the federal cabinet tried again to bribe Riel with rewards, other than money. Again, Trémaudan explains it fully:

> In September, 1884, Riel was called to attend a Conference at St. Laurent. When he arrived at the presbytery, he found: Joseph Forget [government official], Renez, sent by Lieutenant-Governor Dewdney, Monseigneur Grandin, Fathers André, Fourmond, Végreville and Lecocq. They explained that the purpose of the meeting was to offer him [Riel] an advantageous position where he could serve his people better. First, Raoul Breland's place in the North West Council was suggested. Riel asked whether Mr. Breland was not doing a good job. Forget replied that he was. Riel then said: "Then why are you depriving him of his position and giving it to me? That's unjust." Riel was then offered a seat in the Senate. He stated that he doubted very much that they could obtain a seat in the Senate for him. The reply to this was that the governor was very powerful. Finally, Riel said to them: "You want to corrupt me and separate me from my people; well, you won't succeed."[38]

Riel was not for sale. That was Macdonald's final offer to buy off Riel. After September 1884, it is safe to say that Louis Riel's fate had been sealed.

While the trial of Riel held the public's attention, Macdonald's cabinet quietly turned its attention to the recovering economy. A little more than two months after Batoche, a bill was introduced in Parliament granting the C.P.R. syndicate an additional $45,000,000 essential to the completion of the railway. As a result of this grant, C.P.R. creditors were paid, workers were returned to work and paid their back wages, supplies were bought for cash and the construction of the railway got under way once again. Financiers from Britain who had previously stopped putting money into the C.P.R. began investing again. On November 7, 1885, nine days before Riel was murdered, the railway line from the West met up with the line from the East and the C.P.R. was at last completed. A new wave of immigrants moved into the prairies to furnish the land companies with buyers for their land.

Ottawa's invasion of the Northwest Territories cost the Canadian taxpayers $5,000,000.[39] In terms of the Northwest halfbreed population of approximately 5,000 in 1885, this meant that $1,000 had been spent for each Métis man, woman, and child. This sum of money would have given to each average Métis family a sum of approximately $8,000. In 1885 such a sum represented tremendous wealth and would have purchased several hundred acres of land for every halfbreed in the Northwest. Instead, most of this $5,000,000 went to the C.P.R., the Hudson's Bay Company, and other businesses favoured by the government:

> The ill-fated venture with the *Northcote* at Batoche brought a claim for $950 damages to the boat; its owners also collected $14,500 for its rental for fifty-eight days. Traders profited enormously; one of them, I. G. Baker & Company, which collected about $18,000 for freighting and supplies was a Montana outfit.[40]

Once Ottawa had established its dominion over the political and legal institutions of the Northwest, representation in the House of Commons was granted to the districts of Saskatchewan, Assiniboia, and Alberta. Provisions were made so that the Territories would eventually become provinces, but, although they were granted some political concessions, the Northwest Territories nevertheless remained in the grip of the eastern colonialists. Gradually the new legal and political institutions of capitalism became legitimized by the people; police and troops were gradually replaced by teachers and priests. The Catholic and Anglican churches organized a system of missions and schools throughout the Northwest, particularly on reserves and in Métis communities with the result that the people were not allowed to develop a system of education suitable to their particular needs. The hands of the westerners were tied and they were unable to resist Ottawa's economic exploitation of their resources and land. The eastern monopolies maintained high prices on their manufactured goods, especially farm machinery, and the prairies developed an unbalanced wheat-oriented economy — the typical colonial one-crop economy. Industrial development was checked; all raw materials and agricultural products were shipped to Ontario, while manufactured goods were sent to the Northwest from the capital province. Such a colonial system ensured that the prairie provinces remained politically powerless and economically underdeveloped.

By hanging Riel, Ottawa silenced revolutionary and separatist ideas in the Northwest for many years. On November 16, 1885, Riel was murdered on the colonizer's scaffold in full view of curious spectators. It was violence, raw and naked, but the message was clear – the Ottawa régime was now in full command. This highly publicized judicial murder was to serve as a vivid reminder of what happens to patriotic citizens who attempt to establish their own democratic government in a colony. Although there is brutality, suffering, and spilled blood in a political execution, there is also something inspirational and divinely beautiful in the martyred. A quotation from a letter of a witness of the execution reveals this feeling:

> Never before have I beheld a countenance more radiant than Riel's when he prayed as he ascended the scaffold. The beauty of his soul was reflected in his face, and a beam of divine light illuminated his features. His eyes gleamed with an extraordinary brilliance and appeared to be lost in the contemplation of a divine vista. Never, I repeat, had the scaffold afforded a spectacle so sublime, so magnificent. The majesty of the scene impressed the watchers and touched their hearts. Never had any religious ceremony so affected them as the sight of Riel going to his death. The Sheriff, his assistant, even the hangman, were weeping softly. I returned from this hanging, consoled and encouraged when I thought of a similar death [the Crucifixion] while thanking God that I had witnessed it.[41]

Three

The Native Plight in White-Supremacy Canada

White Lives—Red Lives

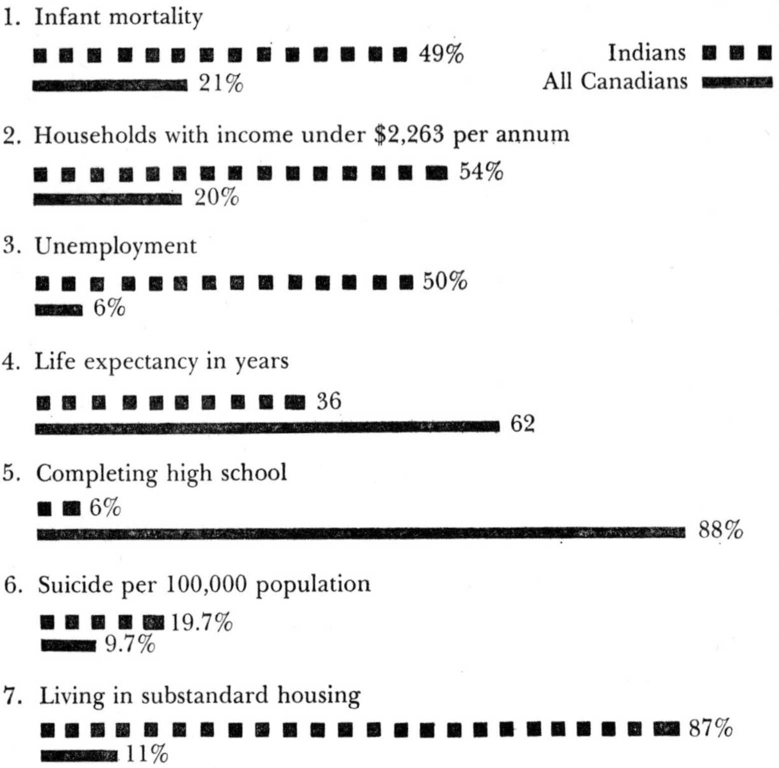

Indians ■ ■ ■
All Canadians ▬▬

1. Infant mortality

■ ■ ■ ■ ■ ■ ■ ■ ■ ■ ■ ■ ■ ■ 49%
▬▬▬▬ 21%

2. Households with income under $2,263 per annum

■ ■ ■ ■ ■ ■ ■ ■ ■ ■ ■ ■ ■ ■ ■ 54%
▬▬▬▬ 20%

3. Unemployment

■ ■ ■ ■ ■ ■ ■ ■ ■ ■ ■ ■ ■ ■ 50%
▬ 6%

4. Life expectancy in years

■ ■ ■ ■ ■ ■ ■ ■ ■ ■ 36
▬▬▬▬▬▬▬▬▬▬▬ 62

5. Completing high school

■ ■ 6%
▬▬▬▬▬▬▬▬▬▬▬▬▬▬▬▬ 88%

6. Suicide per 100,000 population

■ ■ ■ ■ ■ 19.7%
▬ 9.7%

7. Living in substandard housing

■ 87%
▬▬ 11%

1. Based on 1,000 live births: Department of National Health and Welfare Brief to the Senate Commission on Poverty Report #23.
2. Statistic for Indians includes income from welfare and comes from the Indian Affairs Branch Survey in the Senate Commission on Poverty Report #19; statistic for all Canadians includes income from welfare and comes from the *Economic Council of Canada's Fifth Annual Review*, page 107.
3. Statistic for Indians is from the Indian Brotherhood/Indian-Eskimo Association of Canada's Brief to the Senate Commission on Poverty #19.
4. From the Indian Brotherhood/Indian-Eskimo Association of Canada's Brief to the Senate Commission on Poverty #19.
5. *Ibid.*
6. Statistic for Indians from *Report on Vital Statistics*, Department of Indian Affairs and Northern Development for 1968: statistic for all Canadians also for 1968 from *Canada Yearbook 1970–71*.
7. Substandard housing is here considered to be housing without running water. Statistic for all Canadians taken from the 1961 Census; statistic for Indians taken from *Poverty in Canada*, edited by John Harp and John R. Hofley ("*Canada's Indians*" by Jim Harding), page 241.

11 The Underdevelopment of Native Communities

My mother died in 1948 at the age of 52. When I visited her in the hospital in Prince Albert, I knew it was the last time I would see her alive. In the previous couple of years I had discarded my parents; I had even given up visiting them. They reminded me of everything that was halfbreed. I was making it in the white world and I didn't want anything holding me down. All my friends were white, especially girl friends. I had a car and an apartment in the city; I had shaken off the ugliness of Indianness. I couldn't afford the albatross of a halfbreed heritage. One bad move could destroy years of cautious progress into mainstream society. My mother was completely halfbreed. All you had to do was look at her – her appearance, her manners, her clothes, her speech – everything gave her away as a halfbreed, yet she was still the most precious person in the world to me. She had given me the power to love and an appreciation of love in the most profound and sensitive way, and I had cast her aside, denied her existence. Now she was lying on her deathbed in great agony. Those 52 years of hunger and anguish and sacrifice were taking their toll.

Once outside the hospital, I broke into crying, violent crying. I cried so long that I thought I would vomit. Now I hated myself for what I had done – discarding my mother so that I could pretend to be white, free, and happy in mainstream society. I realized for the first time what the white-supremacist system had done to me, how it had perverted my sense of values and twisted the most beautiful relationship between two people. I puzzled over the tragic scene until my head was about to explode. I was tortured. I couldn't explain it to my mother: I thought she wouldn't understand. But perhaps she had understood all the time and had suffered in silence. Perhaps she understood how halfbreed mothers are swept aside for the froth and frills of white mainstream society. But she asked no questions about my absence. She didn't ask me if I had finally returned as her halfbreed son or if I was home to stay or if I was home in spirit as well. She didn't ask me to repent or apologize for rejecting her halfbreed home. She was just overjoyed to see her son – she was the mother I had always known, full of love and forgiveness, who had devoted her life to her family.

Standing in front of that hospital, I suddenly realized the fakery of my "white" life and why I had developed a contempt for my Indianness. It took my mother's death to make me realize what my mockery and ridicule of halfbreed life had done to me. My entire body was in a rage. Somebody had to suffer for this. If I had had a machine gun, I would have raced through the streets of Prince Albert spraying bullets. But were the people on the street to blame? Had they made my mother suffer? Had they tortured her to death? If not, then who was to blame? Does it matter when there is such rage and hostility? To vent that rage is the only important thing and no one thinks about the consequences. Why did my mother have to die at the age of 52? Even so, she had already lived nearly 20 years beyond the life expectancy of most native people.

I remembered the sufferings and violence my mother had experienced. She had shed many tears because her children had to go to bed hungry. I had often seen her cut a small bannock loaf into six equal parts – one for each member of the family, including herself. But she would not eat her piece. Instead, she kept it until all the others had been eaten; then she would further divide her small slice into four parts, one for each of the children, and hand them out. Tears flowed from her eyes during this act of sacrifice and I never knew if they were tears of hunger or pity or shame or the fear of starvation the following day.

Even though I was very young, I remember vividly the serious smallpox epidemic that hit our halfbreed community and our family. My mother's body was completely covered with smallpox swellings; the water and pus from these swellings soaked the bed continuously. Her face was unrecognizable. The pain was so agonizing that it had temporarily driven her out of her mind. No doctor came because doctors never came to the homes of halfbreeds. For days my mother suffered this violent torture, continuously on the brink of death. Although all the members of the family contracted smallpox, no one suffered as much as my mother. I wondered what we had done to deserve such pain. Death hovered over our family for more than two months that spring before it finally left. My mother nursed us all back to health before she herself had fully recovered.

I began to regret every day of the years I had stayed away from my family simply because they were halfbreed. The system had succeeded in turning my love into shame. It had replaced the beauty and love of my Indiannesss with disgust and contempt. But at that time I still did not understand how cultural genocide systematically operated to colonize me. To me, death at 52 meant a violent death – my mother had died at 52 because she was a halfbreed oppressed by Canadian colonialism. I walked over to my car and stood beside it. Only an hour earlier that automobile was beautiful and I was proud of it. Now, suddenly, I hated it. It was a detestable machine, an object of status in a hideous society that had perverted my love into false ambition. I wanted to smash that contemptible gaudy gadget, I wanted a sledge-hammer to beat it into a heap of crumpled metal. I was sure that my mother forgave her enemies, but why should such enemies be forgiven? Every day this cultural genocide is killing people and destroying love, and I felt I had an obligation to work towards the destruction of such a system.

A few days later, I headed back to Vancouver to my clean white-collar job and my sophisticated life as a pseudo-WASP. My head throbbed every mile of that trip. Back at work, I no longer felt smart and affable. I hurt inside. I was part of the genocide scheme and I had contributed to my mother's condition. Betraying my authentic self, I was pretending to a neat, pleasant life away from all the squalor of a halfbreed existence. By pretending, and hiding from my native nation, I had only created an odious veneer. A few weeks later, I received a telegram from my sister in Prince Albert: "Mother passed away early this morning." It was dated November 11. This has always been a personal remembrance day for me. I wondered if I had to avenge the death of my mother: eventually, when the pain lessened, I said no, but her death continued to plague me. The perpetual poverty, ridicule, and violence she and her family had experienced in that primitive house in a remote area of Saskatchewan continued to trouble me. Instead of sleeping I recounted the many times we had been humiliated, degraded, and violated by whites, officials, and the system in general. I clenched my fists in anger. I could not accept the notion that sacrifice was our role, as the priests had tried to make us believe. Memories of the grief I had experienced as a halfbreed refused to go away. I had to know more about the whole system, about how it crushed halfbreeds and kept them chained in poverty until the day they died.

To Indians and Métis the basic cause of poverty is not the psychological or personal weaknesses of individuals but the economic conditions of the capitalist system. In northern native communities nearly 80 per cent of the adults are either unemployed or live in families whose annual income is under $4,000. Any native who opposes the authorities responsible for this oppression is dealt with directly by such means as withdrawal of welfare, harassment by police, or denial of local services. In 1973, a Catholic priest in a northern community threatened the Métis people with a refusal to administer sacraments and confession if they opposed the policies of the local power structure in the community.

Although the poverty of Métis and Indians is ultimately linked to colonial suppression, it is specifically the result of immediate issues such as the availability of jobs. In practically all areas of employment natives are given menial and low-paying jobs which whites do not want, such as picking stones, harvesting beets, and fighting forest fires. Picking stones and beets are done on contracts, which natives must find for themselves. The rate of pay for fire-fighting is very low, and the workers often fight fires 16 hours a day. Although both white and native men can be conscripted into this job, native men almost exclusively are pressed into fire-fighting, often in dangerous tasks for as little as $2.45 per hour. Those who object are jailed.[1] According to Indian and Métis workers, there are few whites fighting fires, except in supervisory positions. In a 1972 report, Indians and Métis claimed that the government's Manpower offices were useless to them:

> Approximately one hundred per cent of the respondents claimed that Manpower offices had done nothing for them in terms of locating jobs. Those respondents who had had some experience with Manpower offices stated they had been racially discriminated against. They claimed they had been assigned to typical Métis and Indian jobs, such as dishwashing, domestic work, unskilled construction, and "dirty" jobs.[2]

These discriminatory practices are followed regardless of the training, education, or skills possessed by Métis and Indian applicants. The majority of jobs given to native people are casual and seasonal, hence they are unable to build any security around such jobs. These employment circumstances force natives into a day-to-day occupational existence. They are unable to plan for a future, or for their children, or think in terms of social mobility within the present employment structure. Even in Métis Farm Colonies,* natives cannot aspire to positions any higher than casual labourers on the farm because all the supervisory positions are held by whites.

*Large farms in Saskatchewan Métis communities owned and operated by the provincial government. The work force, except supervisory and administration staff, is exclusively Métis. Employees and their families live in the housing units on the colony.

How many Métis and Indians are in positions where they are meeting the public, such as sales clerks, bank tellers, bus drivers? Hardly any, and this explains a great deal about Canada's racist society and is a major reason for unemployment among natives. Of course, whites will excuse themselves by saying, "Natives are not qualified for those jobs." However, the other side of the coin is that native people know full well that there is no use in training for such jobs since they will not get them. They are hesitant to take training that will lead to further discrimination, frustration, and disappointment. They are realistic in their outlook; the fact is that Métis and Indians do not get public positions. As a result, the income of natives is severely restricted, both by the type of work and by the rate of pay. The casual, "dead-end" jobs we do obtain have serious psychological effects: they are soul-destroying experiences and force us into hopelessness, frustration, and hostility. Many Indian and Métis families live on social welfare. Since the welfare department does not record payments according to racial origin, it is difficult to obtain accurate figures. However, it is well known that most families on welfare, whether native or white, take it because there is no alternative.

Another cause of underdevelopment and poverty consistent with the colonial pattern is the lack of industrial development in native communities. Even when there are resources within our communities, they are not developed. In the few communities where private enterprise has developed the resources, little advantage has come to Métis and Indians because only a few of them are hired, and then only for the dirty, temporary jobs. Furthermore, native people suffer the secondary aspects of colonialism, such as the denial of creative development. For those born into poverty, little enrichment of the mind can occur, national or cultural identity cannot develop, and there is almost no hope for the expression of individual potential. Instead, insecurity, injustice, and oppression prevail. There is little opportunity for creativity in any area, and almost no incentive to develop mind and talent. People born into poverty learn to adapt themselves to living in ghetto deprivation and their level of expectation is restricted to that particular environment. They have problems adjusting to a more sophisticated, middle-class milieu.

It is difficult to obtain specific data on Métis because government departments do not officially identify us as a particular racial or minority group. The only group of native people officially recognized by the government is the status Indians, also known as treaty or registered Indians. However, there is another group of Indians, probably as large as the status Indians, who, like the Métis, are not officially recognized by the government as Indians. They are commonly referred to as non-status or non-treaty Indians, even though they are full Indians who live the Indian way of life. Their "non-status" has various origins: their ancestors may have been left out of the tribes that entered the reserves in the nineteenth century or they may have disenfranchised themselves, i.e., they may have sold their treaty and reserve rights to the government for a small sum of money, often less than $200. Indian women who marry non-status Indians or whites are also automatically denied their rights as status Indians and there is a large group of Indians in the north who live largely by hunting, trapping, and fishing and have never concerned themselves with treaties and reserves, never having come under Ottawa's jurisdiction. They are unrecognized by the government as Indians. Every status Indian is under the administration of the Indian Affairs Branch in Ottawa. The non-status Indians and Métis are under the jurisdiction of the provincial governments. However, the provincial governments do not have special departments for the Indians and Métis, so both levels of government officially lump the non-status Indians and Métis together with all groups as part of mainstream society. However, in practice, the Métis and non-status Indians are personally identified and discriminated against as a specific racial group. The pretence is made that we are equal co-workers in mainstream society. Most of us are aware of this pretence and find it not only frustrating but repugnant.

A typical example of discriminatory treatment of Métis and Indian workers occurred at Battlefords Provincial Park, Saskatchewan, in 1969. Native workers of this park were being subjected to denial of collective bargaining, unfair wages, and unsatisfactory working conditions simply because they were Métis and Indians. The main complaint of the native workers was that they were subordinated to a park superintendent who abused his authority by discriminatory practices. In June 1969, these workers complained about their working conditions to the Indian and Métis Department at Regina, a department that has since been abolished. They stated that their pay of approximately $250 a month was unsatisfactory. Since park work is seasonal, this amounts to approximately $1,500 per year. Some had worked at the park for several years, yet they were being paid the same rate as when they started. Government officials had promised several times to raise their wages, but this was never done. Higher wages were, however, being paid to white employees who were not any better qualified, and who were doing the same work as the natives. This was further aggravated by the fact that the white employees were recently hired temporary workers who received better working conditions and special privileges.

A Métis worker claimed that the superintendent hired some Métis and Indians, then, in a few days, laid them off abruptly, without reason. As a result of their complaints, native workers were treated with increased and harsher discrimination by the foreman and superintendent. Métis argued that the superintendent and foreman were trying to get them to do something wrong, so they could lay them off or fire them. At the same time, the superintendent hired his young son to work in the park. A mass native meeting was later held in the local community near Battlefords Park to decide on a course of action. Several important facts were revealed. The workers explained how the provincial government, specifically the Department of Natural Resources, was not being honest in its dealing with native workers. From the discussion, it was apparent that the Liberal government was promoting questionable propaganda about native work programs at the expense of native people. The government claimed that it had spent $20,000 a year on an "ambitious training program" in Battlefords Park for natives. According to the Indian and Métis workers, there was no training program in the Battlefords Park at any time. Each summer, natives were given the usual casual labouring jobs of weeding, hoeing, cutting grass, servicing and maintaining the park buildings, and dirty jobs associated with park work, but no systematic training had ever been given.

A significant aspect of this particular conflict was the department's determination to keep native employees out of the union. The Government Employees' Union had a collective bargaining contract with the government, in which there was a "scope clause" that gave the government the right to prevent casual labourers from joining the union. The department had the right to classify workers, and all persons classified as casual labourers were denied membership in the union and collective bargaining rights. Regardless of training and qualifications, the government classified all native employees as casual labourers. During this struggle, the union made little effort to support the native workers or reclassify them. The union was just as discriminatory as the government.

The superintendent of the park apparently discriminated against the native workers individually as well. He claimed that he wanted to hire only "good" Indians. During this struggle, he reduced the wages of some Indian and Métis workers and fired others, at the same time hiring more white workers. The superintendent argued that if the native employees were capable of better work, then they would be given such work. The fact was that the Indian and Métis workers of Battlefords Park were always punctual; they were never absent from work; they were always sober; they were reliable and capable workers and they had the skills to operate efficiently all machines in the park.

When top government officials visited the park with news reporters, all native workers were suddenly sent to the service centre building. Here the workers were given carpenter tools and told to look busy. The contrived show was to give the appearance that Indian and Métis workers had been trained in trades and that they were actually being employed in such work. One Métis worker was even ordered to sit in the superintendent's car and pretend that he was the regular driver of that vehicle. Immediately after the officials and reporters left, native workers were ordered back to their menial labouring jobs in the bush. In the end, although the native workers struggled for some time, no real improvements were made. The same superintendent still administers the park staff according to similar policies, at the time of writing. The government and the union have done very little to improve these discriminatory working conditions.

The standard of living among the Métis, unlike the rest of Canada, is getting worse. Fifty-four per cent of native families have an annual income under $2,300, less than $200 a month.[3] Rents are as high as $100 per month in small Métis towns and villages for shacks with no utilities or furniture. About 20 per cent of Métis families are doubled-up, i.e., two or more families living in a single dwelling. Recently, I visited a Métis home in a small Saskatchewan town where 13 persons were living in a three-room dilapidated shack. The average number of rooms in each Métis home is three, half the average space in a white home. The economic problems of the natives are increasing, for several reasons. Employment opportunities for unskilled workers are rapidly drying up as automation displaces them; while the cost of living skyrockets the income of these workers either remains fixed or increases only slightly. Housing is failing to keep pace with the increase in native population. The worsening of economic conditions has forced native people to identify themselves more as a separate racial group and to organize in fighting these problems. They realize that they are at the bottom of the heap and have little or nothing to lose.

Most of the Métis in Saskatchewan have supported a proposal that a large sum of money be made available to native communities for local development as compensation for the destruction of the native economy. A large percentage of this money would be used to establish light industries and farming within native communities according to the resources of each community and provide jobs in that area. Such enterprises would be initiated, administered, and operated exclusively by local native persons in co-operative communal enterprises with no government bureaucracy or white supervisors. Since the federal government is able to make grants of millions of dollars to underdeveloped countries throughout the world each year, surely it can make similar grants to its own underdeveloped communities. As native people, we resent these large sums of money being sent to other countries to glorify the Canadian government as a generous, kindly, and non-racist government at a time when

Canadian natives are living in conditions of grim poverty that are sometimes worse than in the countries receiving foreign aid. Furthermore, while our people suffer from malnutrition, unemployment, and inadequate housing, the federal government gives billions of dollars of the taxpayers' money as subsidies to rich American and Canadian corporations that employ racist and colonizing practices against Indian and Métis people.

12 Schooling the Redman

The white-supremacist school with its repressive attitudes towards children is the source of the so-called native "school problem". The Métis and Indians with their supposed stupidity and laziness, their so-called lack of industry and ambition, and their apathy to a "progressive" school system are not the problem. The school systematically and meticulously conditions natives to a state of inferiorization and colonization. It does this in a number of ways: most important, however, is that it teaches the language, literature, and history of the colonizer and thus forces the students to deny their language, culture, and essential being. The school and its teachers operate within typical racial stereotypes and coerce students into feeling ashamed and unworthy.

The present formal education program is irrelevant and meaningless to native people. The white middle-class values inherent in classroom instruction mean very little to native students. The curriculum is so strange that students have difficulty relating it to their frame of reference and making it part of their knowledge. Métis and Indian children drop out of school because the program is as alien to them as ballet. At the same time, the school negates native history and culture. If it were not for the white-ideal* operating within native persons, these schools would have little support from natives.

The majority of Métis and Indian students drop out of school because of their lack of interest in the academic subjects. They do not see any relation between the subjects taught in school and practical living in their community. It is more than a gap between curriculum and community; it is a gap between school and native society. In white society, education represents a child's aspirations to occupations and success, whereas in native society education does not represent either of these: natives do not consider it a stepping-stone to employment. Although white children see their elders as lawyers, doctors, teachers, etc., and can realistically aspire to those models, native children do not see their elders in such roles. Indian children perceive those avenues as closed to them because they see their elders in occupations that require very little formal education; the teachers in their classrooms are white, so that even this occupation does not serve as a model for them.

A new economy would have to be established in the native society directly and immediately linked to the educational system before the school would have any credibility. School and economy must develop together. Any patchwork program not based on this principle is bound to fail. The study of ancient history, English literature, or advanced mathematics is meaningless to people who live on a day-to-day survival basis in a racially colonized situation: natives claim school helps them in learning to read and write, but very little beyond that. The present school system is an institution of industrialism, from which native

*Within a native person there is an inclination towards white society. The glorification of whiteness acts as a sort of magnet on the thinking and behaviour of native people.

people have been excluded until recently, and has been imposed on top of the hunting and communal economy still basic to many native communities.

The problem of racism is always present in the schools, particularly with regard to native languages. Many Métis and Indians have been forbidden to speak their native language by their teachers or by official policy. Twenty per cent of those interviewed in the 1972 survey claimed they had been punished for using their native language at school.[1] Others had been forbidden to speak their native language because teachers claimed these students were mocking them. This sort of teacher paranoia only serves to increase the cultural differences that exist between them and teachers. But even though they admit that most white teachers do not associate with natives, the latter often rationalize this discrimination by claiming that "we are of a different culture" and "the teachers are not interested in us".

The vast majority of Indians and Métis do not know who controls the schools in their community, or who decides on the curriculum. Apparently, they are not concerned enough about education to learn about the system of control. Probably they feel it matters little since they would still be powerless to exercise any control once they did know. However, when they do begin to exercise control over their own educational system, changes in white-native relationships in the schools will only take place gradually because of the white-ideal. The rate of change will depend on the rate of decolonization, i.e., on how fast natives can rid themselves of the consciousness of the oppressed. It is therefore unlikely that native people would approve if schooling immediately changed to a completely native operation. Because of the white-ideal, native parents hold certain expectations of success in the white world for their children. Although these are only superficial and surface expectations, nevertheless they do exist and have to be respected. Native teachers would be generally regarded as incapable of preparing native children for white society. Influenced by the white-ideal, native parents feel that white teachers are better able to direct their children to success in mainstream society, even though the majority drop out before reaching high school. Most native parents would probably oppose full native content in the curriculum at the present time. But, as decolonization increases, both native parents and students will develop greater determination and pride in their heritage and nation and more confidence in their own ability and increased skills in community control. This will allow Indians and Métis to move towards a greater degree of native administration and instruction in the schools.

A great deal of the academic content now on the course of studies must not only be de-emphasized but eliminated. Also, time spent in the culturally foreign and repressive classroom must be reduced and more time must be allotted to recreational, cultural, and community projects outside the classroom. The present school system has to be more authentically related to native people and their way of life. Primary-school students need to have native instructors who will teach them Métis and Indian history and culture in their native language. The severe, authoritarian student-teacher relationship at present the norm in the classroom must be altered so that students and teachers can relate to each other as human beings free from social roles and a hierarchy of authority. Students should not be pressured into learning English immediately, or even within a specified time. Great caution must be exercised in teaching English because it is so basic to white supremacy and inferiorization: the standard rule that says it is easier to learn a foreign language when a person is young does not apply to colonized people learning the colonizer's language. The latter inferiorizes the native person and undermines his skills, confidence, and capacity for learning in all areas. Therefore, the longer he postpones learning the colonizer's language in elementary school years the more skillful and capable he is in learning a subject, including English, when he is older. The language of the colonizer is the most powerful device used in colonizing native peoples, and it is not just for reasons of convenience that, in Saskatchewan, "the language of instruction in the classroom must be English".

In some communities of northern Saskatchewan, 30 per cent of the adult native people have never been to school;[2] the majority of Métis and Indians do not go beyond Grade 8. The focus of education therefore has to be on this elementary level and on social education. This does not mean, of course, that high-school education can be completely ignored; in every school program, opportunities for succeeding through the white system should be made available. Gymnasiums should serve as community centres, rather than being the exclusive property of the school, open only from 9:00 a.m. to 4:00 p.m., and operated under the teachers' jurisdiction. Something more than white, middle-class organized games should take place in gymnasiums, for instance multi-recreational programs directed at both native students and adults. Indians and Métis also require social education, including civil rights information, welfare and courtroom knowledge, and so on. This is necessary knowledge for their daily lives. These aspects of social education are very important, not only as practical education, but as education for decolonization. Cultural genocide and childhood inferiorization must be stopped if the native nation is to survive.

Surveys of any significance about colonized people who have been kept systematically uninformed regarding their social environment and excluded from mainstream society are difficult to prepare. Many Métis and Indians know nothing about the government institutions and agencies that control their lives. Not having even a basic knowledge, they do not have a frame of reference for formulating specific ideas about possible changes or how these changes could take place. Nevertheless, they are seriously concerned about schools and the other institutions that affect their lives. Since many natives are unable to express these concerns in specific terms, they become frustrated and resentful, a typical response pattern of native people who have been methodically excluded from decisions on issues affecting their lives and communities.

It is also difficult to ask formal questions and obtain genuine answers that represent the real opinions of native people. Métis and Indians seem to have developed a peculiar kind of "accommodating language" that they use when speaking to white officials: they give answers that do not necessarily coincide with their true feelings and opinions, superficial answers they think will please their colonizers. Apparently, natives reason that to give acceptable answers will serve their best interests and will also result in greater benefits for themselves since they accept the colonizer's superior position of power and authority over their lives. They hope that these accommodating answers will make things run more smoothly in the colonized world and facilitate relationships between colonizing authorities and colonized natives. As a result, answers by Métis and Indians to formal questionnaires rarely represent true opinions about the questions. Since these "slogan" answers reflect white middle-class values, they show that native people are well aware of white values and of their importance in mainstream society. Understanding such "slogan" answers is extremely important in the comprehension of the communications and relationships between native people and white rulers. This is one of the problems that exist within a colonized society, and it may be attributed largely to the state public school system.

One of the most important phenomena in the school system is the colonization of students by the persons of authority who exercise their power arbitrarily and oppressively. Their power is derived from the authority of their position and by the grading that they give children. Their oppressive authority is a source of motivation of student behaviour. Much of the learning that occurs involves manipulation by educators acting according to their assumptions about the authoritarian purposes of education. What is called teaching is in reality eliciting appropriate behaviour from the students. The concept of control, which means the regulation of students, includes assumptions about how students should behave. The image of what is appropriate and successful is a well-disciplined, high-achieving student.

The school is an agency of social and political control. This control is achieved through the public school teacher. During the course of educating a pupil the school requires him to subordinate himself to the teacher, whom the child comes to regard as an authority in education. This authority figure wields control over the pupil very effectively through use of the grading system. As a student progresses through his years of schooling, a belief in the rightness of authority is ingrained in him. When he reaches adulthood this respect for authority is readily transferred to the political administration of the state. Thus the patterns of behaviour delineated by the ruling class authorities are achieved through the use of the public school teacher. Learning what the system wants is part of the pattern of student behaviour.

The manipulative methods of educators include making the student fearful of any behaviour that deviates from the prescribed pattern. The examination method is a concrete illustration of the inculcation of this fear. Students are conditioned to be fearful of failing and not progressing through the system. Another part involves making the student think that his worth and well-being as a person are synonymous with his successful functioning in the school system.

Insecurity and fear are the most harmful effects of schooling, and yet they form the basis of schooling. Fear of failure is the pulse of school life: the fear of failure as a person, the more concrete fear of examinations, the fear of being considered stupid, the fear of not doing the proper thing, the fear of punishment, are all part of the school's network of fears. The student has been made afraid, so that he may more easily be controlled in his behaviour and to get him to do whatever is wanted. Anxiety is a tension that a person experiences within himself, for it stems from his personal conflicts and efforts for success. The fears imposed upon the child become part of the child's nature. This is the process of colonization at work in the classroom.

How fear is used to colonize the student is a very complex question. The status-quo culture uses a person's vulnerability to control him. Firstly, a person is made fearful by making him concerned about, for example, his reputation. Then, once the fear of losing his reputation is established, he can be manipulated by being threatened with some blemish to his reputation. The effect of this fear on the student is to force him to make status-quo choices, and in doing so to limit his possibilities for personal action and growth. Giving in or pleasing the teacher becomes the student's goal. In such cases, the student adopts a subservient attitude, thinking what he is told to think and learning what he is expected to learn. The teachers reward him for this. Frequently the student internalizes this subservient attitude; he actually comes to believe that he personally has all the characteristics associated with the term subservient. A person who adopts a subservient attitude incorporates his fears, his insecurity, his dependency and becomes passive, conforming, and obedient. Acting on his own becomes increasingly difficult and he becomes submissive to the whims of authoritarian persons in the state.

Conformity means an excess of order, more order than is necessary. Order becomes excessive when it is used only for preserving the status quo. Conformity becomes harmful when it prevents people from developing an inner essence and when it stultifies creative energy and action. The presence of excessive conformity, authoritarianism, indoctrination, and fear in the school environment negates the autonomy and the independence of a student. The final product of such schooling is a condition of thorough colonization.

For education to be truly liberating, however, it cannot take place within the present institutions and bureaucracy. Also, it will require more than placing native élites in the oppressor's position. The structures will have to be destroyed and new ones built that embody freedom and humanness as well as political power. Today, schooling is an agency of dehumanization and oppression. Scholars have pointed out very clearly that one of society's problems today is schooling and all the myths that surround it. Schooling leads to alienation, subordination, and conformity. Instead of providing social mobility and serving as an equalizer for its citizens, it rigidly maintains the class system. In addition, it serves to legitimize the capitalist myths, and fails to provide any path to personal or political liberation. It is the dominant social institution in society today and unfortunately has become a serious impediment to personal fulfilment and liberation. A radical theory of educational reform is meaningful only if it is attached to the social relations of production. Under the present conditions schools can do little to improve society in general. However, they can become relevant if they are involved in the forces of decolonization. According to Illich, the schools are exemplary models of bureaucracies geared towards the indoctrination of docile and manipulable consumers.[3] The process of schooling creates institutional values, and insures that all individual needs are transformed into demands for goods and services. The goods become ends in themselves, representing a desired level of consumption. Illich argues that our society is initiated into what he calls "the myth of unending consumption" of services. Consumers can become hooked on the need for more and more of a product.

However, schooling has a much broader function in the capitalist system. Schools engage in political socialization mostly in terms that are highly functional in the prevailing social and political order. In other words, educational institutions at all levels generally fulfil an important conservative role, and act with considerable effectiveness to preserve the status quo in their societies. Today schools deliberately seek to instil into their students conservative philosophy whose themes remain tradition, religion, nationalism, authority, hierarchy, and an exceedingly narrow view of the meaning of democracy. Public education has more than one purpose; but not the least important one is to instil in those subjected to it a submissive acceptance of the social order of which they are destined to form the base. While the emphasis and the content of schooling may vary in each country, the total message is one of attunement to and acceptance of the prevailing economic and social order, and of its main institutions and values. Norman Adler states in his study, *The Learning of Political Behavior:*

> This acceptance of authoritarianism must come from somewhere. Our example of classroom behavior offers one explanation. It is now at least a possible hypothesis that this undemocratic pattern of our schools is not a random or haphazard phenomenon but is in reality functional; that is, it is important for a conservative state to train its citizens to accept authoritarian régimes in case they are needed to maintain order. Since the schools are fulfilling that function, they are supported; and society resists attempts to change schools or to give students power. We must start thinking not only about how undemocratic the schools are, but also about some of the functions that the organization of the school might have in the larger society. In this way the question of what to do in the future becomes not, "How do we stamp out undemocratic features in the schools?" but rather, "How do we make them functionally unnecessary in the larger society?" Then, perhaps, we can make schools the creative, socially relevant, democratic institutions that hold so much promise.[4]

Freire adds to the understanding of the oppressed's educational circumstances.[5] To him the colonized's perception of himself is that of the oppressor submerged in his consciousness. Therefore, the colonized have difficulty in objectifying their oppressor, that is, viewing him from outside of themselves. This view leads to identification with the colonizer, rather than to liberation. This is true for some of the Indians and Métis; their ambition is to be an Indian agent, Hudson's Bay manager, or policeman, rather than be themselves. Freire argues that the colonized have no consciousness of themselves as an oppressed class. If they do acquire the colonizer's position they are worse than the oppressor, because they want to be sure of holding the job, and therefore they exercise greater oppression. The relationship between the colonized and the colonizer follows the guidelines of the latter. Freire argues that the colonized are fearful of freedom because it would require them to reject the image of the colonizer and replace it with autonomy and responsibility. Hence, they resign themselves to a fate of oppression, mostly because of a fear of risks involved – losing welfare, police intimidation, and so on. When a struggle threatens the colonizer, he immediately responds with increased oppression. Severely oppressed people who do not understand their oppression prefer domination. They refuse to listen to the call for freedom. Before they will become involved in a struggle they must be able to perceive liberation as a real possibility and see that society is transformable. The struggle is advanced when they realize that the colonizer cannot exist without them. Once they realize they are the hosts of the oppressor, they begin to struggle.

The colonized and the colonizer are always polarized. Only through comradeship with the colonized can others understand their characteristic ways of living and behaving, which often reflect the structure of domination. The colonized cannot understand the order that serves the colonizer. This often results in violence – striking out at their own comrades. They have a belief in the invulnerability of the power of the oppressor. According to Freire, there is no use attempting to liberate the colonized without a political consciousness. To do so is to manipulate them. The struggle for liberation must be a result of consciousness. It is a struggle for humanity. For Freire, the only effective instrument is a humanizing pedagogy. For him, the strategy of the oppressor has been conquest, manipulation, and cultural destruction. Once they have become oppressed, the colonized are unable to stabilize their social relationships, and so co-operation among them is difficult. At this point, they are below the line of hope; they accept their fate, and this is reinforced by their state of powerlessness. "The important thing," says Freire, "from the point of view of liberation education is for men to come to feel like masters of their thinking . . ."

Although humanization for the colonized is a possibility, it is continuously thwarted by injustice and oppression, exploitation and violence. Becoming more human leads the colonized to struggle against those who have dehumanized them. Through education, the oppressed can be brought to understand that the colonizer is the source of dehumanization. Freire argues that, to achieve liberation through education, "the oppressed must confront reality critically, simultaneously objectifying and acting upon that reality". The reality is the restoration of their common humanity.

13 The White Ideal and the Colonized Personality

I had my first love affair with a white girl when I was 21 years old. One day I walked into a government information office in Edmonton and there at the desk was the most beautiful blonde girl I had ever seen. Flowing golden hair framed her lovely white face. Her pale skin, thin lips, and gorgeous big blue eyes were all radiant. She was so beautiful I felt as if a thunderbolt had hit me. I stood speechless, unable to take my eyes off her. I had never been that close to a white girl who possessed so much beauty. In my mind I had always known what ultimate beauty would be – I had thought of it millions of times. This blonde blue-eyed goddess matched my vision perfectly. I knew immediately that I would pursue this girl until she was mine.

In my dreams I saw her dancing through the sunlight with her golden hair flowing in the breeze. Soon my acquaintance with this white girl blossomed into a love affair.

The sparkle of her bright blue eyes and her expressive smile told me much about dignity and loveliness. Because she was white, she automatically possessed beauty and virtue. I accepted all this without question. She was the white goddess of my dreams. I never questioned why I saw her as completely beautiful and glorious. I did not see her as a real person with faults, as I would see halfbreed girls. Oh no, there was no doubt that she was perfect; after all, there was nothing Indian about her. She seemed too perfect to be real, too perfect for a common, vulgar breed like me. Simply to hold her hand was ecstasy. Yet, even though I was passionately attracted to Bonnie, I stalled over kissing and caressing her. Although I was seeing her often, the friendship was not developing. This worried me because I was afraid of losing her. I seemed unable to caress such a beautiful white girl. Was it because a white girl can only be admired as a goddess from a distance? Was she not meant to be loved passionately as are native girls? The racial barrier stood between us as firm as the Great Wall of China. But when I did kiss her I was kissing white beauty, white dignity, and white civilization. Who but a white woman could do this for me, a halfbreed? By loving me, she proved I was worthy of white love. I was being loved as a white man — I was a white man. Her love had baptized me in the stream of whiteness and led me to seek white success.

Sometimes I was uncomfortable with this beautiful blonde woman. I always felt that she deserved better than a halfbreed. I felt I was not doing her credit or justice; I felt she was too good for me, not only because I was a halfbreed, but because I didn't dress properly, because I didn't have the proper manners for her family and friends, because my life-style was crude and vulgar in comparison with hers. Also, I was haunted by the fact that getting serious over a white girl could lead to disaster. Wouldn't her parents and all society condemn such a relationship? Alone with her, I often felt awkward, uncomfortable, and nervous. I was completely overwhelmed by her beauty and elegance. Her whiteness oppressed me. It crushed me into inferiority; it emphasized my Indianness. I never felt so much a halfbreed as when I was with her. I was sure my Indianness stood out like a beacon. Also, I was seeing, in her, characteristics that were foreign to me – the goals she set for herself, her ambition, her desire for success, and so on. She made me restless. I was losing the peacefulness inside myself.

Gradually, I began to hate everything that was halfbreed. I saw my family, relatives, and the Métis girls as ugly creatures. They were becoming hateful people, mostly because of how they looked. I pushed them farther into the background, I wanted them right out of sight. Any time Bonnie cooled the romance, I felt my Indianness glaring all over like a neon sign and I struggled frantically to extinguish these hideous signs. Quickly, I cut myself off from that despicable island of Indianness and severed connections with all native girls. Every link had to be cut. My only concern was myself, and my love for this blonde. At that moment in my life all native girls became undesirable. I convinced myself that you couldn't trust them like white girls, and that if you did, they wouldn't appreciate it and wouldn't know how to act. In any case I persuaded myself that every native girl hated native men and that, secretly, they all loved white men as I loved Bonnie. It seemed to me that as soon as a native girl was successful she would marry a white man. Native women were the symbol of oppression and white women were the symbol of freedom. Every time I put my arms around a native girl I embraced oppression, but when I hugged a white girl I hugged freedom. I always felt that I would never have complete freedom until I had a white woman in my arms, in my life, in my bed. Until that day came my entire existence would be plagued with oppression.

However, as much as I loved Bonnie, the romance was going nowhere. I was in a dilemma, puzzled and hesitant. It was not an exciting romance because I was always apprehensive, and at times depressed. I was constantly preoccupied with trying to prove to her that I was powerful like a white man and wanted to protect her, but I was concerned about being bold and aggressive for fear of seeming like the "typical brawling halfbreed". I wanted to be powerful and protective, but in the white man's way, whatever way that was, with the result that I paid for my dreams in terms of insecurity and inferiority, by making myself a slave to her. It was a continuation of my lifelong subservience to the white man.

One summer I took Bonnie home to St. Louis to visit my family. My purpose wasn't really to have her meet my parents, it was to display her. I paraded her around the community in front of my friends. I took her to dances and picnics just to exhibit her and her whiteness. I wanted to prove that I could be loved by a white woman, that I was white enough to have a white woman. I paraded my prize like a peacock. Looking back now, I can imagine the contempt the Métis girls must have had for me, and the mixture of contempt and envy the men must have felt. Although my father had married a Métis, as did his father and his father's father, I was sure they all secretly loved white women, but I felt I had more love for this white goddess than all of them put together. I wanted all the white love they had wanted but were never able to get. My desire for this girl was as complete as their failure, and I was sure they had passed all their desire for white women on to me. Many years later when I read *Soul on Ice*, I recognized that Cleaver's experiences and my own were very similar:

> There is no love left between a black man and black woman. Take me, for instance. I love white women and hate black women. It's just in me, so deep that I don't even try to get it out of me anymore. I'd jump over ten nigger bitches just to get to one white woman. Ain't no such thing as an ugly white woman. A white woman is beautiful even if she's baldheaded and only has one tooth. . . . It's not just the fact that she's a woman that I love; I love her skin, her soft, smooth white skin. I like to just lick her white skin as if sweet, fresh honey flows from her pores, and just to touch her long, soft, silky hair. There's a softness about a white woman, something delicate and soft inside her. But a nigger bitch seems to be full of steel, granite-hard and resisting, not soft and submissive like a white woman. Ain't nothing more beautiful than a white woman's hair being blown by the wind. The white woman is more than a woman to me. . . . She's like a goddess, a symbol. My love for her is religious and beyond fulfillment. I worship her. I love a white woman's dirty drawers.[1]

Gradually the affair settled into a comfortable and beautiful romance, and the next two years proved to be among the happiest of my life. Then Bonnie suddenly became restless and wanted to explore other parts of the world. I tried everything in my power to hold her, and offered her everything I could. I was so desperate I was willing to make myself a slave to her. But nothing would hold her and she left for good. My hate for my Indianness was enflamed and I began to hate white women as well. Gradually the wounds healed but the scars have remained.

Every native person has this inclination towards acceptance and success in white society. Because it operates subconsciously, it is not clearly understood at the conscious level. The supposed splendour of whiteness and the ugliness of things non-white deeply affects native people in their thought and behaviour. For example, darker colours corresponding to darker-skinned people are characterized as evil and ugly. A multitude of stereotype images are prevalent in our society demonstrating that non-white people are comparatively repulsive and stupid. Everything white is beautiful and superior. These flattering and pleasing myths reinforce the white man's so-called superiority, but to native people they are degrading and destroy their esteem, confidence, and pride.

Of course, there are Métis and Indian persons who have decolonized themselves and freed themselves from the white-ideal, but they are exceptional. The majority of Métis and Indians still want white officials to hold certain important administrative positions, especially in schools, because white officials can exercise their influence to lead natives into mainstream society. However, the white-ideal mentality is changing in the present native awakening. Now a colonized Indian does not so much want to become a white man as to be in his place and be successful like him. It is necessary to keep in mind that this white-ideal is not rational; it is subconscious. The counteracting force on the white-ideal is the native person's conscious awareness of the racism he experiences in his daily life, and the conflict of these perceptions and desires generates hostility and frustration.

Indians and Métis realize that they are identified as natives by their appearance because these are indelible characteristics. But, paradoxically, most native people are reluctant to acknowledge to white people that discrimination happens to them, because to do so would emphasize that one is not white. By admitting discrimination, a person is stating that he/she looks Indian, and that people distinguish him/her immediately as an Indian. Most native people are unwilling to admit this fact publicly. They try to hide from their Indianness and dissociate themselves from everything that would classify them as members of the native society, even though their physical appearance and life-style still show them to be Indian.

Racial discrimination is not solely a white-native problem. It is difficult to bring the Métis people together as a single group and even more difficult to unite Indians and Métis. Some Métis may have a white appearance and will try to pass as members of a European ethnic minority group. They will then not identify or associate with anything Indian or Métis. Since the whites are inclined to hold full Indians in greater contempt, and since Métis sense this sliding scale of discrimination, they sometimes make sure they are as distinct as possible from full Indians. In Saskatchewan, there are two native organizations, the Federation of Saskatchewan Indians, which is exclusively for treaty Indians, and the Métis Society, which includes the non-status Indians and Métis. They emerged as two separate organizations largely by historical accident because status Indians are under federal government jurisdiction and non-status are under provincial jurisdiction. However, it would be difficult to group all Métis, status Indians, and non-status Indians in a single organization. Because of the white society's racial images, the Métis consider themselves superior to Indians. One of my maternal aunts has refused to allow me in her house or to speak to me because I stated publicly that my mother was of Cree ancestry. On the other hand, many status Indians consider themselves superior to halfbreeds because they are true Indians and have a noble heritage. Native people all along the continuum of Indianness are sensitive to and react to the colonizer's portrait of themselves which obstructs the building of harmonious relationships among the members of native society. These aspects of racism allow local white rulers to manipulate native social conflicts to their own advantage.

In their attempts to escape from themselves, natives try to destroy the characteristics that mark them as Indians, but their imposed inferiority and insecurity are revealed when they struggle for status in the white society, and they become consumers of material goods that represent prestige symbols. These native persons are seeking recognition from the white world and lead a sham existence that leaves them disappointed and more frustrated than they were before. At some point in their lives, they refuse to identify with the native masses and pretend to feel sorry for those who are "stuck at the bottom". They will not take part in any civil rights activities or liberation struggles because they claim that they are treated equally with whites. According to their new philosophy, the struggle is only for "those Indians and halfbreeds down there – not me, I've made it". Such persons express contempt for the rank-and-file natives who are struggling against racism and colonialism. Although these colonized people try to reach a "respectable" social status, they live in constant fear of losing the little status they have gained. Indians and Métis have practically no social status in mainstream society, but some still struggle for a recognition that can never be more than charity, patronage, and condescension. They drive luxurious automobiles, associate with "bigshots", and lead an extravagant social life. Regardless of their display of wealth, Indians and Métis will still be rejected by white society because the basis of discrimination is racism. Elitist natives nevertheless feel that they are a sophisticated part of mainstream society and, as a result, they make other minority groups, such as Ukrainians and French Canadians, the object of their discrimination. The white-ideal becomes the master of these middle-class natives. While pretending to be Indian, they ridicule and condemn Indian characteristics; they never use the term "halfbreed" because it sounds vulgar and crude. Obviously, they have internalized the attitudes of whites towards Indians. They belittle and mock other natives who achieve status in leadership positions. Within a colonized society, there is fierce competition for status, because there is so little to start with.

The power of the white-ideal becomes obvious when young Indian and Métis people who have succeeded academically reject their own culture and seek their success in the white world. They have internalized the institutional racism of the college and its instructors, and a future in the native nation now appears bleak and hopeless to them. Because of the white-ideal in educational institutions, higher education cannot be considered as a solution to the problem of Métis and Indians: instead, it firmly entrenches white-supremacist attitudes and the white-ideal in the minds of native students.

There is a general behaviour pattern common to all Third World people.[2] Many of them cannot read or write; many are heavy drinkers of cheap liquor. These people have a deep sense of submissiveness and readily accept their condition of misery and poverty. Colonized people apparently are not troubled by their state of deprivation and have little ambition or hope to rise above it. Gradually, they allow themselves to drift into loose marriage relationships that often fail. They lack initiative and industry, and develop an ineradicable sense of indifference. The spirit of gambling, from bingo to sweepstakes, becomes part of their lives. The men incline towards physically aggressive behaviour, such as wrestling and boxing, and when they drink they brawl. The restricted environment and lack of intellectual challenge make colonized people very personal and trivial in their concerns: jealousies and conflicts engulf much of their lives and consume most of their energies. Envy arises quickly because of the low opinion they have of themselves.

In all colonies, segregation induces shame for the natives' degraded position. However, at the same time there is resentment. Indians and Métis, particularly young people, are sensitive to their condemned, racial position. They conceal their anger from white officials, and show a superficial humility. They know that the white man communicates with them on the basis of his stereotypes, so they learn to conceal their resentment and relate to him only on the surface. This resentment is the negative aspect of their desire for personal esteem. Because their pride has been eroded they are also inclined to be jealous of fellow natives who achieve success. This is systematic colonialism operating the way it was intended to operate. Sometimes, when a native person gains social recognition, other natives may attempt to undermine him through gossip or destructive schemes worked out with local white officials.

It is useless for us to become involved in a struggle to improve our image, because native people did not create these images, and they should not be concerned with trying to improve them so that whites will respect them. The society would simply create new racist images for us to work at and we would be continuously involved in image betterment while remaining colonized. Because racial images in Canada are part of the economic system, whites will not change their attitude towards natives until the economic system is changed. Romantic images, such as "they love the simple life", "they're good hunters", "carefree", "wants are easily satisfied", and "they can't hold their liquor", will persist as long as the present colonial system continues.

An effective method of distorting the social relationships between white and native people is through the myth that Indians need to be protected. By persuading whites to believe this illusion, colonizing governments are able to get away with suppressive and abusive control of natives. Such protection only serves to imprison Indians and Métis more severely. In Canada, schemes of protection are enforced by the Royal Canadian Mounted Police, the treaties, the reserves, and the Indian Act. The economic dependency connected with these schemes fosters distorted social relationships and life-styles. A century ago it was rations; today, it is welfare, which prevents occupational independence and allows the government to control native people as wards and "children". Rather than developing independence and confidence, the protection scheme creates a false sense of security and encourages attitudes of supplication. The small white-power structure in each native community is allowed to dominate the large native population through protective administrations that stifle normal relationships. Because colonizing officials are nervous about the threat of native mass movements, they are increasing protection in their dealings with Indians and Métis.

Sometimes a native father deserts his family in despair because his role and rights as a man and as a breadwinner have been completely eroded. Because of the colonial system, worthwhile employment is denied him, and he is prevented from being restored to his status in the family. He turns to desertion or alcohol to escape from his failures. Giving way to their feelings like this can often get natives into more trouble than they were in before; as a result they become distrustful of emotional experiences, develop "stoical" attitudes, and caution themselves in their responses, emotions, and personal relationships. This, in turn, makes it difficult for them to relate honestly to other people, including members of their own family.

Discrimination and its brutal effects in early life leave scars of hostility and a self-consciousness about ourselves that is difficult to overcome. We feel our self-hate, but, instead of dealing with it honestly, we project it into the entire native race. A Métis fellow I met at a bus depot one day expressed this self-hate when he said, "It's when you see someone very dark, Indian-looking, vulgar, dressed like a bum at the bus station, and you see him acting like all stupid halfbreeds; that's when I could just kill him and all the halfbreeds."[3]

Priests, nuns, and schoolteachers do their share in fomenting hate among native people. By suppressing the native children, these authorities condition them to be quiet, unresponsive, and detached. The children are further conditioned to believe that they are powerless to change anything within the system and instead are directed towards the white middle-class society, a goal that is sure to result in self-hate. A native child can never become a white adult. If an Indian or Métis person succeeds, he is considered by whites as a "pushy", "phony", or "professional" Indian, while the natives say to him, "You've made it, why bother with us": they are somewhat suspicious of a "successful" Métis or Indian.

Métis and Indians define and understand their situation in simple terms according to concepts that differ from those of the whites. Natives discuss issues related to culture and race from their immediate experience, not from abstract theories. They are obliged to live at a subsistence level, so their philosophy is a practical one dealing with immediate concerns. Many are unable to give detailed explanations of racism; instead, they can only give direct examples supported by the phrase, "I just know." Indians and Métis have the feeling that everyone should know that racism is obvious and blatant – to ask them to document discrimination is an insult because racism surrounds them constantly.

Four

Towards Liberation

14 The Failure of Native Leadership

In all the twenty years that I spent at my halfbreed home, a bed was known as a "paillasse" (*pa-jas*). Doughnuts made by Métis women were called "la bange". There were many other words and phrases that were peculiar to our Métis language that remained part of my vocabulary for a long time.

When I first went into mainstream society my Métis ways were ridiculed and my language of "Metchif patois", a combination of English, French and Cree, was openly mocked. I was fully aware that I was struggling in an alien culture, and it was impossible to explain to whites that my native culture had a different frame of reference and a different value system that made it extremely difficult for me to cope with a sophisticated, urban way of life. In mainstream society I began to believe I actually was inferior because of my inability to cope with this totally alien culture, and, consequently, success did not come easily in highly competitive situations against sophisticated whites. Because of the arrogance of white supremacy, there was no attempt on the part of white people to understand my position. It seemed impossible for them to realize that a separate and different native culture existed in Canada; not only were they ignorant of this culture, but they weren't at all concerned to learn more about it.

While I was at university in Berkeley, California, I began to realize my deep feeling for my native heritage. I attended Berkeley for three years and there I met students from many different parts of the world. This international association made me conscious of myself as a Canadian, yet being Canadian did not satisfy or explain fully my nationality. It was only when I acknowledged to myself my Indian ancestry that I was fully satisfied with my national identity. Through my participation in the black people's civil rights struggle I could see myself struggling beside my people at home for the same freedom. The parallels between the black people of America and the native people of Canada are obvious, since they both live in a white-supremacist society: like the Indians and Métis of Canada, black people face discrimination, economic oppression, and political powerlessness. I felt very strongly about their oppression and consequently as colonized natives we understood one another immediately – there was no need to explain our causes to each other.

The more I became involved, the clearer colonialism became. I was very moved when I heard Malcolm X speak to the students about black nationalism. Afterwards, I wanted time to think of the beautiful things he had said. The ideas he expressed about black nationalism were so important that I could not put them out of my mind. I kept trying to fit them into the Indian/Métis situation at home. Nationalism seemed to be the spirit that motivated the black people to a new sense of pride and confidence. Like the black people, I began to reject my feeling of inferiority and shame, and to become proud of my Indian heritage and native nation. In Berkeley I read everything I could find on the Métis and Indians of Canada. I spoke with pride of my Indian heritage. By the time I had finished my doctorate I was very anxious to return to Canada and particularly to Saskatchewan where I would be at home among my Métis people.

Shortly after I went to work for the University of Saskatchewan, I realized that there was an awakening among the Indians and Métis. On a trip through the northern part of the province in 1966 I spoke with many of the native people. They were aware of their oppression and of the critical racial problems in their communities. They were anxious to discuss their problems of inequality and discrimination and they had a sense of pride in their recent struggles against white colonizers. These feelings were representative of Métis and Indian communities throughout the north, I am convinced.

My adventure into white middle-class society had inevitably affected my way of thinking and behaving. I had become much like the white man – sophisticated and urbanized, concerned about the physical comforts of life, and concerned about social mobility and achievement. I suppose the one thing that kept me conscious of being a halfbreed was my childhood experiences of inferiority and discrimination. I had never forgotten the racist abuses I had suffered in my youth, and the hostility that results from such encounters does not die. I had shared the poverty, shame, oppression, and brutality inflicted on us by white supremacy. Because I had made a resolution as a child that I would never turn the other cheek, it was easy for me to become part of the native struggle again. I realized immediately that I belonged in the Indian/Métis society and that my passions and loyalties were with them.

Now that I was able to understand the white-ideal and the profound effect it had on my life, I was able to appreciate the beauty of my own people. The women were indeed beautiful and they possessed a warmth and charm of which I had previously been unaware.

From my experiences in the black civil rights struggle and the Berkeley campus revolt, I had learned a great deal about civil disobedience – boycotts, demonstrations, picketing, sit-ins, and so on. Now that I was back home in my native society of Saskatchewan I offered the skills and benefits of my schooling to my people in their struggle for equality and liberation. Experience in the civil rights struggles had provided me with the political skills essential to organizational work among colonized people.

"Divide and rule" is a basic method of oppressive action that is as old as imperialism itself. Since the colonizer subordinates and dominates the rank-and-file natives, it is necessary to keep them divided in order to remain in power. The oppressor cannot permit himself the luxury of tolerating the unification of indigenous people, which would undoubtedly cause a serious threat to the status-quo rule. Accordingly, oppressors prevent any method and any action by which the oppressed could be awakened to the need for unity. Concepts such as unity, organization, and struggle are immediately labelled as dangerous. These concepts are dangerous to the oppressor because he knows they are necessary for actions of liberation. It is in the interest of the colonizer to continuously weaken the oppressed, to isolate them, to create and deepen rifts among them. This is done by various means, from repressive methods of police action to forms of cultural imperialism and community action programs. The colonizer manipulates the people by giving them the impression that they are being helped, e.g., community development programs, free education, etc.

One of the characteristics of oppressive cultural action that is almost never recognized is the emphasis on a local view of problems rather than on seeing them as parts of a larger whole. In community development, the more a region or area is broken down into local projects, the more alienation and powerlessness is intensified. The more isolated and individualized people are, the easier it is to keep them divided. Intensifying the local and individual way of life of the oppressed hinders the colonized in perceiving reality critically, and keeps them isolated from the common problems of oppressed people in all Third World areas.

The same dividing effect occurs in connection with the so-called "leadership training courses", which in reality co-opt the leaders, isolating them from the masses. These courses are based on the naïve assumption that one can promote the community by training selected leaders. This suggests that it is élites that promote community action and not the masses. Those members of the communities who show sufficient leadership capacities and who are chosen for these courses reflect and express the aspirations of the colonizer's community. They are not in harmony with the way of living and the view of reality that characterizes their people. As soon as they complete the course and return to the community with skills they did not formerly possess, they either use these skills and resources to control the submerged consciousness of their people, or they become strangers in their own communities. Hence, their former leadership position is often threatened. In order not to lose their leadership status, they will tend to continue manipulating the community and the members, but in a more efficient manner, and all in the interest of the colonizer.

When cultural action, as a mass process, begins in a community from the bottom upward and not among its leaders, the former leaders go along agreeably with everyone else, or they are replaced by new leaders who emerge from the rank and file. The result is a new social consciousness of the total community. The oppressors do not favour promoting the community as a whole, but selected leaders, whom they pick. By preserving a state of alienation, they hinder the emergence of political consciousness. And, without this consciousness, it is difficult to achieve the unity of the oppressed as a class.

Class conflict is another concept that upsets the colonizer, since he does not wish to consider himself as part of an oppressive class. Unable to deny the existence of social classes, the oppressors and the supporting middle class preach the need for understanding and harmony between whites and Indians, between management and labour. However, harmony with the oppressed is only possible when its members are engaged in the struggle for liberation.

All actions of the colonizer manifest his need to divide in order to facilitate the preservation of the oppressed state. There are ways of dividing the colonized in order to preserve the system that favours the ruling class. There are forms of action that exploit the weak point of the oppressed, their basic insecurity; they are insecure because they come to believe that the oppressor is omnipotent, and the system is invincible. Under these circumstances, the oppressors take advantage of these weaknesses and perpetuate divisive action. This basic insecurity is thus directly linked to their oppression.

If men in the world of work are to be totally dependent, insecure, and permanently threatened; if their work does not belong to them, men cannot be fulfilled. Work that is not free ceases to be a fulfilling pursuit and becomes an effective means of dehumanization. Every move by the colonized towards unity indicates other actions; it means that sooner or later they will perceive their state of powerlessness and depersonalization. They discover that as long as they are divided they will always be easy prey for manipulation and domination. Unity and organization can make it possible for them to change their weakness into strength.

Since it is necessary to divide the people in order to preserve the colonial government and thereby the power of the colonizer, it is essential for the oppressors to keep the colonized from perceiving a united strategy. In this way the colonizer convinces the oppressed that they are being "defended" against evil people, e.g., whiskey traders, land speculators. In order to divide and confuse the people, oppressors call themselves builders of progress, and accuse the colonized of being obstructive and destructive. History, however, often distorts historical facts. It is the oppressed who are the heroes, not the ruling-class oppressors who use their power to divide and rule.

It is common practice of imperial governments to use middle-class native élites to provide support for their administration. Middle-class society, which shares the same value system and ideology as the ruling class, provides political stability for the capitalist system. Therefore, as soon as natives start action towards liberation, governments make serious efforts to bring native leaders into middle-class society. Attractive offers are made to co-opt them into the mainstream so that these natives see a future there instead of in native society. After these leaders are co-opted, they become supporters of the government and of the colonial rule that suppresses their people and serves to disrupt and weaken native nationalism.

Until recently, the Indian and Métis nation was relatively free from the middle-class élite and the Uncle Tomahawks. However, immediately after the red awakening in the mid 1960s, Indian and Métis organizations rose up in almost every province of Canada, as well as at the national level. Some of these were old organizations revived under different leaders, others were completely new. Since the governments provide generous grants for the operation of these organizations, they direct their policies and programs and even the ideology for the leaders. Most native leaders, however, would deny this. Governments did not get into the business of supporting these organizations until the 1960s when the restlessness of native people and red power posed a potential threat to their administration.

The native groups were structured along the same lines as white bureaucratic institutions. All have a president – in Indian organizations he is called a chief – several vice-presidents, a board of directors and sometimes a senate. They have an executive that is the decision-making body of the organization. Meetings are held in accordance with parliamentary rules and great emphasis is placed on rules and procedure. At a native brotherhood meeting I attended in 1974, I was struck by this tremendous faith in proper procedure – the meeting was more a ritualistic ceremony in praise of Robert's *Rules of Order* than a forum for debate. The natives were so preoccupied with procedure and ritual that discussion on serious social and political issues never arose. They could not relate to each other as people. This is the result of counselling by white advisers and by those native collaborators who want to imitate sophisticated white leaders. Such meetings are useless because they smother rather than develop political and national consciousness. Native people must be perceptive enough to recognize when they are being led down blind alleys by their oppressors, red or white.

Before money is given to native organizations, governments insist that such organizations have legal constitutions. Annual meetings are often spent debating constitutional changes and bylaws. This kind of discussion prevents any political debate on native colonialism. The two national organizations – the National Indian Brotherhood and the Native Council of Canada – are typical middle-class bureaucracies that are not at all representative of the native masses. In some native organizations, the influential decision-makers are white consultants and, in the case of the Indian Brotherhood organizations, even employees of the Indian Affairs Branch – the colonizer. Discussion at the meetings revolves around the internal structure of the organization, its principles, aims, and priorities. The chief concern is to communicate with the federal or provincial cabinets and exert pressure on government policy-makers, because they operate on the assumption that government is going to solve all the problems of the Indian and Métis people. To these native leaders, the matter is essentially one of making officials aware of native problems. The Native Council of Canada in 1972 submitted a brief to the Secretary of State in Ottawa with a demand typical of these native élites:

> We would like to see native representation on several key Federal Agencies and Boards. We refer to the CRTC [Canadian Radio-Television Commission] and the CBC [Canadian Broadcasting Corporation] where we feel that the presence of a native appointee would not only be good for these Boards but would serve as a communications link between us and them.[1]

It would be hard to imagine anything more remote and irrelevant to the Métis and Indian people than the C.R.T.C. and C.B.C., apart from a couple of programs specifically directed at native people. The CBC is the epitome of snobbish middle-class culture, and is not even remotely connected with native society. Another request the Native Council made was for a Métis senator. "We also seek the appointment to the Senate of any one of a number of eminent and distinguished Métis Canadians."[2] Yet today, many whites are talking about abolishing the Senate, not adding to it. Our real struggle is in the streets and in the native ghettos, fighting with our people against colonialism, not seeking prestigious but powerless positions.

These organizations do not represent the grass-roots people. In Saskatchewan, where approximately 60,000 Métis live, only 1,350 are members of the Métis Society of Saskatchewan, slightly more than 2 per cent. Whenever these native organizations establish committees to negotiate with the government, they make them so bureaucratic and complicated that they are virtually useless to the people. Basically, élites work only for better public relations with cabinet ministers, and think too much of their own personal position, prestige, and salary. Yet governments continue to give recognition to these national and provincial organizations as the official voice of native people and grant them millions of dollars annually.

Some native leaders get to the top through compromising their position. The right person receives a lot of promotion and publicity in the news media; "right" means the leader who works within the colonial system of the government and who leads his people to meaningless and trivial achievements. Such leaders often appear to be militant and progressive, but inside the native communities they are reactionaries and "sell-outs". Considerable publicity is given them and as a result they attract a certain following of young, determined, radical youth. They promise great things to the native people with all the flair and rhetoric of colonizing politicians, yet their prime concern is for their public image and income. These leaders are supported by government on the basis of their rhetoric and public image, not on the basis of their support from the native people. When they are co-opted, the leaders also cause most of their followers to be co-opted and in this way they have victimized many native followers who are desperately seeking serious improvements. Since these élites do not have mass support and government officials are notoriously fickle, their political positions are extremely vulnerable. These leaders are useless to the native people.

From their dominant positions the collaborators smother all new and potential leadership among the masses. Because they play the role of messiah, they suffocate the native movement and curb mass involvement. Some of these men give themselves handsome salaries and expense accounts that often exceed $30,000 a year. They spend lavishly on luxurious automobiles, houses and furniture, mod clothes, costly entertainment, and expensive hotels. They are far removed from the actual circumstances of the masses of native people who live in poverty and wretchedness. The real function of these collaborator leaders from the government's point of view is to prevent any mass radical movement from developing and to check social action that would embarrass or threaten the government. Budget programs occupy almost all of their time, so they seldom become involved in any social action that might affect their finances.

They use revolutionary rhetoric about national liberation, but they always do so in safe places like university auditoriums and the ballrooms of luxurious hotels. Their rhetoric is never spoken to the restless and oppressed Indians and Métis who are serious about social action. Because they operate mostly in white society, their impact is almost entirely limited to that area. Having a mentality and life-style like the white businessman, these leaders follow the same colonizing pattern. For example, provincial and national native organizations are attempting to take over the colonial functions of the Indian Affairs Branch and the provincial Métis departments as neo-colonialist administrators. Through this kind of leadership and organization, the native movement is prevented from advancing to serious political and liberation struggles.

It is only a matter of time before Indians and Métis will restructure themselves on a firm political basis for a new movement. There is presently a growth of political awareness among the Indians and Métis, due partly to dissatisfaction with native organizations and partly to the people's involvement in civil rights struggles in their neighbourhoods. Native people are beginning to understand that local social and economic problems are linked to civil rights and liberation struggles. However, native organizations fail to provide any proper political direction for the people.

At the top of the native organization is the executive, which consists usually of president, vice-president, secretary, and treasurer. They are elected by the delegates at the annual meeting. Governing the organization is the executive together with a board of directors. Each director represents a specific geographical area of the province who is supposed to be elected by the people of that area. There are several directors, the number varying for each province. Together, the executive and the board of directors form the supreme governing body. This makes it very centralized and authoritarian. It may be possible for organizations to function democratically and efficiently within this kind of structure under normal circumstances. However, when large, unaccountable government grants that exceed $3,000,000 annually enter the organization, then its entire operation is opened up to manipulation and corruption.[3]

Since most organizations have no training programs, new employees are simply put on the payroll and told to "go out and do your thing". The majority of these recruits have little or no concern for the plight of the native people, or how the native problems can be resolved. Nevertheless, this sudden change in life-style and status has serious psychological implications for colonized employees. The new status immediately isolates the worker from the masses of native people, which is what it is intended to do. Because the colonized's esteem has been so underdeveloped, the new status practically immobilizes him or her for effective communication with the rank-and-file natives at the local level. Without a personnel policy, much of the hiring is done through patronage, or through hiring the threatening critics. Since voting is done through voting delegates from various communities, the employees use their influence to get the "right" delegates elected, who will guarantee support for the Uncle Tomahawk establishment. In some cases, employees themselves are the delegates representing certain locals. Abuses arise easily in such situations. It has been found that some locals were non-existent as in the old "rotten borough" system in England. Through this method the collaborators are assured of re-election.

It is understandable why colonized persons will be subservient to an authoritarian native organization. They are the neo-colonial oppressors. The colonized have changed only from the white bureaucrat to the red bureaucrat; except that the new red oppressor is more absolute, exploitive, manipulative, and brutal. And the people have bought this scheme as a liberating and liberalizing experience for the native people, when in fact the material conditions have become much worse. In this fashion, the advanced capitalist system has integrated its racial problem into the sophisticated liberal system to the satisfaction of the white population, and particularly to the satisfaction of the white radicals. Because they are afraid of falling back on welfare, these collaborators will not oppose each other regardless of the detrimental effects on the masses of native people.

Practically no accountability is demanded by the governments for the $3,000,000 in grants. Thus, it is inclined to attract persons who are opportunists, drifters, hucksters, uncommitted and non-political workers. The flow of easy money and its unaccountability generate a basic rip-off philosophy. Because there is no real direction or purpose in the jobs, a "free loading" philosophy develops.

Although these native leaders talk continuously about political awareness, it is only rhetoric. Most of the workers are politically illiterate on civil rights struggles, colonial oppression, liberation, and social movements. Being able to verbalize a militant language of liberation, they create an impression of radical anti-capitalist activists.

Generally, these native organizations are inclined to provide services to those few persons who are part of the favoured group. Over the last few years, these native organizations have shown how it is possible to create a seemingly democratic and just organization for oppressed people, for their benefit, but behind the scenes and underneath the surface, there is severe discrimination, injustice, and oppression – worse than any white colonizer. Liberal capitalism has successfully integrated Mafia and "goon squad" sub-systems to administer its own ethnic groups. Economically, the Indian and Métis communities remain seriously underdeveloped. Politically, the Métis and Indians remain powerless.

Governments fully comprehend the political principles that operate behind massive grants to native organizations. They understand that racial groups, blacks in the United States, coloured people in Third World colonies, can be a disruptive force in the capitalist system. Therefore, governments continuously attempt to integrate these racial groups into mainstream in order to prevent disharmony. So far, governments have found that co-opting native organizations and their leaders is the most effective method of integrating them, yet keeping them in their same "caste" position. Watergate has given ample evidence of how governments try to stabilize their positions through spying and corruption. Or, whenever necessary, harsher methods are used. Governments understand how they control colonized natives and how they can utilize élitist collaborators to oppress the others, and if necessary terrorize them into submissiveness. Judging by governments' reactions to complaints against the injustices of native organizations, it seems that governments' intentions are not to benefit the masses. Instead, they are to reward the co-opted leaders who will keep the others in their places through vague promises and manipulated token programs. At the same time, the organizations smother all potential indigenous leadership at the local level, and suffocate potential movements that might embarrass or disrupt the establishment.

Of course, government bureaucrats are anxious to solve all "misunderstandings" through a quiet, rational discussion at the office. This is echoed by the élites of the native organizations. Naturally, it is to the advantage of the colonizer to negotiate when he has control of all the power, wealth, and resources. And the native élites who get the crumbs from this wealth usually suggest that the solution to our problem is through the "established and proper legal channels". It is a nice motherhood appeal to suggest that Indians and Métis become Members of Parliament and improve the legislation for native people.

Liberation will not take place through the present native leaders and organizations. The native masses must come to understand that these native élites are working together with the colonizing rulers who hold all the power and decide on the rules of the game. We know only too well the shocking results of working together with our colonizer through his legitimate channels; from 60 to 90 per cent of the inmates in Canada's jails are Indians and Métis.

15 Decolonization and Nationalism

One of my early experiences as an employee was a job with a prosperous white farmer in a neighbouring district. It was my initiation into working for colonizing bosses. He was a fierce man – from the moment he said "Hello" I felt that he owned me, body and soul. He looked at me as part of the "Indian problem". He was both patronizing and oppressive, yet if I had had the courage I could have scared him with a threat of scalping, because I could see that he regarded halfbreeds in terms of the typical racist images. According to his mentality, he had the right to treat me as a powerless and dependent creature, to exploit me and pay me less money. His attitude told me that he saw all halfbreeds as lazy and irresponsible. I found myself totally subservient to him; even my "Hello" was subservient. I was too servile to ask about the wages – I would take whatever he gave me and be grateful for it. His voice rang with contempt. I was fearful to ask any questions, regardless of how necessary they were, because I knew that his answers would only humiliate me. To a simple question of how many sheaves to each stook, he terrorized me with a shout of "Eight, you stupid Indian." He completely crushed me, but, at the same time, hostility arose in me. I felt like punching him in the guts, but instead I stood like a cripple in front of this great white boss.

He was like most racist bosses, ruthless and brutal, completely without understanding or sensitivity. I thought he was trying to figure out how he could cheat me out of my wages, but secretly I plotted my revenge: I would burn down his whole damn wheat crop. I wondered if he was ordering me around just because I was a halfbreed worker, or did he do that to all workers – white or red? I felt he degraded me so that he could hold absolute control over me, not because he was cruel, but because he was greedy. I kept asking myself why it was that he had so much power and the halfbreeds had none. Could I ever become a powerful boss, like him? I saw myself in his eyes – dirty, drunken, and irresponsible. Obviously, he would work me like a horse, and I also knew that I was too submissive to refuse. Maybe he'd work me to death. It would serve him right to have my death on his conscience for the rest of his life. But then again, he didn't seem to have any conscience. In those hot autumn days I stooked till I thought my back would break.

When I got bored and angry I played games and pretended the sheaves were the boss. I'd punch them, kick them, throw them on the ground, jump and spit on them. I'd call them filthy names, insult and debase them in front of all their sheaf friends. I'd shame the "boss" sheaf so badly he wanted to die, but I wouldn't let him die – I made him live to suffer. At other times, I would slowly crush the head of a wheat stem, the symbol of his profit, under my heavy workboots. I'd crush it like a worm. One day, the boss drove over to the field and brought my lunch which I had forgotten. Had the old boy really changed? Was he now going to treat me like a human being? That thought was short-lived. He came to give me hell for leaving the field without his permission and for supposedly bothering his neighbours. He didn't ask *me* if I had walked across the neighbours' fields. Oh no. He automatically took whitey's word against mine. What could I expect, though: I was only a sneaky halfbreed. I wanted to spit right into his fat face, but instead I bowed my head and said, "I'm sorry, sir, I won't do it again," even though I hadn't done what he thought I'd done. He warned me that I had to respect private property. This land was private and sacred to my racist boss but he couldn't appreciate the fact that this land originally belonged to my ancestors and that it had been precious to them. It was sacred to him because it was his means of profit.

I would stook until nearly dark, then walk back to the house for supper. As I got close to the door, the boss's wife would open the door and place a bowl of fricassee and bread on a table outside the house. That was my supper. She always dashed back into the house before I got close enough even to thank her. She too had racist ideas about halfbreeds, I figured she was afraid I might rape her. For the fun of it, I was tempted to frighten her by racing at her but then I realized the old man might be ready with the gun. And it would be easy for any white man to justify the killing of an "oversexed" halfbreed by saying that he had shot in self-defence. After all, the judge would be a colonizer and part of the same oppressive class. As I slowly ate my fricassee I wondered how much happier those rich people were in that beautiful house. Did they really have more fun and happiness than the halfbreeds in their shacks? I never heard them laughing. In fact, I never saw anyone around that farm even smile. As I walked away from the house after returning the bowl and spoon to the outside table I heard someone step outside, pick up the utensils, dash back in, and slam the door. I lived like a phantom, except in the field. But maybe they thought they had a right to treat me like a vicious savage because a couple of halfbreeds I knew had got very drunk one night and "rearranged" things in their farmyard. These two had given a bad name to the whole native community. But why the hell should a couple of halfbreeds stigmatize the whole nation? Such things didn't happen to whites.

My first evening there, I approached the boss as he walked

from the barn, hoping I would have enough nerve to ask him about wages. But before he came even close to me he started to blame me for not stooking faster. He warned me that there were a lot of young breeds hanging around town looking for stooking jobs. It was true. But he was attacking my ability as a worker: I knew how to stook, I had done it before and, in fact, I took pride in my stooking. As I stood there in the semi-darkness listening to him insult me, my anger rose. I wondered if it would boil over. I slowly took off my sweaty gloves, wrung them out, stretched them to full length and pondered. Should I slap this white "couchon"* silly with my stooking hands? Should I stuff his grumbling mouth with my sweating gloves and let him choke on the sweat of a working man? No. I was a true halfbreed, so I calmed down and said obediently, "I'm sorry, sir. I'll work harder tomorrow." He told me I'd find a bed in the barn. In the darkness I found a couple of rough boards with a few filthy rags covered in bird manure. I scraped off the boards and straightened out the rags, took off my boots and stretched out. The stench of manure was so powerful and piercing it almost choked me. I decided to ask the boss about wages tomorrow; in the meantime I was grateful for the bed.

I was a fully colonized native at that time, pathetically subservient and silently hostile. I accepted my inferior place as an Indian. There was no desire or confidence to stand up to this powerful boss, confront him, and struggle for justice. I wanted to do my work, quietly collect my pay, and sneak back home. Although my hostility seethed, I controlled it and submitted to racial indignities. Because I postponed any confrontation with this white oppressor, I postponed decolonizing myself. Is there a right time for decolonization? I don't know. It depends very much on the conjunction of personal feelings and political circumstances. This judgement is hard to arrive at, because of the personal unworthiness and social inferiority a native person experiences with regard to himself and his people.

Decolonization in the Third World colonies of Africa and Asia has meant violent confrontations. As long as ruling forces continue to use brutality, then the colonized people will have

*Local variation of *cochon*, pig.

to counter violence with violence. This situation only spirals. Acts of violence by liberation forces become justified when there is no other way of bringing an end to colonizing governments. If revolutionary violence does become a necessary and legitimate weapon for a national liberation struggle, what form should it take and against whom should it be directed? Would a single act of terrorism aimed at a particular white bureaucrat, or would a collective effort directed towards the entire system be more effective? The success of liberation violence will depend largely upon the determination and commitment of the native people. According to Franz Fanon, violence will free them from their sense of inferiority, despair and inaction.[1] Unfortunately, centuries of hidden hatred have often been directed inwards against fellow natives in the form of beatings, stabbings, and shootings. Right now there is a high murder rate amongst native people, but there comes a time when this hostility and violence must be directed outwards for change, against the external forces that continuously oppress us.

How much longer can native people be expected to endure violence and injustice? Should the children continue to tolerate insults and humiliation at school? Simply because they are native people, should they die of malnutrition in this so-called affluent Canadian society? Why should their life-expectancy be 36 years, compared to 62 for whites? Yet all these forms of abuse and violence have been tolerated by the Indians and Métis themselves as a natural part of their lives.

It might be possible to achieve liberation in an orderly, systematic manner. First, it must be recognized that attempts to decolonize Indian and Métis by integration into mainstream will only be self-defeating, because white supremacy and the white-ideal reinforce and perpetuate colonization and inferiorization. When the white-ideal is gradually destroyed, a reformed education system, a re-created economy, and a spirit of purpose could be regained. This would lead to a genuine sense of confidence, personal skills, and self-esteem. From there, social action could begin in a meaningful way to restructure native society.

An important force in liberation is nationalism, which is difficult to define or explain because it is neither objective nor tangible: on the contrary, it is subjective, spiritual, ideological, and surrounds people continuously. Nationalism gives spirit and content to a community of people by bringing them together under a common history and state of mind. Under ordinary conditions, nationalism will be a positive and rewarding force, giving its members a sense of belonging and pride and serving to educate people both culturally and politically. It can also provide the spirit necessary for independence.

There are clearly many kinds of nationalism. In former Third World colonies such as Cuba and North Vietnam, it is revolutionary nationalism that has formed the basis of the native liberation movement. The means of achieving liberation has been violent, in line with the oppression suffered by the people; a "nation", as defined by their nationalism, is territorial in addition to being economic, cultural, and political. Revolutionary nationalism in this sense is not applicable to the native people of Canada. They are simply not numerous enough to be able to overthrow the government of the country and recapture the entire land according to their justified aboriginal claims, nor are they powerful enough to form a separate state within the dominion. Their nationalism is therefore best defined as "radical nationalism"; their goals are economic, social, and cultural autonomy, and control over all political affairs concerning the natives as a nation, beginning with complete local control of Indian reserves, Métis communities, and native urban ghettos. As long as capitalism remains the dominant ideology in Canada, these segregated Métis and Indian areas will probably have to remain separate and autonomous. A single community of all peoples in Canada with true equality and justice may not be possible until a new order emerges, most likely under socialism. It is also necessary to keep in mind that nationalism is based on the unique historical development of a particular nation. In their present awakening, Indians and Métis are becoming concerned about their heritage and culture in relation to the larger Canadian society and its colonialism; since natives identify themselves as separate from white mainstream society, Canadian bourgeois nationalism means very little to them because it fails to provide a meaningful native identity.

Radical nationalism is activated through a deepening of

social and political consciousness. Such nationalism is linked to, or contains within itself, a progressive political ideology that serves to advance the social awareness of oppressed native people regarding their colonized circumstances, as well as directing the cultural revolution. Beginning at the neighbourhood level, nationalism helps to unite the social actions of native people through mass participation, and therefore grows naturally from the struggles of the people, not from indoctrination through a ruling-class ideology. Radical nationalism is created by the people, who, by participating in the struggle, make the nation a reality to everyone, and, in turn, make the nation part of their personal experience. Nationalism cannot exist if it has not been taken up with full understanding and enthusiasm by the masses, nor can it remain in a static or fixed state; it has to adjust continuously to the changing developments of the people. A nationalism worked out by leaders or by a ruling class does not belong to the people and has no meaning for them.

The growing nationalism among Indians and Métis that specifies that we are a distinct group with our own interests and aims has been accelerated by our political awakening. The examples of Third World liberation struggles have also fostered this native nationalism. We must be careful, however, that our efforts towards political and social advancement do not imitate those of mainstream bourgeois society. We need to define our native ethic according to those principles inherent in our culture that are strongly opposed to the capitalistic profit ethic. This will inevitably mean native separatism for a temporary transitional period. Dignity to a colonized nation under capitalism cannot be restored as long as a white-supremacist society dominates or influences it. In this case, however, separatism means nothing more than allowing the present segregation of reserves, colonies, and ghettos to continue as they are today, with the exception that autonomy and local control must be given to them. Two essentials are needed: constitutional authority and economic independence, since integration into a white-supremacist society for native people causes disintegration of their nation. At the same time, this segregation under radical nationalism will mean greater class consciousness. It develops the understanding that a native liberation struggle is essentially the same struggle as that of the working class and all oppressed people against a capitalist ruling class. In this way, Indians and Métis can build alliances with workers and other oppressed and colonized groups of white society. The struggle today centres on local grievances such as discrimination, poor housing, unemployment, etc. There is virtually no red bourgeoisie in the native society, and the colonizers are trying their best to de-fuse such local resistance as exists by establishing such a class through government programs that attempt to promote service stations, souvenir shops, restaurants, and small industries. However, the influence of the major political parties on the masses of native people in terms of bourgeois politicization and nationalism has been almost nil.

Indians and Métis will need to fight for independence and self-determination like other Third World peoples. We have to recognize that our rights are what we take, that it requires power to take rights and preserve these rights after they have been taken. Freedom will never be freely given. As soon as our struggle begins to gain momentum, ruling authorities will declare that natives are racist and violent. However, it is impossible for minorities to practise racism effectively because they do not exercise any influence on the society that determines the ideology and attitudes of that nation. Under radical nationalism the masses are the leaders and not the Uncle Tomahawks, or the self-appointed representatives, or the élites. Liberation demands are based on obtaining autonomy in native communities and throwing off the domination of government bureaucrats.

Under the colonial society that has imprisoned native people, practically all creativity and intellectual development have been smothered. Radical nationalism provides opportunities for exploring and expanding creatively because the excitement and potential of an awakening nation generates rich, flourishing ideas. Red nationalism revives those native cultural traditions that give stability and security to the nation and discards those that oppress the people. The native nation, in a state of archaic suspension for the last hundred years, will break out of its colonial moulds. Nationalism will usher in a new humanism and harmony that will set native culture in motion once again and open the doors to new cultural developments. This revival of culture will not be refined or sophisticated but it will be vigorous. Formalism and ritualism will be abandoned in favour of new forms of expression that will depict struggle, freedom, vitality, and hope.

Since red nationalism is essential to Indian/Métis liberation, it must be a spearhead force for the native movement, as well as providing the machinery for educating the masses politically. Since the cultural awakening is only one stage of liberation, steps must be taken to ensure that the national consciousness will develop its political aspects as well. There is danger in nationalism if this transition is not made at the right time, because colonized people can quickly become involved in cultural nationalism, which is a move backward to further oppression. They must also be on guard against bourgeois nationalism as well as cultural nationalism. Bourgeois nationalism, however, is easily recognized: it is simply a code of patriotism imposed by a ruling class through authoritarian officials and channels, such as the schools – it is a purely ritualistic and empty exercise, performed only because one is obligated to participate in displays of patriotism.

Cultural nationalism is a reactionary nationalism that forms part of the ideology of imperialism. It is adopted by or imposed on Third World people in their colonized state and it involves the revival of indigenous native traditions and tribalism. Today, in our awakening, many Indians of Canada are returning to native religion and tribal rituals. The danger in this is that it might begin to sever any links with a progressive liberation ideology. The idea that a return to traditional Indian customs and worship will free us from the shackles of colonial domination is deceptive – a return to this kind of traditional worship is a reactionary move and leads to greater oppression, rather than to liberation. Cultural nationalism is more than behaving and believing as traditional Indians; it is a return to extreme separatism in the hope that colonial oppression will automatically go away. The emphasis is upon worship and the performance of ritual behaviour, not upon politics and liberation. Because cultural nationalism insists on excluding political issues, Indians and Métis accept their colonized political conditions without challenging them. It perpetuates the racist idea of "Indians in their place", and does not allow them to develop a radical consciousness or a reorganized culture that would be in harmony with liberation.

Given official encouragement and support, cultural nationalism can entrench itself deeply in the ideology of colonized Indian society and in this way assist imperial governments to control colonized native people. This type of cultural imperialism is spreading rapidly among Canadian Indians, thanks to the generous support of the Indian Affairs Branch. Each year, the Branch sponsors extravagant Indian cultural conferences that are programs designed specifically to bring about a return to tribalism and ritualism. Politics is rigidly excluded from these conferences, and, in fact, any native cultural conference or festival that excludes politics furthers cultural imperialism. The reinforcement of colonization through the encouragement of non-political native cultural activities is not the only form of cultural imperialism. Capitalism has its own supportive culture which it imposes on natives. A good example is the Indian Ecumenical Conference held each summer at Stoney Reserve, Alberta, sponsored by Canadian churches and attended by hundreds of Indians from across Canada and the United States.

Some Indian and Métis studies departments at universities are cultural imperialist programs. They are administered by paternalistic authorities who for the most part support the status quo. The federal government has several such colonial programs in various universities throughout the nation. In 1973, the Indian Culture Centre of Saskatchewan was given a grant of about $500,000 by the Indian Affairs Branch to promote cultural nationalism. Ottawa knows what it is doing. Half a million dollars is a small price to pay for the smothering of radical nationalism among the Indian people of Saskatchewan. This form of cultural nationalism also allows the rulers to create dissension among the various groups of native people. A particular kind of segregation is urged whereby only certain groups of Métis and Indians are allowed to participate in designated tribal festivals, pow-wows, and cultural ceremonies. This is a highly effective method of dulling political consciousness.

Unfortunately, the radical nationalism of the native people is still in the infant stage in Canada. This is largely because colonialism has seriously mutilated the native culture and ideology and has left it with weakened traditions, institutions, and philosophy. At the present time, there is not a great deal of creativity and vigour in the native nation; however, there are signs at the local level that a genuine red nationalism is beginning to emerge.

16 The Struggle for Liberation

Indians and Métis are generally inactive in elections and voting, because when they attempted to negotiate with the federal government before 1885 they were answered with gunfire. A conquered people learns to shun the politics of the conqueror. Through the years, parliamentary government has done very little to improve our social and economic conditions. Under both Liberals and Conservatives we have lived in poverty, without decent jobs or political rights. The New Democratic Party is very much like the other two bourgeois parties, except that it brings about small reforms in health, welfare, car insurance, etc.; it is equally a part of the capitalist system and therefore unable to bring about any real and basic changes in society. All governments regardless of their political affiliations have discriminated against native people and denied them their rights as full citizens.

Parliament is an instrument of the ruling class and its main purpose is to support and protect the ruling class. For example, in the years 1967-75, the federal government gave "a total of $10 billion to the corporations, most of them large and wealthy"[1] in the form of grants, subsidies, and income-tax concessions. Real changes and improvements for native people cannot be obtained through Parliament. It is misleading to think that a capitalist government will ever bring any real freedom and equality to natives: the ballot box is a fraud that tricks us into believing that the next election can relieve us of our oppression. This kind of thinking prevents the development of radical ideas and actions, and it is destructive to urge Indians and Métis to participate in "parliamentary democracy".

All courts and laws are under the control of the ruling-class government and are changed or cancelled to suit their own interests. An example of this occurred in October 1970, when Ottawa forced the War Measures Act on the people of Quebec, thus depriving many citizens of their civil rights. Ottawa did the same thing to the native people of Saskatchewan in 1885 when our ancestors were imprisoned and their valuable lands taken. The ruling class can take these actions whenever we present an obstacle to their plans. The illegal seizure of Indian lands recently near James Bay, various quasi-legal expropriations of reserve lands near Caughnawaga, and illegal attempts to conscript Indians into the army are modern examples of continuing white oppression in the mid and late twentieth century. We have no guarantee that the federal government will not again send in soldiers and guns as it did in the West in 1885.

Some natives of Saskatchewan ran an Indian candidate in the Meadow Lake constituency during the 1968 federal election. This candidate received fewer than 700 votes. Nevertheless, the natives felt that such activity in party politics helped to awaken native people to an understanding of their political situation. Elections can be used to educate people regarding the politics of oppression. When their attention is focused on candidates and elections, they are in a good position to understand the faults of the capitalist system and the way it suppresses native people. But is that enough? The ballot box is clearly not the way we are going to achieve liberation. Our past experiences tell us that the Canadian system is much too racist to ever allow the election and seating of native persons who truly represent their people and not a political party. Louis Riel's expulsion from the House of Commons in 1874 proved that Parliament is a useless exercise for native people. The Members of Parliament voted to deny Riel his House seat even though the people of Manitoba had democratically chosen him to be their representative. Obviously, the wishes of the people mean nothing when capitalist rulers do not want certain individuals in their parliament.

A similar situation occurred in Saskatchewan during the 1972 Athabasca provincial by-election. We native people wanted to nominate a Métis as a candidate for one of the political parties. To vote in the nomination, people had to have a membership in that political party. This cost three dollars. Since we knew that most native people would support a Métis for the nomination, we sold party memberships among our own people. Since many were too poor to afford three dollars, we loaned some of them the money. Enough Indians and Métis bought memberships so that our Métis candidate was assured of winning the nomination. Racism, however, was stronger than we had expected. As soon as the local executive of the party realized that our candidate would win, they developed a scheme to disqualify him. Instead of holding the nomination election, the party executive suspended our Métis candidate on the grounds that our loans to buy memberships were "irregular", if not illegal. Charges were fabricated against our candidate and natives were used to give evidence against him. The Athabasca experience tells us that political parties in a capitalist society will never truly serve native people. Although Canadian society encourages us to get natives into Parliament, the political parties will not accept us when we represent liberation. The token Indians and Métis who are elected to Parliament voice the thoughts of their particular political party and not the demands of native people. We can be sure that all political parties are the same in their policies towards native people. As Indians and Métis, we must reject parliamentary elections as useless in the struggle for native equality and autonomy. Party politics mocks us and exploits us on election days. To overcome this, we must work outside the so-called "established and usual channels" of Parliament. We can make greater progress using civil-rights methods such as picketing, demonstrations, boycotts, sit-ins, as well as confrontations and guerilla activities.

A liberation movement must always deal with the question of reform politics. When Indians and Métis pressure the government through civil-rights action, the government will sometimes make slight reforms. However, we must be cautious about such token reforms because the government changes as little as possible – just enough to quiet the people. Regardless of how great the reforms seem to be, they will still serve to perpetuate the capitalist system and in some cases they may even improve the efficiency of the system that suppresses us. A few years ago, native people established welfare committees in Métis local communities, whereby committee members went with our needy people to welfare offices to ensure that they would receive fair and just treatment from welfare officials. To counteract this decolonization activity, the Liberal government offered to hire native people to work as welfare assistants in their offices to deal with the needy Métis. If native workers had accepted these positions they would have become bureaucrats with a vested interest in their jobs, salaries, and prestige. At the same time, they would have become decision-makers over their own people. Such co-opting schemes cause disagreement among us because those who are politically unaware see these jobs as excellent opportunities. They do not realize that they are being manipulated into the scheme of Métis oppressing Métis. It is important that natives develop a sense of unity and a sense of brotherhood about such matters. Petty differences and ambitions must be put aside in order to concern ourselves with the masses of native people. Above all, Indians and Métis must stop trying to be accepted by white society. A strong native movement cannot be built by people who are ashamed of their Indianness, lying to themselves, and "sucking up" to the so-called important white people.

According to Canadian society, Indians and Métis have two alternatives: integration or segregation. But does integration exist as a possible reality? Not if the person bears the indelible print of Indian appearance. For centuries, Canadian ruling authorities have forced segregation upon Indians and Métis. It was their way of hiding Canada's racial problems. With the spread of colonial uprisings in the world after 1945, schools became recognized as an important socializing agency towards integration. The prime function was to get native children to accept the capitalist system and their position in it. Schools became the main agency for integration. Teachers, who are status-quo oriented, taught that "life is fun in a smiling fair-skinned world". Integration for native people means becoming part of the dominant WASP society. However, such integration is a possibility only for those Indians and Métis whose appearance is white enough to allow them to pass as non-Indian people. Only a small percentage of the native population will be successful in such integration.

Integration gives increased support to the white-supremacy system and stabilizes it rather than promoting a fundamental transformation of it. Doubtless, thousands of fair-skinned Métis have integrated into mainstream and have become part of the status quo. However, at the same time they have denied their Métis background and will forever remain silent about it. There are some Métis in every generation who cross the racial barrier and integrate as deeply as possible into mainstream where they hope their background will never be discovered.

However, for the masses of natives, whose appearance is clearly Indian, their destiny is almost certain to be the ghetto. There are, of course, those exceptions who will deny their ancestors and succeed in a pseudo-integration. Their route is through higher education, luxurious cars, suburban homes, mod clothes, and lavish social entertainment. Such pseudo-integration relies upon the whims of patronage and paternalism. Since Canada is a white-supremacy country, the white-ideal will continue to attract Indians and Métis to integration. However, for the rank-and-file native people there is no alternative to segregation. One of the certain results of conquest is the ghetto, because it is a reaction of the conquered to the new imperial rulers. In the colonial process, the native people are conditioned to a servile and oppressed status, which is part of the culture of the ghetto. It perpetuates itself from one generation to the next, because of the particular kind of economics that operate within the capitalist system. Although middle-class values and their importance in the larger society are known by ghetto people, these people concern themselves mostly with their own ghetto neighbourhood. It seems to provide a certain sense of security. The natives who have integrated encounter a dilemma because there is little likelihood of their being allowed back into the ghetto. Integration implies a rejection of those who remain. Within the ghetto there is a certain friendship and generosity that provides security and comfort, in spite of the poverty and wretchedness.

Federal and provincial governments have been trying rather desperately to integrate Indians and Métis through education, upgrading programs, small business enterprises, etc. However, these programs have so far met with little success. Obviously, the governments are fearful of the black ghetto violence that took place in the United States. But the racism in Canada is too deeply entrenched to permit mass integration of the Métis and Indians. Token integration is the most the Canadian society will allow and that is not enough to prevent racial problems. It seems that the Indians and Métis have little choice but the ghetto in one form or another. The ghetto does not have to mean continuous disintegration and political immobility. Instead, it can serve as a base for civil-rights action and liberation. In the last few years a movement of red nationalism has developed slowly, with which the native people have identified to some degree. As soon as ghetto people have a social consciousness beyond their state of colonization, they begin to explore for participation in some form of social action.

It is quite impossible for Indians and Métis in their present condition to experience any real liberation within the present capitalist society in terms of gaining control of reserves and communities, being free from discrimination and racism, obtaining full employment, acquiring a decent standard of living, or becoming free and equal people. We need to liberate ourselves from the courts, ballot boxes, school system, church, and all other agencies that command us to stay in "our colonized place". This oppression of the native people is so deeply rooted in the capitalist system that it cannot be completely eliminated without eliminating capitalism itself. The Indian/Métis struggle for self-determination against the ruling class has some potential because of the occupational structure of the native people. Those Indians and Métis who have jobs are almost exclusively labourers and very few are of the professional classes or the petit-bourgeoisie. Because of racism we are the most exploited and oppressed of all the workers. At the moment the success of the native movement depends on its ability to develop a radical thrust and upon the strength of its red nationalism. Mobilization of the masses of Indians and Métis is still centred around local community struggles. However, as the struggle widens, social class features will gradually become more prominent and the movement will turn into a class struggle. Indians and Métis will come to see that the different class struggles throughout Canada are not separate and unrelated.

This analysis takes into account the fact that it is not only the native society that is colonized, but Canada and all of its citizens. White Canadians and Indian/Métis are in similar states of colonization. Canada has always been a colony, first of France, then of Britain, and now of America. Although Europeans came to Canada as settlers, they in turn were colonized by the mother country. In 1837 Canadians attempted a struggle for independence, but they were defeated by English imperialists; consequently, the social institutions, legal and political structures, and ideological framework remained under the control of the Imperial government in London and later under the colonial bourgeois administration in Ottawa. Canada is now a colony of America, and what applies to Indians and Métis to some extent applies to white Canadians who have their own national liberation struggle against the empire of the United States. Like Indians and Métis, white Canadians must acknowledge their colonized situation and then direct their national liberation movement from that point. At the same time, Canadians in general will need to develop their radical nationalism. Such a nationalism is beginning to emerge, but work must be done to make sure that it does not remain bourgeois nationalism. The major difference between whites and reds in their colonization is that natives have been moulded into a pseudo-apartheid system. Their struggle is therefore a double one: the first and most immediate struggle is against the colonialism of the federal and provincial governments; the second is against the imperialism of the United States. The struggle against the government of Canada is the most immediate because its agents occupy our native communities and dominate our daily lives.

Among the Métis and Indians, nationalism has helped to create a certain unity and political consciousness. However, if it does not develop into a realistic attack on imperialism, it can only become a false consciousness, a breeding ground for cultism, adventurism, and opportunism. We must not let the middle-class native élites mislead us into believing that our people can achieve freedom and justice through assimilation, integration, a good education, small business ownership, etc. We must expose these reactionary leaders as collaborators of the imperialist rulers. They depend on the government for their privileges, not on the masses in the native world. A class of red bourgeoisie provides an important means to continue colonialism and oppression. As long as governments continue to use Indian and Métis élites, it will be difficult for us to obtain our liberation from this kind of neo-colonialist rule over our people. Because these leaders pretend to be radical and militant, the result of their leadership is that the masses are kept in a state of agitation and expectation. This projects the erroneous idea that the native people are about to rebel, and for the last few years these middle-class Indian and Métis leaders have made demands on the government, threatening them with the possibility of native violence if their demands for financial grants are not met. The result has been increasing opportunism and corruption in the native organizations: the restlessness of native people has been exploited to advance the personal ambitions of opportunistic élites and the development of a neo-colonialist rule.

In the last few years the Indians and Métis have explored many different possible solutions to their problems, ranging from petitions to confrontations. However, all these methods have been relatively unsuccessful. In the meantime, governments have promoted schemes for solving the so-called "Indian problem". These schemes have included the following:

1. Physical integration into white society. This attempt has been largely through the "integrated school" policy where

Indian and Métis children are bused into public schools in neighbouring towns. This has failed, in most cases because Indian parents are now having new Indian schools built on the reserves where their children are not forced into white society and mainstream. Also, government upgrading training programs and attempts to relocate Indian and Métis in the towns and cities have failed. These plans have met with little success simply because employment is not available at the end of the training program and these native people are obliged to return to their communities.

2. Red capitalism, particularly in Alberta. Red capitalism has failed as a solution because it includes so few native persons that it has not assisted the rank-and-file Métis and Indians. By tradition and heritage, native people are not inclined to private enterprise. The financial assistance provided by governments for these business enterprises is too small to make them successful. Furthermore, an Indian or Métis businessman is no less exploitive of native labour than a white businessman.

3. Government self-help programs. These community development programs have failed largely because they have been allocated to and administered by the native organizations. As a result, most of the funds have been ripped off by the native administrators before they get to the communities. Consequently, these programs rarely reach the native masses and hence do not benefit them.

4. Educational and cultural programs. The provincial and federal governments know about the colonizing effects of the cultural programs they support and promote among the native people. An example of cultural imperialism was the "Back to Batoche" Métis festival in 1974. The provincial government gave a $40,000 grant to the Métis Society on the condition that *no* politics would be allowed during the festival. This kind of cultural imperialism is very effective in directing the native masses into greater oppression. Likewise the Cultural College of the Federation of Saskatchewan Indians with its emphasis on Indian legends is a white-liberal

concern that assists in impoverishing the Indian culture even further.

5. Promotion of native organizations. Native organizations are the "hidden hand" of the government's bureaucratic oppression. These organizations have become more effective in controlling and suppressing the Indian and Métis masses than any government agency. Governments have found that these organizations are exceedingly co-operative, although at times, for the sake of their credibility with the native masses, these organizations stage professional civil-rights actions, such as sit-ins. All in all, these native organizations are for the most part opportunistic and élitist, serving to keep the native masses oppressed and at the same time giving the governments a liberal, democratic image, as if they were seriously concerned about the situation of the Indian and Métis people.

Native people have also been encouraged to believe that their problems will be solved if they will elect more native politicians to Parliament. None of these programs has produced any real or permanent improvements; however, they have helped to mobilize a social force of a few thousand native activists across the nation. Such programs have also forced us to reject many illusions: the illusion that mass integration is possible; the illusion that party politics is the answer; the illusion that peaceful methods and moral appeals will bring results; and the illusion that native élites and revolutionary rhetoric adequately represent native aims. It is now clear that the problems of native people cannot be solved by native organizations or by government programs or by increased welfare. Faced with these realities, the native movement is now painfully evaluating its past actions and seeking a plan for the future. In the meantime, the native movement has been brought to the public attention as part of Canadian politics.

Within the context of Canadian society, the Indian and Métis liberation problem is complicated by the fact that our social lives and material conditions are bound up with those of the colonizer and his system. Although we have lived relatively separated and isolated from mainstream society in our reserves, colonies, and ghettos, we are tied to the capitalist system by such things as religion, material consumption, and social success. Although we have been denied the major benefits of industrialism, we were the original source of labour that created the wealth of this country and thus we contributed to the development of the existing colonial system. Consequently, it is quite impossible to separate the development of Canadian society from the growth of our colonized conditions. Therefore, if the society is to be changed to meet the needs of the Indian and Métis people, the problems of the entire society will have to be resolved at the same time. The native movement cannot avoid tackling the basic problems of the entire Canadian society. In this way our liberation struggle automatically involves the Canadian whites.

Realistically, our decolonization has to be developed through our role as revolutionary people in the present colonial system. No longer are we needed as a labour force to meet the needs of economic development. Indians and Métis, particularly the young, are a potential revolutionary force inside Canada, yet we have not acknowledged the need for the revolutionary organization, ideology, and action that must be developed if we are ever to be free. We are reluctant to tackle the responsibility of revolutionary politics. We share the Canadian tendency to avoid looking at reality, hoping to find easy solutions to complex problems.

Indians and Métis cannot count on any support from the white working class in their struggle against imperialism, at least not at this time. Part of the working class and its union aristocracy have disappeared into the capitalist ranks. Some unions and workers appear to be primarily concerned with getting a greater slice of the economic pie rather than with promoting a revolutionary struggle. Their energies are directed towards internal organization and economic gain within the capitalist system, such as higher wages, pensions, etc. Because they have been absorbed into the system as an integral part of capitalism, they have reduced their effectiveness in struggling against it. Historically, white workers of the imperial nation generally have much better working conditions, higher wages, and a higher standard of living than the workers of the colonies.

The white workers' good conditions are due partly to the crude exploitation of the native workers in the Third World. Generally, white workers are inclined to oppose liberation and independence for native colonies. White workers tend to identify themselves with the colonizing society, and white supremacy is as much a part of the working class as it is of the ruling class. As jobs become increasingly scarce, white workers react more severely against native workers. The poorer the white worker, the more he is threatened by the native worker, and the stronger are his racist feelings. Since white workers are inclined to see developments in the native struggle as a direct threat to them, they often support the reactionary appeal to enforce "law and order". In this way, they serve the forces of counter-revolution. It is understandable that Indians and Métis identify more with the colonized coloured people of the Third World than with the white working class of their own nation. Instead of struggling against capitalism, the majority of workers are inclined to accept it as the best of all possible systems; they believe it only needs to be reformed so that they will receive greater privileges and benefits. Those workers who have become integrated into the capitalist system are not at present a potential source of support for revolutionary change. There are exceptions, of course: many workers and unions in Quebec are in the forefront of struggles against the capitalist system. Nevertheless, there comes a time when all oppressed people must join together in a united struggle and form a new revolutionary class. It appears that this new class will comprise women, youth, natives, and workers. At the same time, the ruling class must be prevented from isolating any one group from the remainder, as they did in 1885 and again in 1970 during the Quebec crisis.

The Indian and Métis movement must focus primarily on the destruction of imperialism and on the process of decolonization. There is no longer any question of whether the native struggle should pursue a capitalist or socialist path of development. Liberation can take place only within a true socialist society. However, we must not let ourselves be turned against socialism by weak or oppressive examples of it in other countries. We need the socialism that leads to the liberation of oppressed racial groups and a democratic society for all people. It is certain that the New Democratic Party does not stand for true socialism. We know also that the Labour Party in England has a pseudo-capitalist ideology, and that the Union of Soviet Socialist Republics is an imperialist nation that oppresses minority groups. Only when the native people have been politically awakened to a new socialist society will the struggle expand to a full revolutionary movement. The support of the masses is an absolute necessity before a complete transformation of society can be made.

Support from the people will come as soon as they can see the possibility of improvement in their conditions and have developed a desire to change the system. When this point has been reached, the people will have a clear understanding of the aims and purposes of the struggle. One of the greatest tasks is to organize around local grievances in order to improve the people's circumstances and educate them politically at the same time. The basis of such organizations should be the local native communities, reserves, or urban ghettos. In each of these a committee or council should be established by the residents. These local councils must make it possible for the greatest number of people to unite and take an active part; they will come into existence only when the local people themselves decide on such action. There is nothing complex or mysterious about a local council; it is a very simple and flexible organization of people in a large committee. There is no official executive: the people select a person to take the chair for a limited period of time, as required. This person acts as spokesman for the group and is responsible for the details of administration. All major decisions are made by the whole group or by committees established for specific functions. Every effort must be made to prevent power from being invested in one person and, similarly, the group must not become dependent on one or several individuals to make the decisions and do all the work. The position of secretary should also be rotated. Although the council is flexible, totally co-operative, and democratic, it is not disorganized or chaotic. Discipline is exercised by the individual, according to his or her commitment and loyalty. By their involvement, the masses of people will become politicized, and the first step towards liberation comes through this type of local organization and action.

All struggles must be about specific local issues that people feel are significant to them. Each struggle must relate to the people's daily existence. It is up to the local people to say how and where they are to struggle and what kind of confrontation they will employ. Since the movement must be kept flexible so that local communities are able to take action immediately and independently, no head office or central leadership can be allowed to direct the movement. Each community must follow its own distinct pattern. Central leadership only preserves and stabilizes the present capitalist system. Likewise, local councils should guard against the formation of any kind of hierarchy or bureaucracy or any distinction by age, sex, or education. A continuous exchange of ideas and information must take place among all local people as equal members in the struggle. We have to learn for ourselves through experience, rather than being dependent on the teaching and information of so-called specialists and experts.

The revolution has to be brought about by the masses through the unique struggles that embody their politics and culture. It is from locally based struggles that true revolutionary theory evolves, a revolutionary theory functional for those people who must liberate themselves. Similarly, the local people will create new kinds of social institutions so that they can relate to one another in a human and dignified way. By starting with local struggles in which the chances of winning a small measure of power are good, the people will develop a sense of hope and determination. Later, they will widen the struggle and challenge the larger structures of society. As the movement advances they will develop increased enthusiasm and allegiance to their struggle against oppression. People soon learn that political maturity comes from direct and immediate acts of liberation.

These local communities must always be free to engage in spontaneous revolutionary activities at any time. They know better than any central authority the right time and the right place to rupture the system. The development of confrontations must be the sole decision of the local people, based on their own experiences and priorities. Such decentralization allows the masses to organize their own tactics and to engage their people in serious political struggles that will advance consciousness, skills, leadership, decolonization, and liberation. Self-determination for each community means working at the level where the community and the people actually exist so that the masses become involved in decision-making.

The Métis community at Ile à la Crosse in northern Saskatchewan is a good example of how the local people can take control of local institutions. There, the native people gained control of the public school in June 1973. Their success was partially due to the people's readiness to seize control and to exploit the opportunities when they presented themselves. A portion of the school had burned down and a few months later the government was about to receive tenders for the reconstruction of the school. At this point the local Métis people decided that they should be employed to rebuild the school, since there were skilled tradesmen among them who were unemployed. Later, they also decided that they should take control of the school's administration and the selection of teachers. Since the community is populated almost entirely by Métis people, they hold the power, at least in numbers. They realized this fact and used it as a lever in their struggle. The methods they used to achieve their goal were mass meetings, continuous campaigning in the community, and persistent bargaining.

During this period the provincial government was in the process of transferring authority over the school from the Department of Education to the newly created Department of Northern Saskatchewan. Consequently, legislation on education in the north was in a state of flux. The natives of Ile à la Crosse took advantage of this situation and demanded that authority over the school be legislated to the local people. Again they were successful. They were now in control of the local school administration and the selection of teachers, and all this was accomplished without any violence or threat of violence. Through their elected local committee they kept the community organized and well informed. Developments did not all take place automatically or smoothly. There were temporary setbacks, and there will be many more before the native people get full control of their community, but resistance from the teachers, white officials, Catholic priests, and Hudson's Bay employees kept the native people united and mobilized. After the Métis had taken control of the school, the white power structure reacted negatively. The parish priest threatened to deny the Catholic native people sacraments and confession. The school principal made a public statement that "someone would be killed". These threats did not stop the native people from restructuring the school into an educational, recreational, and cultural institution that would serve all the people of the community. They are now defining new goals of education with a broader and more human meaning by making the curriculum more relevant to their daily lives.

Only through persistent struggles for control of local situations such as these can a mass liberation movement develop. The Métis of Ile à la Crosse have shown that it is possible to take over local institutions in native communities and re-create them so they serve the liberated native people and not the imperialist agents. They did receive valuable support from two key government officials and in a way this could be called protection, but we must use whatever allies are willing to support us at such critical times. This is not the time for a call to violence. In the Quebec crisis of 1970, the government showed itself completely willing to use violence and jail against people who attempt liberation through violent means, and they would crush a native people's liberation struggle with even greater brutality than they did in 1885. A call to arms by the native people at this stage would be a call to martyrdom. However, as the native movement develops together with the struggles of other oppressed groups in Canada, there may come a time when guerilla violence will be necessary and appropriate, and we must not hesitate to use it.

Indians and Métis know that the present institutions have failed them, and that they have a right to take control of these institutions and change them. The greater the number of institutions that are liberated from white bourgeois control and turned into liberated zones, the greater will be the base for expanded control. Once we gain control of such institutions, we will resist giving them up. At this time the local councils will form a base of native power and will serve as the native people's local government. The larger and more united are the local councils throughout Canada, the more powerful the native movement will be. The time is long overdue for Indians to take over their reserves but, instead of liberating themselves from the Indian Affairs Branch departments, they are becoming managers of social service and community programs that remain under white colonial control within the capitalist system. The successful development of the native movement, particularly in the advanced stage, will depend upon the development of the revolutionary struggles of other groups in Canada. However, in this present early stage of the movement, the native people are able to fight as an independent group because they are not seriously threatening the ruling forces.

To link the local communities together, a provincial co-ordination committee could be created from among the representatives of the local councils. However, this co-ordinating committee would not be given any authority over local organizations. Its primary function would be to channel information to local communities and to develop political analyses that would contribute to the understanding of the Indian/Métis liberation. It could synthesize the activities of the various local councils and broadcast them at a provincial or national level, but the co-ordinating committee would have no authority over the direction of the movement or over any local council. There is no room for an élite leadership.

In the struggle for liberation, the native people are asked to put their confidence in the good intentions of the colonizers. While it is true that certain decolonization is taking place, it is false to pretend that it is the result of the changing nature of man and of the state. The optimism that prevails today for liberation is not based on the fact that capitalism is becoming more humane or that colonialism is becoming more just. It is simply that the advanced liberal corporate state is able to co-opt native nationalism and revolutionary consciousness. Even our own revolutionary rhetoric has become an integral part of advanced capitalism.

We are told that the enemy, colonialism, is the historical oppressor. But we must make no mistake that our oppression is in the forms and institutions of colonialism, and in its manifestations, such as racial stereotypes, Indian bureaucracies, welfare, prisons, etc. Only by transforming the objective conditions can we put a final end to colonialism. For example, we must change the authoritarian schools and government departments, the economic élite who control the masses and the government, the chauvinist relationships that exist between men and women.

The Indians and Métis are now concerned with giving a native dimension to their lives and actions because identity helps in the struggle against colonialism. This struggle for liberation is a long and arduous one, yet it is for this reason that it must be fought without respite and without compromise. We have to do this by working at all levels in the liberation struggle. For instance, some members are able to work at the neighbourhood level in simple organizational and education work, while others can work in a broader way, mobilizing for civil-rights actions and extra-parliamentary confrontations. Finally, there must be a group of natives who are willing and able to work at the sophisticated level of guerilla warfare, both urban and rural. The racism and colonialism of capitalism will always hold us captive in misery, violence, and exploitation. It is time that we recognized our own power and faced the fact that our solutions lie within ourselves. Revolution can be made only by those who are in a state of revolution.

Appendix A

CASUALTIES OF INDIANS AND MÉTIS IN 1885 BATTLES

I. Executed by judicial system: 9
II. Indians and Métis killed in military action: 49
III. Indians sentenced to prison: 23
IV. Métis sentenced to prison: 21
V. Indians and Métis wounded during battles: Unknown, but estimated to be in the hundreds.

I. NATIVE PERSONS MURDERED ON THE SCAFFOLD

1. Louis Riel
2. Papamahchakwayo – Wandering Spirit
3. Nopface – Iron Body
4. Wohwahnitch – Man Without Body
5. Manachoos – Bad Arrow

6. Wawaase — kovees — Dressy Man
7. Charles Ducharme, Charlebois, Itca
8. Kittamaque — Miserable Man
9. Apischikoos — Little Bear

II. INDIANS AND MÉTIS KILLED IN MILITARY ACTION

1. André Batoche
2. Isidore Boyer
3. François Boyer
4. Damase Carrière
5. Michel Desjarlais
6. Charles Ducharme
7. Isidore Dumont
8. Ambroise Jobin
9. Auguste Laframboise
10. Joseph Mountour
11. Jean Baptiste Mountour
12. José Ouellet
13. Donald Ross
14. John Swain
15. Calixte Tourond
16. Elzéar Tourond
17. Joseph Trottier
18. Michel Trottier
19. Pierre Parenteau
20. José Vandal
21. José Vermette

And an additional 26 men, one 14-year-old girl, and one infant.
TOTAL: 49
TOTAL NUMBER OF INDIANS AND MÉTIS KILLED IN 1885 WAR: 58

III. INDIANS SENTENCED TO PRISON FROM TWO TO 20 YEARS

1. Kaykewipahtow
2. Ooskatatask
3. Ahtomisscomcoahwahsce
4. Okadoka
5. Wahmahditota
6. Cahrutamahitchi
7. Konahmahchee
8. Papumakesick
9. Wahsahgamap

10. Mussinass
11. Copinouwaywin
12. Kaphayakastocum
13. Big Bear
14. Poundmaker

And nine additional Indians.

TOTAL: 23

IV. MÉTIS SENTENCED TO PRISON FROM ONE TO SEVEN YEARS

1. Pierre Parenteau
2. Pierre Gariépy
3. Pierre Henry
4. Emmanuel Champagne
5. Maxime Lépine
6. Albert Monkman
7. Joseph Delorme
8. Phillipe Gariépy
9. Joseph Arcand
10. François Tourond
11. Alexandre Cayen
12. Patrice Tourond
13. Jim Short
14. Alexandre Fisher
15. Baptiste Vandal
16. Ignace Poitras
17. Pierre Vandal
18. Joe Pilon
19. Baptiste Rocheleau
20. Moïse Parenteau
21. Maxime Dubois

TOTAL NUMBER OF INDIANS AND MÉTIS IMPRISONED FROM 1885 WAR: 44

(NOTE: It is difficult to get accurate figures and names on wounded and killed warriors of the Indians and Métis. Like all guerilla fighters, they always gathered their dead and wounded before the federal troops could identify them. The above information comes partly from the priests and partly from the native leaders after the hostilities.)

Bibliography

1. ORIGINAL SOURCES

Canada, Parliament, *Select Committee to Collect Evidence on Hudson's Bay Company*, 1857.

Claims to Land by the North-West Half-Breed Grant by Settlers Along the South Saskatchewan and Vicinity, Ottawa, 1886.

Dominion Parliament, Debates in the House of Commons, 1875, 1876, 1885, and 1886.

Epitome of Parliamentary Documents: Northwest Rebellion 1885, McLean, Roger & Co., Ottawa, 1886.

Interviews with some elderly Métis and Indian persons of Saskatchewan.

Jackson Papers, University of Saskatchewan Archives, Saskatoon.

Ledoux, Isidore, 100-year-old Métis of Leask, Saskatchewan.

Macdonald Papers, Public Archives of Saskatchewan, Saskatoon.

Mika, N. *The Riel Rebellion: A Documentary History,* Belleville, 1972.

Northwest Rebellion 1885, Canada, Department of Justice, Ottawa, 1886.

Oliver, E. H. *The Canadian Northwest: Documentary History,* King's Printer, Ottawa, 1914.

Prince Albert *Times,* 1883-5.

"Reminiscences of Louis Cochin", *Canadian Northwest Historical Society,* Vol. 1, No. 11, Battleford, 1927.

Report of the Select Committee on the Causes of the Difficulties in the Northwest Territory in 1869-1870, Ottawa, 1874.

Saskatchewan *Herald,* North Battleford, 1883-5.

Sessional Papers, Department of the Interior, Vol. 19, Nos. 6 and 12, Ottawa, 1886.

Toronto *Globe,* 1884-5.

The Treaties between Her Majesty, Queen Victoria, and the Indians of British North America, Queen's Printer, Regina, 1961.

2. COLONIALISM AND RACISM

Boggs, J. *Racism and the Class Struggle,* Monthly Review Press, New York, 1970.

Casas, B.de las. *History of the Indies,* Harper & Row, New York, 1971.

Cockroft, J. D. *Dependence and Underdevelopment,* Anchor Books, New York, 1972.

Cox, O. C. *Caste, Class and Race,* Monthly Review Press, New York, 1959.

Fanon, F. *The Wretched of the Earth,* Grove Press, New York, 1966.

———. *A Study in Dying Colonialism,* Penguin Books, London, 1970.

Goshal, K. *People in Colonies,* Sheridan House Press, New York, 1948.

Green, F. *The Enemy: What Every American Should Know about Imperialism,* Vintage Press, New York, 1971.

Hobson, J. A. *Imperialism,* University of Michigan Press, Ann Arbor, 1965.

Howitt, W. *Colonization and Christianity,* Negro University Press, New York, 1964.

Jalée, P. *Pillage of the Third World,* Monthly Review Press, New York, 1968.

Leonidov, F. *Racism: An Ideological Weapon of Imperialism,* Foreign Languages Publishing House, Moscow, 1968.

Magdoff, H. *The Age of Imperialism,* Monthly Review Press, New York, 1969.

Memmi, A. *The Colonizer and the Colonized,* Beacon Press, Boston, 1965.
———. *Dominated Man,* Beacon Press, Boston, 1968.
Miller, N. *National Liberation,* Free Press, New York, 1971.
Morel, E. D. *The Black Man's Burden,* Monthly Review Press, New York, 1969.
Nkrumah, K. *Neocolonialism,* International Publishers, New York, 1965.
———. *Class Struggle in Africa,* International Publishers, New York, 1970.
Winks, R. *The Age of Imperialism,* Prentice-Hall, Englewood Cliffs, N.J., 1969.
Woddis, J. *Introduction to Neocolonialism,* International Publishers, New York, 1967.
Worsley, P. *The Third World,* Weidenfeld & Nicolson, London, 1967.
Wright, L. B. *Religion and Empire,* Octagon Books, New York, 1965.

3. INDIANS AND MÉTIS

Davis, A. K. *A Northern Dilemma,* Vol. 2, Western State College, Bellingham, Washington, 1965.
Engels, F. *The Origin of the Family* (translation), Foreign Languages Publishing House, Moscow, 1942.
Farb, P. *Man's Rise to Civilization,* Dutton, New York, 1968.
Forbes, J. *The Indian in America's Past,* Prentice-Hall, Englewood Cliffs, N.J., 1964.
Giraud, M. *Le métis canadien,* The Institute of Ethnology, Paris, 1945.
Howard, J. K. *Strange Empire,* James Lewis & Samuel, Toronto, 1974.
Jenness, D. *The Indians of Canada,* King's Printer, Ottawa, 1932.
Meyer, W. *Native Americans,* International Publishing House, New York, 1971.
Morgan, H. *Ancient Society,* Charles Kerr, Chicago, 1877.
Novak, G. *Genocide against the Indians,* Merit Publishers, New York, 1959.
Osler, E. B. *The Man Who Had to Hang, Louis Riel,* Longmans, Green, Toronto, 1961.
Patterson, E. *The Canadian Indian,* Collier-Macmillan, Toronto, 1972.
Robertson, H. *Reservations Are for Indians,* James Lewis & Samuel, Toronto, 1970.
Roe, F. G. *The North American Buffalo,* University of Toronto Press, Toronto, 1970.

Trémaudan, A. H. *Histoire de la nation métisse dans l'ouest canadien*, Lévesque Publishers, Montreal, 1936.
Waubageshig, *The Only Good Indian*, New Press, Toronto, 1970.

4. CANADIAN HISTORY

Begg, A. *History of the Northwest*, Hunter Rose, Toronto, 1894.
Bergeron, L. *The History of Quebec*, NC Press, Toronto, 1971.
Brown, L. and C. *An Unauthorized History of the R.C.M.P.*, James Lewis & Samuel, Toronto, 1973.
Easterbrook, W. *Canadian Economic History*, Macmillan, Toronto, 1956.
Innis, H. A. *The Fur Trade in Canada*, University of Toronto Press, Toronto, 1930.
Innis, H. A., and Lower, A. R. M. *Select Documents in Canadian Economic History, 1783-1885*, University of Toronto Press, Toronto, 1933.
Lamb, R. E. *Thunder in the West*, Pageant Press, New York, 1957.
Morton, A. S. *A History of the Canadian West to 1870*, Nelson, Toronto, 1939.
———. *Under Western Skies*, Nelson, Toronto, 1937.
Morton, W. L. *Manitoba: A History*, University of Toronto Press, Toronto, 1957.
Myers, G. *The History of Canadian Wealth*, James Lewis & Samuel, Toronto, 1972.
Rich, E. E. *The Fur Trade and the Northwest to 1857*, McClelland & Stewart, Toronto, 1967.
Ryerson, S. B. *The Founding of Canada*, Progress Books, Toronto, 1960.
———. *Unequal Union*, Progress Books, Toronto, 1968.
Stanley, G. F. G. *The Birth of Western Canada*, University of Toronto Press, Toronto, 1961.
Thomas, L. *The Struggle for Responsible Government in the North-West*, University of Toronto Press, Toronto, 1956.
Wright, J. F. C. *Saskatchewan: the History of a Province*, McClelland & Stewart, Toronto, 1955.

Source Notes

CHAPTER 1

1. O. C. Cox, *Caste, Class and Race,* Monthly Review Press, New York, 1959, p. 330.
2. *Ibid.,* p. 335.
3. L. B. Wright, *Religion and Empire,* North Carolina Press, Chapel Hill, N.C., 1943, p. 86.
4. *Ibid.,* p. 93.
5. *Ibid.,* p. 96.
6. Cox, p. 335.
7. *Ibid.,* p. 334.
8. *Ibid.,* p. 336.

CHAPTER 2

1. James Walker, "The Indian in Canadian Historical Writing", *Canadian Historical Association*, 1971, pp. 21-51.
2. Rupert Costo, *Textbooks and the American Indian*, Indian Historian Press, San Francisco, 1970, p. 11.
3. N. Miller, *National Liberation*, Free Press, New York, 1971, p. 104.
4. R. McLachlan, *Indians*, Longmans, Green, Toronto, 1959, p. 4.
5. P. Farb, *Man's Rise to Civilization*, Dutton, New York, 1968, p. 124.
6. J. Forbes, *The Indian in America's Past*, Prentice-Hall, Englewood Cliffs, N.J., 1964, p. 16.
7. *Ibid.*, pp. 16-17.
8. *Batoche National Historic Site*, Department of Indian Affairs and Northern Development, Queen's Printer, Ottawa, 1972, p. 7.
9. S. B. Ryerson, *The Founding of Canada*, Progress Books, Toronto, 1960, p. 35.
10. A. Josephy, *The Indian Heritage of America*, Bantam, New York, 1968, p. 120.
11. *Ibid.*, p. 121.
12. *Ibid.*, p. 118.

CHAPTER 3

1. L. J. Burpee (ed.), *Journals and Letters of La Vérendrye*, Champlain Society, Toronto, 1927, pp. 179-80.
2. H. J. Moberly, *When Fur Was King*, J. M. Dent, Toronto, 1929, p. 31.
3. *Ibid.*, p. 38.
4. "Report upon the Present State of the Great Manitoulin Island etc.", *Journals of the Legislative Assembly*, Province of Canada, Appendix 21, 1858, pp. 15-16.

CHAPTER 4

1. Canada, Parliament, Sessional Papers, Vol. 19, No. 45c, 1886.
2. Wright, p. 87.
3. *Ibid.*, p. 88.
4. *Ibid.*, p. 89.
5. Jean de la Pérouse, *A Voyage Round the World*, Johnson Company, London, 1789, p. 205.
6. A. H. de Trémaudan, *Histoire de la Nation Métisse dans l'Ouest Canadien*, Albert Lévesque, Montreal, 1935, p. 425. (An unpublished translation is in the author's possession.)

7. H. Merivale, *Lectures on Colonization and Colonies*, Longman, Green and Roberts, London, 1861, pp. 487-8.

CHAPTER 5

1. *The Indian Act*, Queen's Printer, Ottawa, 1970, Section 83, p. 4287.
2. J. L. Humfreville, *Twenty Years among our Savage Indians*, Hartford Publishing Company, Hartford, Conn., 1897, pp. 52-3.
3. Saskatchewan *Herald*, North Battleford, May 12, 1883.
4. "The Treaties of Forts Carlton and Pitt", *The Treaties between Her Majesty, Queen Victoria, and the Indians of British North America*, Part II, Queen's Printer, Regina, March 1961, p. 5.

CHAPTER 6

1. *Report from the Select Committee on the Hudson's Bay Company*, British Parliament, London, 1857, p. 323.
2. Trémaudan, pp. 98-9.
3. *Report from the Select Committee*, p. 389.
4. G. Myers, *A History of Canadian Wealth*, James Lewis & Samuel, Toronto, 1972, pp. 123-4.
5. *Ibid.*, p. 139.
6. *Ibid.*
7. Trémaudan, pp. 125-6.
8. *Ibid.*, p. 125.
8. E. E. Rich, "Trade Habits and Economic Motivation among Indians", *Canadian Journal of Economics and Political Science*, Vol. 26, 1960, p. 46.
10. G. F. G. Stanley, *The Birth of Western Canada*, University of Toronto Press, Toronto, 1936, p. 47.
11. Myers, pp. 145-6.
12. *Ibid.*, p. 240.
13. *Ibid.*, p. 146.
14. Trémaudan, p. 182.
15. *Ibid.*, p. 200.
16. Stanley, p. 84.
17. Trémaudan, p. 199.
18. One Who Knows, *The Gibbet of Regina*, Thompson and Moreau, New York, 1886, p. 45.
19. J. K. Howard, *Strange Empire*, Morrow, New York, 1952, p. 131.
20. *Ibid.*, p. 132.
21. S. B. Ryerson, *Unequal Union*, Progress Books, Toronto, 1968, p. 387.

22. Stanley, pp. 110-13.
23. Trémaudan, p. 240.
24. *Ibid.*, p. 244.
25. *Ibid.*, pp. 258-9.
26. *Ibid.*, p. 266

CHAPTER 7

1. Josephy, p. 123.
2. Sessional Papers, Vol. 19, No. 8, *Detailed Report Upon All Claims to Land and Right to Participate in the North-West Half-Breed Grant*, Ottawa, 1886, pp. 1-2.
3. *Ibid.*, p. 4.
4. Saskatchewan *Herald*, February 23, 1883.
5. "The Treaties of Forts Carlton and Pitt", p. 13.
6. Saskatchewan *Herald*, February 25, 1882.
7. Toronto *Daily Mail and Empire*, November 24, 1909.
8. "The Treaties of Forts Carlton and Pitt", pp. 16ff.
9. *Ibid.*, p. 17.
10. *Ibid.*, p. 18.
11. Stanley, p. 214.
12. Saskatchewan *Herald*, August 4, 1883.
13. *Ibid.*, June 30, 1879.
14. "Reminiscences of Louis Cochin", *Canadian North West Historical Society*, Battleford, Vol. 1, No. 11, 1927, p. 38.
15. *Ibid.*
16. Saskatchewan *Herald*, February 8, 1880.

CHAPTER 8

1. Stanley, p. 190.
2. Prince Albert *Times*, June 20, 1883.
3. *Ibid.*, November 15, 1883.
4. R. E. Lamb, *Thunder in the North*, Pageant Press, New York, 1956, pp. 137-8.
5. Howard, p. 317.
6. Public Archives of Saskatchewan, Macdonald Papers, Macdonald to Dewdney, July 18, 1884.
7. Stanley, pp. 300-1.
8. "The Cree Rebellion of 1884", *Battleford Historical Publications*, Vol. 1, No. 1, 1926.
9. Stanley, p. 270.
10. *Ibid.*, p. 271.
11. Trémaudan, p. 415.

12. *Ibid.*
13. *Ibid.*, p. 417.
14. London *Advertiser*, March 31, 1885.
15. Macdonald Papers, Kennan to Crozier, September 26, 1884.
16. "Copy of the Laws and Regulations Established for the Colony of St. Laurent on the Saskatchewan", *Documents and Articles about Métis People*, Indian and Métis Department, University of Saskatchewan, Saskatoon, 1972, p. 42.
17. Prince Albert *Times*, September 19, 1884.
18. Stanley, p. 301.

CHAPTER 9

1. Lamb, p. 139.
2. Howard, p. 366.
3. Trémaudan, p. 427.
4. *Ibid.*, p. 413.
5. *Ibid.*
6. *Ibid.*
7. Howard, p. 373.
8. *Ibid.*, p. 376.
9. *Ibid.*
10. Trémaudan, pp. 291-2.
11. *Ibid.*, p. 411.
12. Macdonald Papers, Kennan to Crozier, September 26, 1884.
13. Sessional Papers, Vol. 19, No. 43, 1886, pp. 12-13.
14. Trémaudan, p. 392.
15. Howard, p. 383.
16. E. B. Osler, *The Man Who Had To Hang, Louis Riel*, Longmans, Green, Toronto, 1961, pp. 229-30.
17. Stanley, p. 324.
18. Howard, p. 374.
19. Toronto *Globe*, March 26, 1885.
20. Trémaudan, p. 298.
21. *Ibid.*, p. 411.
22. Toronto *Globe*, March 28, 1885.
23. Winnipeg *Times*, June 11, 1885.
24. Trémaudan, p. 305; and interview with Isidore Ledoux, 100-year-old Métis of Leask, Saskatchewan, on August 10, 1973. Ledoux claimed that the goods left behind by the Mounties were heavily soaked with coal oil.
25. *Batoche National Historic Site*, p. 7.
26. J. M. Gibbon, *The Romantic History of the Canadian Pacific*, Tudor Publishing Company, New York, 1937, p. 285.

27. *Ibid.*, p. 288.
28. Trémaudan, p. 322.
29. *Ibid.*, p. 325.
30. G. F. G. Stanley, "Dumont's Account of the North West Rebellion", *Canadian Historical Review*, Vol. 30, 1949, p. 266.
31. Trémaudan, p. 336.
32. Toronto *Mail*, June 19, 1885.
33. House of Commons Debates, speech by Mr. Royal, May 28, 1885.
34. Trémaudan, p. 416.
35. *Ibid.*, p. 417.
36. *Ibid.*
37. Stanley, *The Birth of Western Canada*, p. 367.
38. D. Morton, *The Last War Drum*, Hakkert, Toronto, 1972, p. 109.
39. "Reminiscences of Louis Cochin", p. 40.

CHAPTER 10

1. *Queen vs. Riel*, Queen's Printer, Ottawa, 1885, p. 375.
2. *Ibid.*, p. 374.
3. *Ibid.*, pp. 377-9.
4. *Ibid.*
5. Provincial Archives of Saskatchewan, Saskatoon, "The Trial of the White Rebels", *Saskatchewan History*, Vol. 25, Spring 1972, p. 44.
6. Trémaudan, preface.
7. Sessional Papers, Vol. 19, No. 43, 1886.
8. Stanley, *Canadian Historical Review*, Vol. 30, 1949, pp. 259-62.
9. Sessional Papers, Vol. 19, No. 43, 1886.
10. Montreal *Daily Witness*, July 14, 1885.
11. Sessional Papers, Vol. 12, No. 43H, 1886; and G. F. G. Stanley, *Louis Riel*, Ryerson Press, Toronto, 1963, p. 276.
12. *Father Végreville's Journal*, University of Saskatchewan, Saskatoon, 1885. (The translation is the author's.)
13. *Ibid.*, p. 1 (of the author's translation).
14. *Queen vs. Riel*, p. 116.
15. Myers, p. 147.
16. Howard, p. 508.
17. *Ibid.*
18. Public Archives of Canada, Macdonald Papers, No. 44779.
19. Howard, p. 131.
20. *Ibid.*, p. 132.

21. *Ibid.*, p. 2.
22. *Ibid.*, p. 4.
23. *Ibid.*, p. 6.
24. *Ibid.*
25. *Ibid.*, p. 8.
26. Trémaudan, p. 427.
27. Sessional Papers, Vol. 19, No. 43, 1886.
28. Trémaudan, pp. 350-3.
29. Toronto *Globe*, March 26, 1885.
30. Lansdowne Papers, Macdonald letters, Macdonald to Lansdowne, July 17, 1884.
31. Toronto *Globe*, April 13, 1885.
32. *Ibid.*, April 20, 1885.
33. *Ibid.*, March 26, 1885.
34. Trémaudan, p. 266.
35. *Ibid.*
36. *Ibid.*, p. 418.
37. *Ibid.*
38. *Ibid.*, p. 419.
39. Stanley, *The Birth of Western Canada*, p. 378.
40. Howard, p. 502.
41. Trémaudan, p. 431.

CHAPTER 11

1. Prairies and Forest Fires Act, Statutes of Saskatchewan, Chapter 364, Section 21.
2. H. Adams, *An Educational Survey of Métis and Non-status Indians*, unpublished report, Métis Society of Saskatchewan, Regina, 1972, p. 46.
3. *Maclean's* Magazine, May 1973, p. 29.

CHAPTER 12

1. Adams, p. 22.
2. *Ibid.*, p. 33.
3. I. Illich, *Deschooling Society*, Harper & Row, New York, 1972.
4. N. Adler, *The Learning of Political Behavior*, Scott, Foresman, Glenview, Ill., 1970, p. 191.
5. P. Freire, *Pedagogy of the Oppressed*, Herder and Herder, New York, 1970.

CHAPTER 13

1. E. Cleaver, *Soul on Ice*, McGraw-Hill, New York, 1968, p. 159.

2. A. Memmi, *The Colonizer and the Colonized,* Beacon Press, Boston, 1965, pp. 79-89.

3. Author's conversation with a Métis in Saskatoon.

CHAPTER 14

1. Letter to the Secretary of State from A. E. Belcourt, president of the Native Council of Canada, July 6, 1971. (In the author's possession.)

2. Letter to P. E. Trudeau from A. E. Belcourt, June 30, 1971. (In the author's possession.)

3. Audited Statement of Revenue and Expenditures for the Period April 1, 1972, to March 31, 1973, Secretary of State Budget, Métis Society of Saskatchewan, Regina, 1973. (In the author's possession.)

CHAPTER 15

1. Franz Fanon, *The Wretched of the Earth,* Grove Press, New York, 1966.

Index

Acknowledgements

The author is grateful to the following for permission to reproduce copyright material:

Cox, Oliver C., *Caste, Class and Race*, Monthly Review Press, New York

Farb, Peter, *Man's Rise to Civilization*, Dutton, New York

Howard, J. K., *Strange Empire*, Morrow, New York (reissued by James Lewis & Samuel, Toronto, 1974)

Myers, Gustavus, *A History of Canadian Wealth*, James Lewis & Samuel, Toronto

Josephy, A., *The Indian Heritage of America*, Bantam, New York

Wright, Louis, *Religion and Empire*, North Carolina Press, Chapel Hill, N.C.

Gibbon, J. M., *The Romantic History of the Canadian Pacific*, Tudor, New York

Cleaver, E., *Soul on Ice*, McGraw-Hill, New York

Adler, N., *The Learning of Political Behavior*, Scott, Foresman, Glenview, Ill.

Burpee, L. J. (ed.), *Journals and Letters of La Vérendrye*, Champlain Society, Toronto

Costo, Rupert, *Textbooks and the American Indian*, Indian Historian Press, San Francisco

Maclean's Magazine, May 1973, p. 29, for information reproduced on p. 150.

Stanley, George F. G., *The Birth of Western Canada*, University of Toronto Press, Toronto

Forbes, Jack D., *The Indian In America's Past*, Prentice-Hall, Englewood Cliffs, N.J.

Moberly, H. J., *When Fur Was King*, J. M. Dent, New York

Miller, N., *National Liberation*, Free Press, New York

Ryerson, S. B., *The Founding of Canada* and *Unequal Union*, Progress Books, Toronto

Fanon, Franz, *The Wretched of the Earth*, Grove Press, New York

Morton, D., *The Last War Drum*, Hakkert, Toronto

McLachlan, R., *Indians*, Longmans, Green, Toronto

Osler, E. B., *The Man Who Had To Hang, Louis Riel*, Longmans, Green, Toronto